Visual Data Storytelling
with Tableau

The Pearson Addison-Wesley Data and Analytics Series

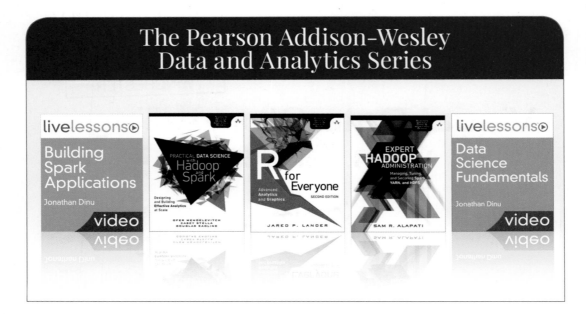

Visit **informit.com/awdataseries** for a complete list of available publications.

The **Pearson Addison-Wesley Data and Analytics Series** provides readers with practical knowledge for solving problems and answering questions with data. Titles in this series primarily focus on three areas:

1. **Infrastructure:** how to store, move, and manage data
2. **Algorithms:** how to mine intelligence or make predictions based on data
3. **Visualizations:** how to represent data and insights in a meaningful and compelling way

The series aims to tie all three of these areas together to help the reader build end-to-end systems for fighting spam; making recommendations; building personalization; detecting trends, patterns, or problems; and gaining insight from the data exhaust of systems and user interactions.

Make sure to connect with us!
informit.com/socialconnect

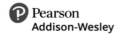 

Visual Data Storytelling
with Tableau

Lindy Ryan

Addison-Wesley

Boston • Columbus • Indianapolis • New York • San Francisco
Amsterdam • Cape Town • Dubai • London • Madrid • Milan • Munich
Paris • Montreal • Toronto • Delhi • Mexico City • São Paulo
Sydney • Hong Kong • Seoul • Singapore • Taipei • Tokyo

Library of Congress Control Number: 2018932444

ISBN-13: 978-0-13-471283-3
ISBN-10: 0-13-471283-3

1   18

Editor-in-Chief
Greg Wiegand

Executive Editor
Debra Williams

Development Editor
Chris Zahn

Managing Editor
Sandra Schroeder

Senior Project Editor
Lori Lyons

Copy Editor
Paula Lowell

Project Manager
Dhayanidhi Karunanidhi

Indexer
Erika Millen

Proofreader
Jeanine Furino

Cover Designer
Chuti Prasertsith

Compositor
codemantra

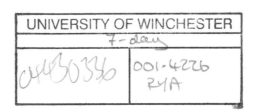

For all my students—past, present, and future

Contents at a Glance

Contents

FOREWORD

Data visualization is about presenting data in a way to help humans interpret, analyze, learn from it, and most important in a business context, take action on it. More than just objectively showing a result of data discovery or analysis, visualization can point a user in one direction or another based on the data chosen, the techniques used, and the creator's focus. This book focuses on the narrative part of data visualization. It's an excellent addition to this series, which has mostly focused on the infrastructure and algorithms of data and analytics. Visual representation is the end result of all that work on the back end, which means this book closes the loop on the overall analytics story. Despite its focus on Tableau as a tool, the concepts and methods discussed throughout are applicable to any data tool, be it Excel, custom visualizations, or other products that give analysts and data scientists the ability to tell a story through data.

Lindy has deep experience in analytics, communication, and data visualization. She led research in visual analytics, among other things, at Radiant Advisors before moving into academia where she now teaches on data analysis, communication, and visualization at both Rutgers University and Montclair State University, as well as actively researches in the field at Rutgers Discovery Informatics Institute. She brings her depth of experience to this book with explorations and analysis of some famous and well-known data visualizations in addition to lessons on choosing different visuals, color palettes, data preparation, charts, and more.

Two of the three primary takeaways from this book are broadly applicable to any developer, business analyst, executive, journalist, or student regardless of which tool they use. Specifically, the first takeaway focuses on giving the reader the knowledge to evaluate visualizations for their effectiveness and determine how best to tell a story with their data. The second focuses on how to present this data and focus on the audience for maximal impact. Finally, the third takeaway of the book is to use Tableau as a tool to produce compelling visualizations from diverse data sources and types. This book is a great addition to the series for any reader wanting to learn how to create the most impactful stories possible around their data, and to apply hands-on skill learning with today's best data visualization tools.

—**Paul Dix**, Series Editor, Addison-Wesley Data & Analytics Series

PREFACE

For as long as I can remember, I have always been fascinated by the power of a good story (see Figure P.1).

Figure P.1 A young me, reviewing the available data on weekly sales.

As a young girl I was an insatiable reader. I read it all, from fanciful children's classics, to the weekly Sunday newspaper, to novels way beyond my budding adolescent intellectual band-width. In those early days I approached a new book as one might approach a new relationship: if I could get my hands on one and it could hold my attention beyond the first few sentences, then I would read it from cover to cover and let it tell me whatever story it wished. It was a win-win scenario.

I read voraciously, inhaling stories that entertained, inspired, and educated me. I read without discretion, never worrying over parameters of genre, or length, or subject matter—those pesky ingredients that blend together inside the lines of a great piece of writing. I moved through stories with the same speed and determination as might a starving person (or perhaps a late-night cruise line passenger) move through a buffet of delicious foods: greedily and indulgently. I *devoured* stories. Along the way, I discovered those I liked and those I didn't. More importantly, I discovered story frameworks and storytelling voices that called to me, and met those special few authors whose powerful prose I would approach for the first time, fall immediately in love, and continue to read their books over and over again until their pages became soft and their spines so bent they required surgical repair with Scotch Tape. It might not surprise you that I began my collegiate career with an eye on a major in literature.

Like taste buds, my taste for stories evolved over time, both in terms of format and content. I moved from flea market paperbacks, to glossy novels, and have now managed to go almost entirely digital in the way I seek out and consume informational storytelling, preferring online articles and satellite news radio over newsprint and cable TV journalism (although, to be honest, if you find yourself tagging along in my company at a rare bookstore, it would be advisable to come equipped with an overnight bag and at least one prepackaged meal, just to be safe—a few people have learned this lesson the hard way). Likewise, my appetite for stories that entertain and inspire have become more complex and multi-faceted; my desire for stories that educate require them to be more dynamic, data-rich, and interactive.

My personal evolution in story preferences parallels a similar journey that we, as a collective, take as our taste for stories mature. Our storytelling appetite changes alongside age, experiences, and interests, yet still the desire for a good story persists.

So it is with data stories. As we learn to communicate the results of our analysis—the hidden secrets carefully plucked from within the rows and columns of our data and curated into insight—we mature from being okay with being told something, to wanting to see it for ourselves, and, eventually, to wanting to interact with it. We need more—more information, more context, more action, and more substance. It's not "see Jane run" anymore, it's "let's talk about how fast Jane ran from Point A to Point B and, more important, why (and if) that's actually important."

And sometimes, we learn something entirely new and unexpected. Maybe Jane was being chased by a bear.

We crave stories; it's part of our design. As a species, humans are intrinsically hungry for a good story. Without getting into the weeds, we can leave it simply at this: We *need* stories. They entertain us, they educate us, and they provide ways to transmit knowledge, information, and experiences. They don't even have to be in written form. In fact, we're rather non-discriminatory about how we receive stories—in fact, we might even prefer stories that move us and touch our senses (there is certainly enough scientific evidence to support this, as discussed in a later chapter). Think about movies, radio, Broadway performances, or screening your favorite film accompanied with a live one hundred-piece orchestra contributing the soundtrack.

Today, the concept of data storytelling is reshaping stories of all forms, from news media and journalism, to boardroom reports and conference presentations, to even how we script documentaries and educational programming. If you have seen any conference presentations over the past couple of years, or watched a TED talk, or read an article out of the *New York Times*, or listened to National Public Radio, or watched an episode of *Cosmos*, then you have witnessed data storytelling in action. It's a trend that we—from the classroom to the boardroom—are jumping on with more velocity than you might imagine. Students from grade school to graduate school are working hands-on with data and changing the way they learn about and communicate about information. Business analysts, managers, and executives are moving away from static, statistic-laden reports and toward interactive, visual data dashboards. Journalists and news editors the world over are using data storyboards and engaging, often interactive, infographics to share information with society-at-large—in print, online, and across form factors.

Visualizing our data helps us to see trends and patterns. Telling stories about our data helps us to connect with it. Combined, visual data storytelling pushes beyond the boundaries of simply analyzing information to providing the capacity to communicate it in ways that leave a meaningful, lasting impact. Together, these converge into what I've termed the "visual imperative," a paradigm shift that is radically reshaping how we work with and seek to understand our data, big and small. This visual imperative is reforming our expectations of information, changing the question from "what can we do with our data" to "what can our data do for us." And, it's making its mark on every aspect of a progressively data-driven culture, too. From traditional business intelligence and data discovery, to the personal analytics on our smart devices and wearable technologies, to the manner in which we are using data recipes to cook up our new favorite television shows (I'm looking at you, Netflix), we are becoming more data-dependent and data-driven than ever before. Data has changed from being gold, to being the oil of the century, to what one witty columnist decided to combine and dub the "black gold" (a.k.a., oil) of the century, to being the oxygen of the most innovative and disruptive companies.

In a nutshell, this was the premise of my first book, *The Visual Imperative: Creating a Visual Culture of Data Discovery*, which arrived in bookstores in 2016. Written primarily from an analyst's perspective, this book focuses on how the data industry-at-large has been undergoing a beautiful period of disruption, and how this innovation and transformation has affected society across the blurred boundaries of customer to consumer. It discusses how the emergent visual revolution of the last several years has changed the language of data discovery across industries; how this has affected modern data architectures, governance expectations, and practices; and explores several of the advancements in data visualization that I expect to see over the upcoming years.

In my years as an analyst, the use of visuals to convey incredible insights into data captured my interest immediately. This led me to focus my research on data visualization and visual analytics, and, eventually, on visual data storytelling. I learned how critical data visualization truly is to communicating the results of data analysis and discovery to enrich the intelligence that is provided to decision makers and leaders within any organization and how a compelling visual narrative can transform insight into action. Then, as I transitioned from industry into academia, I recognized firsthand the importance of careful planning and foresight in communicating data, as narratives begin to take form and we build visualizations to support story arcs. More specifically, as I watched education translate into application, I recognized this isn't an intuitive and obvious process. It takes work, it takes understanding, and it takes a *lot* of practice.

If my previous book was the use case to support the visual imperative, then this book is the how-to guide to put it into action with visual data storytelling. For lack of a better phrase, I'm done pontificating: it's time to get our hands dirty.

Three Core Takeaways

This book focuses on giving you the foundational knowledge, contextualized learning, and hands-on skills you need to be successful in leveraging the power of data visualization to tell compelling data stories. The goal is not to inundate you with academic lessons in the science of data visualization or story composition, nor to provide a full-scale training experience on any particular software or technical application, but instead to provide guidance as you build the necessary skills to produce visual data narratives within the context of business communication. Therefore, this book concentrates on helping you learn how to organize your data and structure analysis with stories in mind; to embrace exploration and the visual discovery process; and to articulate your findings with rich data, purposefully curated visualizations, and skillfully crafted narrative frameworks. Ultimately, these presentations can help you to deliver your business message while satisfying the needs of your audience. By the time you've reached the end of the text the expectation is that you will have earned the three core takeaways represented in Figure P.2.

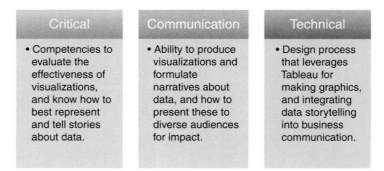

Figure P.2 The core takeaways.

What You'll Learn in This Book

In data visualization courses, students learn how to present data in visual form. This involves working with data, learning how to apply visual design principles, and—often—learn new software. This book is intended to tackle all three. What you will learn from this book includes the following:

- ✔ Why we tell stories and what visual data storytelling is
- ✔ The difference between data visualization for analysis versus presentation
- ✔ How to tell visual stories that communicate insights and make an impact
- ✔ How to leverage questions to design logical and fruitful data collection and analysis
- ✔ How to create important graphs in Tableau and know which chart to use
- ✔ How to utilize concepts of design in data visualization and storytelling
- ✔ How to best storyboard your story for your message based on your audience
- ✔ How to direct your audience's attention to the most important parts of your data story
- ✔ How to design effective business presentations to showcase your data story with Tableau

Who This Book Is For

This book is for anyone who has data and wants to use it to communicate something to someone else in an engaging and memorable way. This includes, but is not limited to:

- ■ Analysts sharing the results of their data discovery or analysis
- ■ Students communicating data for reports or presentations
- ■ Teachers helping learners (of any age) to cultivate visual data literacy
- ■ Executives and business managers reporting data-driven results or metrics
- ■ Journalists giving data the starring role in their editorials

Essentially, if you have some data and want to tell a story about it to someone else, then this book is for you. So, from the most savvy of data users to students just beginning to learn about the power of data visualization in business communications, as long as you are interested in becoming a better visual data storyteller, then you're in the right place!

There are no prerequisites for this book. In fact, it might actually be preferable if you're coming into this text with fresh eyes and a fresh perspective. We start with the basics and build incrementally on concepts and to move through the data storytelling process from beginning to end.

Don't let the topic overwhelm you: Whether or not you have been practicing data visualization and visual analysis for some time or are just beginning, you don't have to be a statistician or a computer scientist, a graphic designer, or even a well-trained writer to learn how to navigate the art and science that is data visualization or to become a master data storyteller. Likewise, you do not need to be a data visualization expert or come armed with deep technical expertise in visualization software packages. Although this book utilizes Tableau as the primary mechanism for data visualization, you need not be a power user or expert prior to getting started—you don't even have to have a purchased license on your machine! You can simply download a free trial of Tableau Desktop version 10 or higher to get started—and we'll go through that process together, too. Finally, you don't even need to bring your own data to play just yet (although you certainly can). The sample datasets used in this text, as well as information on where you can find other free datasets, are available to you through the resources listed at the end of this book. Tableau also provides a large selection of sample datasets that you can work for practice, too.

I realize that the idea of visual analysis or data storytelling might sound intimidating to many and that learning new software is always a challenge. Therefore, this book is designed in a way that a professor or a tutor might teach visual data storytelling (and in fact is the approach I take in my classrooms for undergraduate- and graduate-level students) using what I call the 1-2-3 Method (see Figure P.3). This breaks down like this: (1) grounding easy-to-understand principles (2) reinforcing these through real-world examples, and (3) guided hands-on work to incrementally develop skills. By the time you have worked your way through each of the chapters and exercises in this book you will walk away with something tangible: competency as a visual data storyteller using your own data in your own dashboards and presentations. And you'll have some great visuals on your Tableau Public profile that you can add to your resume!

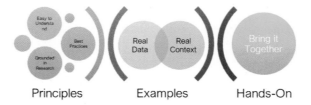

Figure P.3 The 1-2-3 Method.

Assumptions

To write a comprehensive text on any of the topics covered in this book would take several volumes and the combined mind power of multiple subject matter experts and scholars across industry and academia. Thus, this book makes some assumptions about the skillset, expectations, and needs of its audience to limit the scope to the most valuable content. My goal is to distill complex topics to the most effective level of detail necessary to help you learn how to communicate business-relevant implications of data analyses using the visualization and storytelling capabilities of Tableau. Additional learning resources to expand on the concepts covered in these chapters are provided at the end of this book.

First, this book is focused primarily on storytelling and presentation. While analysis is an intrinsic part of this, in this book you work from a perspective of communicating insights rather than statistical analysis—data explanation rather than exploration, if you will. Thus, the way you curate visualizations for storytelling purposes may be slightly different than how you would approach these tasks if you were designing analytically accurate data representation not intended for presentation. Additionally, while I will touch on subjects like data preparation and wrangling tasks associated with getting data ready for analysis, the full scope of what is involved in all the steps necessary to transform raw data into a workable format is beyond what is covered in this book. Instead, I provide some basic information on these tasks and lean on the capabilities of Tableau as well as other available software, such as Alteryx and Excel.

Last, but not least, this book assumes that the reader has access to Tableau Desktop 10, which is currently available to install on either Windows or Mac operating systems Free trials are available for business users or general audiences, while students and educators can take advantage of the Tableau for Teaching program, which offers free licenses to the full desktop version, as well as the Alteryx for Good program, which is similar.

note

Here are a few caveats and notes:

- Versions of Tableau prior to version 10 support much of the same functionality as version 10. However, the interface is notably different and may affect navigability of instructions in this text.

- Alteryx runs solely on Windows; Mac users will need to install Parallels or a similar program (most offer free trials) to follow along.

- All sample data files are provided in Excel-ready formats; SPSS files may also be available.

- Data not available for public use or sharing will be noted as such.

Why Tableau

If you browse the shelves of your local bookstore, you'll find several wonderful books available that teach data visualization and data storytelling skills in a tool-agnostic manner. (I've included some of these titles in the recommended reading resources in Chapter 10.) There is a good reason for this. To borrow the aptly stated words of Cole Nussbaumer Knaflic, author of *Storytelling with Data: A Data Visualization Guide for Business Professionals*, "No matter how good the tool, it will never know your data or its story like you do." With any software there will always be weak points to balance out the strong ones. However, my goal in this book is to not only give you the information you need but the application to use it. For that, we need a tool.

Many software packages are available on the market that would serve as capable platforms to support this book, including Excel, which is still the most ubiquitous, if unexciting, analysis tool, with the capability to functionally create basic charts and graphs. However, although many of the more advanced available technologies meet the rigors of building beautiful data visualizations, few provide the end-to-end capabilities that Tableau does. What we're looking for is a best-of-breed tool that delivers an approachable, intuitive environment for self-service users of all levels to prepare, analyze, and visualize data, as well as delivery platforms like dashboards and story preparation. All of these are native to Tableau.

Today, Tableau is the world's leading data visualization analytics software company with 57,000 customer accounts ranging from small to large organizations across all industries and 160 countries (as of Q1 2017[1]). Tableau provides a suite of licensed and free software products—including a recently released mobile product called Vizable—and excels at displaying data visually, using a drag-and-drop canvas on top of embedded analytics to help users explore their data. Although Tableau can mimic Excel by providing the capability to analyze rows and columns of numbers, its focus is on interactive, visual data exploration through complex analytical capabilities as well as dashboarding and storytelling features not found in other tools. For more advanced users, Tableau supports a complete formula language and robust data connections: Tableau's live query engine enables users to connect to more than forty difference data sources; its in-memory data engine leverages the complete memory hierarchy from disk to L1 cache and shifts the curve between big data and fast analysis. And according to Tableau's aggressive product roadmap, the fine-tuning of some of these capabilities as well as several worthwhile new features are on their way.

Another aspect of Tableau that I find impressive and worthwhile to a larger data storytelling movement is its focus on building a community of data users. I encourage you to join the Tableau Community and connect with the resources and peers you will find there.

---

1. https://www.tableau.com/about/press-releases/2017/tableau-reports-first-quarter-2017-financial-results

How to Use This Text

Like traditional classroom instruction, this book's chapters are organized as individual modules that will be your guide as you learn how to go beyond the dashboard to communicate business-relevant implications of data analyses using the analytic, visualization, and storytelling capabilities of Tableau. Some chapters provide complete coverage of a story, from data collection to a completed storyboard. Others are organized as granular exploration of a single concept.

Although you are not limited to working through this book cover to cover, it is recommended that you do so for incremental development of learning and reinforcement of skills. Each module builds on concepts and skills discussed in the preceding one, and may include advancements on working through an end-to-end data project that are necessary before taking the next steps forward.

> **note**
>
> With the exception of a very few, all visualizations and screenshots in this book are created using Tableau version 10 for Mac. Differences in operating system versions are negligible.

Supporting Materials

Beyond the modules of this text, I have developed several companion materials to support ongoing skills development and learning. These are intended to go beyond the confines of these chapters and to attempt to keep pace with innovations in Tableau functionality as well as review some of its more nuanced advanced features that are out of scope for this book. These resources are suitable for the workplace, although special attention has been given to classroom use:

- **Companion website (www.visualdatastorytelling.com):** Includes presentation materials and an ongoing blog, as well as a library of visual data stories contributed by storytellers from industry to academia
- **Educator portal:** Provides lecture materials as well as in-class assignments and rubrics for individual and group projects, as well exams that support student learning at the undergraduate and graduate levels
- **Recommended reading:** A list of additional reading, organized by topic
- **Glossary:** Provides a list of terminology and definitions used throughout this text

Contents of This Book

Each chapter in this book is intended to achieve two purposes:

- Provide a foundation of knowledge that forms the basis for education on the concepts we'll be covering. These are the chapters grounded in best practices and empirical evidence.
- Give you the opportunity to get hands on with the data in Tableau and begin to develop these skills for yourself. These chapters provide step-by-step instruction with accompanying screenshots and examples of outputs to verify your work.

The following list provides a brief description of each of the chapters.

- **Chapter 1: Storytelling in a Digital Era**

  This chapter sets the context for the book with an introductory discussion on data visualization and visual data storytelling, how these two concepts are similar and different, and how both practices have transformed in the digital era, propelled by new technologies and more data. The chapter explores the value of visual data storytelling for data communication and establishes how data storytelling is the necessary skill that bridges the business-IT gap.

- **Chapter 2: The Power of Visual Data Stories**

  This chapter uses real-life and quintessential examples to analyze the power of visual data stories to communicate discoveries and insights hidden in data. You ground these lessons by taking time to understand what makes visualization and stories so powerful to the human brain from both a cognitive and an anthropological perspective by comparing the brain on data versus the brain on stories.

- **Chapter 3: Getting Started with Tableau**

  This chapter shifts focus to begin exploring the Tableau ecosystem. It reviews the different software products and provides a detailed tour of the new and improved Tableau user interface. Finally, you will walk through the Getting Started process to begin working hands-on in Tableau and review what users need to know about bringing data into Tableau to prepare for the analytic and visual process.

- **Chapter 4: Importance of Context in Storytelling**

  This chapter describes the importance of understanding data's context and its role in helping data storytellers ask the right questions to build a story framework. It discusses exploratory and explanatory analysis; gathering stakeholder requirements; and strategies for successful storytelling, including repetition, narrative flow, considerations for spoken versus written narratives that support visuals, and structures that can support your stories for maximum impact. You will also explore helpful techniques in Tableau that guide you to crafting effective data narrative structure.

- **Chapter 5: Choosing the Right Visual**

  This chapter introduces the common types of visuals used to communicate data in a business setting, discusses appropriate use cases for each, and highlights their use through examples built from the catalog of charts available in Tableau. The chapter also covers techniques to help you assess when to use these graphs, when to avoid certain types of charts, and how to generate them according to best practices, along with some of the special features in Tableau designed to help you get the most from your visual.

- **Chapter 6: Curating Visuals for Your Audience**

  This chapter dives into human cognition and visual perception to frame the contribution of pre-attentive attributes like size, color, and position and how important they are to the storytelling process. You will explore how to use these strategically to help direct audiences' attention and create a visual hierarchy of components to communicate effectively. This chapter provides the framework for curating story arcs and layouts with visualizations in Tableau that the following chapters explore in-depth.

- **Chapter 7: Preparing Data for Storytelling**

  This chapter covers the very beginning of the data storytelling process with the processing steps necessary to ready messy data for visual analysis and storytelling in Tableau. You will leverage the lessons learned thus far in the text by working through preparing data for analysis, connecting to data, and beginning to visually explore it in Tableau. The chapter walks you through this process beginning with exporting raw data from survey platforms, through manually preparing it in Excel, to using Tableau 10 and other external tools to get data just where it needs to be so you can start building a compelling visual data story.

- **Chapter 8: Storyboarding Frame by Frame**

  This chapter picks up where the previous chapter left off and looks deeper at the process of constructing a data narrative by covering how to build purposeful visualizations and organizing them to tell a story. It offers a closer look at building a sequence of data visualizations, reviews how to build dashboards and organize them as well as individual visualizations in story points, incorporating features like annotations and highlighting, and covers how to revisit earlier discussions on context to present a compelling visual data story.

- **Chapter 9: Advanced Storytelling Charts**

  This penultimate chapter explores advanced strategies for visual data storytelling beyond the basic charts and graphs provided in Tableau's core functionality. It covers how to create advanced charts that require additional formatting and calculations, including timelines, Likert scale charts, lollipop charts, and more.

- **Chapter 10: Closing Thoughts**

  This chapter recaps the main lessons covered throughout the text. As a resource kit for life beyond the book, this chapter provides checklists of best practices and practical suggestions for continuing to master data storytelling, as well as discusses additional resources available to support the text.

Good luck! Let's get started.

ACKNOWLEDGMENTS

Although only one name appears on the cover of this book, innumerable others have contributed in ways both big and small to the creation of this text. It is with utmost sincerity that I say that without these people much of this work would not have been possible, or half as interesting.

First and foremost, my deepest thanks go to my colleagues in academia at Rutgers University, Montclair State University, and City University of Seattle: Drs. Manish Parashar and Deborah Silver at Rutgers; Rashmi Jain and Richard Peterson at Montclair State University; and Pressley Rankin, Greg Price, and Kelly Flores at City University of Seattle. A special thank you also to Dr. Mark Berenson for gifting me two splendid books on "antique" data visualization, and for spurring my thoughts on visual storytelling through the ages. I am eternally grateful for all of your support of my research, for your belief in me as an educator, and for your guidance and mentorship over the years.

To my former second-half at Radiant Advisors, John O'Brien, for having exposed me to the world of data visualization and giving me the courage to venture out on my own and pursue my passions, both within industry and out.

To Robert "Dr. Bob" Brownlow for being a consistent source of wisdom and encouragement every day, from that fateful first phone call in 2011 when I began work on my graduate thesis to now, and every moment in between.

To my friends at Tableau and the entire Tableau Academic Team: Thank you for everything you do and continue to do, for data visualization and for students of all ages! Additionally, many thanks are due to some of my most inspirational friends in the data science industry, among them Anne Buff, Josh Howard, Nate Halko, and Stephen Faig.

To Debra Williams, Chris Zahn, and the entire editing, review, and design team at Pearson, for making this project possible, for seeing it through, and for bringing a beautiful new book into the world. It has been an honor to work with you.

To my partners at New Jersey Public Schools and Sussex County, who have contributed the data used to create some of the tutorials and visuals in this text and afforded me the opportunity to work together on meaningful research.

Much appreciation is owed to several former and current students and research assistants: Sierra Gratale, Gerald Wrona, and Chantel Diaz for your hard work and diligence, and to Craig Moran for volunteering time, ideas, and constructive feedback. I am privileged to have worked alongside you, and I hope you have taken away as much from your time with me as I have from my time with you.

Of course, I am grateful for the love and support of my family: my parents, Lydia and Paul, John and Viktoria; my in-laws, Dave and Korla; my son and personal sunshine, Wake, for being the most amazing person in the entire world. And, of course, I've saved the best for last: to my husband, Mike, for unconditional love and support.I love you all.

Finally, to all my students—past, present, and future—who I am humbled and grateful to have the pleasure of teaching and learning from:

Sweet Circle of Thanks
My sincerest gratitude to the mentors, friends, colleagues, students, and family who have made this journey so special!

ABOUT THE AUTHOR

Lindy Ryan is passionate about telling stories with data. She specializes in translating raw data into insightful stories through carefully curated visuals and engaging narrative frameworks.

Before joining academia, Lindy was the Research Director for research and advisory firm Radiant Advisors from 2011 through 2016. In this role Lindy led Radiant's analyst activities in the confluence of data discovery, visualization, and visual analytics. She also developed the methodology for the Data Visualization Competency Center (DVCC), a framework for helping data-driven organizations to effectively implement data visualization for enterprise-wide visual data analysis and communication. Her tool-agnostic approach has been successfully implemented at a variety of organizations across several industries and with multiple visualization technologies, including Tableau, Qlik, and GoodData. She remains a respected analyst in the data visualization community and is a regular contributor to several industry publications as well as a speaker at conferences worldwide.

Lindy began her academic career as an associate faculty member at City University of Seattle's School of Applied Leadership where she taught graduate courses in business leadership from 2012 to 2016. In early 2016 she joined the ambitious team at the Rutgers Discovery Informatics Institute and began contributing to multidisciplinary research focused on designing solutions for the next generation of supercomputers tasked with enabling cutting-edge extreme-scale science. Currently, Lindy leads RDI[2]'s research on understanding and preventing cyberbullying behaviors in emerging technology users through advanced computing approaches.

Today, Lindy teaches courses in visual analytics and data visualization in Rutgers University's Professional Science Masters program and in Montclair State University's Business Analytics program. She is a recipient of the MSU Professing Excellence Award, which recognizes professors' teaching excellence, particularly those who inspire and motivate students. This honor is especially meaningful to Lindy because in addition to her passion for teaching, her research includes a commitment to STEM advocacy, and she spends time on research related to increasing gender equity in CS&E and finding new and novel ways to nurture visual data literacy skills in early STEM learners.

Lindy is an active committee member of the New Jersey Big Data Alliance, a partnership of New Jersey-based academic institutions that serves as the State's legislated consortium on research, education and outreach in advanced computation and big data. She is the author of "*The Visual Imperative: Creating a Culture of Visual Discovery*" released by Morgan Kaufmann in 2016, and the owner of Black Spot Books, a traditional, analytics-driven small-press publishing house.

Learn more about Lindy at www.visualdatastorytelling.com. You can also follow her on Twitter @lindy_ryan or view samples of her work on her Tableau Public page at https://public.tableau.com/profile/lindyryan#!/.

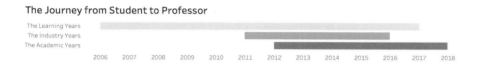

The Journey from Student to Professor

CHAPTER 1

STORYTELLING IN A DIGITAL ERA

This chapter sets the context for the rest of this book with an introductory discussion on data visualization and visual data storytelling. It explores how these two concepts are similar and different and how both practices have been transformed in the digital era by new technologies and bigger, more diverse, and more dynamic data. Lastly, the chapter explores the value of visual data storytelling for data communication, and establishes how data storytelling is the perfect skill to bridge the very broad and expansive business—IT gap.

A Visual Revolution

A data revolution is happening across the globe. From academics to politics and everywhere in between, the world's stories are being told through their data points. Although using visualization to tell stories about data isn't particularly new (in fact, as you'll soon discover, we've been doing it for quite some time), we are now telling them in more influential and impactful ways than ever before.

Today, the resurgence in the power of data visualization—alongside a virtual gold rush of bigger, more diverse, and more dynamic data—is providing new tools and innovative techniques to help us transform raw data into compelling visual data narratives. Propelled by this newfound horsepower in data visualization, we are recreating the entire analytic process. We're also making it increasingly more visual—from how we explore data to discover new insights all the way to how we curate dashboards, storyboards, and interactive visualizations to share the fruits of our labor. We are always looking for new ways to show off the messages hidden within our data, and we're getting pretty good at it, too. Charts and graphs created five years ago in Excel do not compare to the incredible visuals we are now producing with best-of-breed tools like Tableau, or scripting with dynamic JavaScript libraries like D3.js (see Figure 1.1).

Our newest breed of data visualizations are moving beyond the classic bar, line, and pie charts of the past, and pushing beyond the boundaries of traditional information displays to powerful new territories of graphic representation. With determination and a healthy spirit of curiosity and adventure, we are visually representing our data on everything from massive, mural-sized visualizations like the Affinity Map,[1] a 250-square meter visualization produced by the Swiss Federal Institute of Technology in Lausanne, to interactive visualizations like Trendalyzer,[2] a statistical animation visualization developed by the late Hans Rosling's Gapminder Foundation, to streaming visualizations that bring data to life with real-time movement, to fluid, customizable dashboards that toggle between form factors from the desktop to the smartphone with pixel-perfect rendering. If Gene Roddenberry, creator of the science fiction series *Star Trek*, had scripted today's visual analytics movement, he might have said we are boldly going where no viz (visualization) has gone before—and he'd be right.

However, all of these visualizations, from the most dynamic to the most static, need more than just data to make the leap from information representation to resonation. They need a story—something to show, or, more aptly, to "tell" visually—and finding this tale isn't always obvious when digging through a data set. It takes exploration, curiosity, and a shift in mindset to move from creating a data visualization to scripting a data narrative. They are similar, but not identical, skill sets.

---

1. https://actu.epfl.ch/news/the-world-s-largest-data-visualization/

2. https://www.gapminder.org/tag/trendalyzer/

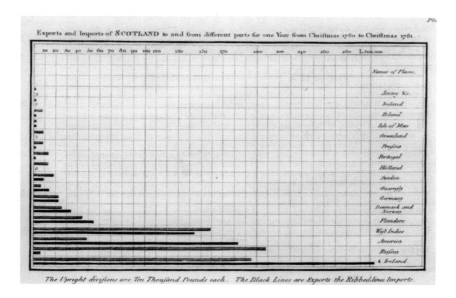

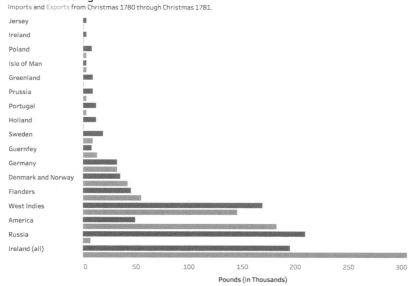

Figure 1.1 An example of "old" data visualization compared to its modern equivalent.

Scripting a data narrative might sound like a vague or even an overwhelming process. After all, many of us would consider ourselves analysts first, "data people" before storytellers. We enjoy numbers and analytics and computation more so than the artsy craft of writing stories. Nevertheless, the two are fundamentally intertwined: We must know our data, its context, and the results of analytics in order to extrapolate these into meaning for an audience who doesn't. That's all a story is, really—one person sharing something new and unknown with another in a way that is easily understandable and relatable. The good news? There's no single way to do it. We can use several proven narrative frameworks to design a data storyboard, and numerous quintessential examples exist where a data storyteller has exercised a generous amount of creative liberty and done something entirely new. After all, like any kind of story, data stories require a certain amount of creativity—and although tools and technology can do much with our data for us, creativity is a uniquely human contribution to any narrative (see Figure 1.2). We'll take a look at some of these examples as we go forward.

> ### note
> Data *visualization* is the practice of graphically representing data to help people see and understand patterns, insights, and other discoveries hidden inside information. Data *storytelling* translates seeing into meaning by weaving a narrative around the data to answer questions and support decision making.

Data visualization and data storytelling are not the same thing; however, they are two sides of the same coin. A true data story utilizes data visualizations as a literary endeavor would use illustrations—proof points to support the narrative. However, there's a little bit of a role reversal here: whereas data visualizations provide the "what" in the story, the narrative itself answers the "why." As such, the two work together in tandem to translate raw data into something meaningful for its audience. So, to be a proper data storyteller you need to know how to do both: curate effective data visualizations *and* frame a storyboard around them. This starts with learning how to visualize data, and more importantly, how to do so in the best way for communication rather than purely analytical purposes. As discussed later in this book, visualizations for analysis versus presentation are not always the same thing in data storytelling.

One of the most common clichés in the viz space is that "data visualizations are only as effective as the insights they reveal." In this context, effectiveness is a function of careful planning. Any meaningful visualization is a two-pronged one. It requires analytical perfection and correct rendering of statistical information, as well as a well-orchestrated balance of visual design cues (color, shape, size, and so on) to encode that data with meaning. The two are not mutually exclusive.

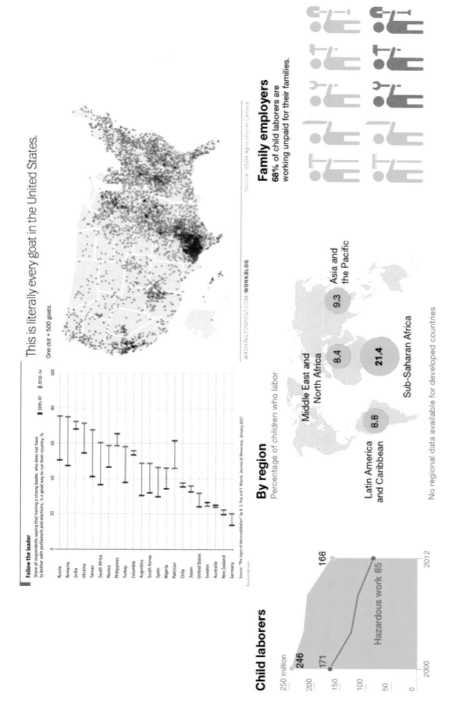

Figure 1.2 A sampling of great data stories in recent headlines by statisticians and data journalists.

Data visualization is a place where science meets art, although the jury is still out on whether the practice is more a scientific endeavor or an artistic one. Although experts agree that a compelling visual requires both, it tends to be something of a chicken and egg scenario. We haven't quite come to a consensus as to whether science comes before design or we design for the science—and the decision changes depending on whom you ask, who is creating the visualization, and who its audience is. That said, whichever side of the argument you land on, the result is the same. We need statistical understanding of the data, its context, and how to measure it; otherwise, we run the risk of faulty analysis and skewed decision making that, eventually, leads to risk. Likewise, our very-visual cognition system demands a way to encode numbers with meaning, and so we rely on colors and shapes to help automate these processes for us. An effective visual must strike the right balance of both to accurately and astutely deliver on its goal: intuitive insight at a glance.

This might sound like an easy task, but it's not. Learning to properly construct correct and effective data visualization isn't something you can accomplish overnight. It takes as much time to master this craft as it does any other, as well as a certain dedication to patience, practice, and keeping abreast of changes in software. In addition, like so many other things in data science, data visualization and storytelling tend to evolve over time, so an inherent need exists for continuous learning and adaptation, too. The lessons in this book will guide you as you begin your first adventures in data storytelling using data visualizations in Tableau.

From Visualization to Visual Data Storytelling: An Evolution

With all the current focus on data visualization as the best (and sometimes only) way to see and understand today's biggest and most diverse data, it's easy to think of the practice as a relatively new way of representing data and other statistical information. In reality, the practice of graphing information—and communicating visually—reaches back all the way to some of our earliest prehistoric cave drawings where we charted minutiae of early human life, through initial mapmaking, and into more modern advances in graphic design and statistical graphics. Along the way, the practice of data visualization has been aided by both advancements in visual design and cognitive science as well as technology and business intelligence, and these have given rise to the advancements that have led to our current state of data visualization.

In today's data-driven business environment, an emerging new approach to storytelling attempts to combine data with graphics and tell the world's stories through the power of information visualization. For as far back as we can trace the roots of data visualization, storytelling stretches further. Storytelling has been dubbed the world's oldest profession. Likewise, it is now and has always been an integral part of the human experience. There's even evidence of the cognitive effects of storytelling in our neurology. It's a central way that we learn, remember, and communicate information—which has important implications when the goal of a visualization or visual data story is to prepare business decision makers to leave a data presentation with a story in their head that helps them both remember your message *and* take action on it. We'll discuss the cognitive and anthropological effects of stories more in later chapters.

Graphing stories is the intersection of data visualization and storytelling. American author Kurt Vonnegut is quoted as having famously said, "There is no reason that the simple shapes of stories can't be fed into a computer—they have beautiful shapes." Likewise, we could restate this to say that data stories provide the shapes to communicate information in ways that facts and figures alone can't. Just as much as today's approach to data visualization has changed the way we see and understand our data, data storytelling has equally—if not more—been the catalyst that has radically changed the way we talk about our data.

Learning to present insights and deliver the results of analysis in visual form involves working with data, employing analytical approaches, choosing the most appropriate visualization techniques, applying visual design principles, and structuring a compelling data narrative. Also, although crafting an effective and compelling visual data story is, like traditional storytelling, a uniquely human experience, tools and software exist that can help. Referring back to Vonnegut's quote, stories have shapes. In visual data storytelling, we find the shape of the story through exploration of the data, conduct analysis to discover the sequence of the data points, and use annotations to layer knowledge to tell a story.

To visualize the data storytelling process, consider the graphic shown in Figure 1.3. This is the process we'll follow throughout this book. It's worthwhile to note that this process isn't always as straightforward or linear as it might initially appear. In reality, this process is, like all discovery processes, iterative. For example, as a result of analysis we might need to revisit data wrangling (for example, if we find that we are missing a required attribute that we need for our proposed model). Further, as we find insights we might need to revisit the analysis or adjust the data. Finally, as the story unfolds we might need to revisit previous steps to support claims we did not originally plan to make.

Figure 1.3 The storytelling process, visualized.

From Visual to Story: Bridging the Gap

Before we move into building skills and competencies in visual data storytelling, let's take a moment to pause and think about why we are doing this. We've danced around this already in previous conversations, and while we could make a convincing argument that mastering new tools and ways to interact with data is an inevitable result of the big data era, that would only be half of the reason. Data will continue to grow, technologies to adapt and innovate, and analytical approaches to chart new territory in how we work with and try to uncover meaning and value hidden within our data. The real value in becoming a data storyteller is to amass the ability to share—to communicate—about our data.

So far, I've put data visualization first and communication second, because that is the order you follow when you structure your visual analysis—you have to explore and build something before you can tell a story about it. However, we shouldn't underestimate the communication that happens before you ever touch your data. Communication skills are a prerequisite listed on every job description, but just how important are these skills in data analysis and visual data storytelling—and why?

In 2012, academic researchers with the AIS Special Interest Group on Decision Support, Knowledge, and Data Management Systems (SIG DSS) and Teradata University Network (TUN) formed the Business Intelligence Congress 3 to survey and assess the state of business intelligence and analytics. They surveyed more than 400 recruiters from technical companies, asking what skills and competencies they looked for in new analytic hires.

Their number one answer? Communication skills[3] (see Figure 1.4).

The BI Congress survey isn't the only piece of data to pinpoint the importance of communication skills in analysis. A second recent piece of research comes from data research and advisory firm Gartner.[4] It conducted a research study to determine why big data projects fail—specifically, what percentage of big data projects fail due to organizational problems, like communication, and what percentage fail due to technical problems, like programming or hardware? Only about 1% of companies responded that technical issues alone were the fail point of their data analytics problems. The other 99% of companies said that at least half of the reasons their data analytics projects failed were due to poor organizational skills, namely communication, and not technical skills.

3. Wixom, Barbara; Ariyachandra, Thilini; Douglas, David; Goul, Michael; Gupta, Babita; Iyer, Lakshmi; Kulkarni, Uday; Mooney, John G.; Phillips-Wren, Gloria; and Turetken, Ozgur (2014). "The Current State of Business Intelligence in Academia: The Arrival of Big Data," *Communications of the Association for Information Systems*: Vol. 34 , Article 1.

4. http://www.gartner.com/newsroom/id/2593815

How Important are Communication Skills?

According to a survey of recruiters, managers, and practitioners in analytics: very important.

SOURCE: The Current State of Business Intelligence in Academia: The Arrival of Big Data, 2014

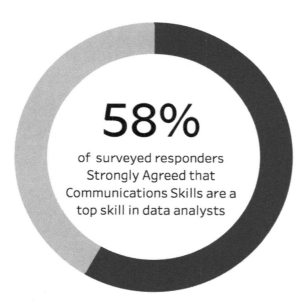

58%

of surveyed responders
Strongly Agreed that
Communications Skills are a
top skill in data analysts

Figure 1.4 According to the BIC3 Survey published in 2014, communication skills outrank technical skills for getting a business analysis job.

Of course, there isn't a perfect correlation between organizational skills and communication, but the reality is that one of the most important organizational skills *is* the ability to communicate—hence its inclusion in every business academic program and on every aforementioned job posting. Although communication skills might live on the softer side of things in terms of skillsets, it is nonetheless a skill that is critical for success, particularly when helping others to see the story within data. However, sharing a story isn't enough. Anyone can do that. If we can't communicate, we can't inspire change or action. Real communication is a two-way dialogue between a sender and a receiver, or receivers. It prompts an action, supports a decision, or generates understanding.

When we discuss the importance of communication skills within the context of data storytelling we are looking at it from an audience-first perspective. This means putting the audience's needs ahead of the storytellers. Successful communication hinges on the ability to influence the people who matter the most—the stakeholder to your analysis, be that an executive, a teacher, the general public, or anyone else. Ultimately, how data—visual or otherwise—is interpreted is fundamentally influenced by context. Context is a multifaceted thing. It is driven in part by your audience, but just as important to your story is the part of the context driven by you—your assumptions, your goals, and what you already know.

Understanding the importance of context is the focus of Chapter 4. For now, to answer the question I posed earlier—how important are communication skills in visual data storytelling?—they are paramount.

A NOTE ABOUT "DESSERT CHARTS"

After more than 200 years of use (the first being credited to William Playfair's *Statistical Breviary* of 1801) what have come to be called "dessert charts"—those circular visualizations including pie and donut charts that "slice" data into wedges reminiscent of our favorite sweets—have had a bit of a fall from grace. Although still widely in use, many visualization experts and educators preach against the use of these types of charts, myself included. However, it should be noted that hatred of pie charts is not merely an opinion, and there is empirical research that provides the basis for why these types of charts just don't work analytically. That said, there are ways to use them productively—particular as mechanisms for data storytelling—if a few words of caution are followed. We'll take a deeper look at how to best curate "dessert charts" for visual data storytelling in Chapter 7, "Preparing Data for Storytelling."

DATA SCIENCE EDUCATION GETS ON THE MAP

By now we are all in agreement: The business of data is changing. Business users are more empowered to work with data; IT is shifting its focus to be less about control and more about enablement. New data science job descriptions—like data scientist and visual data artist—are springing up as companies look for the right people with the right skill sets to squeeze more value from their data. Data itself is getting bigger, hardware more economical, and analytical software more "self-service." We've embraced the paradigm shift from traditional BI to iterative data discovery. We're depending on data visualization and data storytelling to see, understand, and share data in ways like never before. It's the visual imperative in action.

As you might expect, these changes have a significant effect on how people work in data science, be they executives, data scientists, researchers, analysts, or even data storytellers. There are a lot of skills available and a very big toolbox to choose tools from, and we are all learning together. Adding to that, over the past few years we've been reminded that data workers are in high demand, and we've seen firsthand how limited the current supply is. There's the familiar U.S. Bureau of Labor Statistics estimate that expects 1.4 million computer science jobs by 2020. Another familiar statistic from the McKinsey Global Institute estimates that there will be 140,000 to 180,000 unfilled data scientist positions in the market in 2018. That's a lot of empty seats to fill. So, we are faced with two challenges: 1) we need more capable data people and 2) we need them with deeper, more dynamic skillsets. This means we have to start thinking about cultivating talent—rather than recruiting it—and training an incoming workforce isn't something that an industry can do alone, no matter how many specialized software training programs, MOOCs, conferences, and excellent publications we produce. To enact lasting change and a sustainable funnel of competent data workers suited to the new era of the data industry, we need to move further down the pipeline to that place where we all discovered we wanted to be data people in the first place: the classroom.

That's exactly what we're doing. The academic community has been tasked with developing new educational programs that can develop the skills and education needed by new data science professionals. These university information science programs—called business analytics, data science, professional business science, or the dozen or so terms used by academia—are only just beginning to be sorted out. However, they are growing exponentially across the country, and so far enrollment is promising.

Different universities are taking different approaches to structuring a new kind of data science education. Some are developing entirely new pedagogy focused on the fluid and dynamic fields of data science. Others are reshaping existing curricula by unifying across academic silos to integrate disciplines of study, particularly among business and IT domains. Others are forming academic alliance programs to give students learning experiences with contemporary industry tools and creating projects that expose students to analytical problems within real-world business context.

Nevertheless, all universities are listening to campus recruiters, who are clearly saying that we need people with more data skills and knowledge, and they're working hard to fill that gap. More importantly, there are a few things that these programs have in common. They're focused on real-world applications of data problems. They're doing their best to keep pace with fluid changes in technology adoption, new programming languages, and on-the-market software packages. They're also putting a premium on data visualization and data storytelling. Vendors like Tableau with its Tableau for Teaching program are helping, too.

So just how big is data science education? Over the past couple of years, the number of new business analytics program offerings has significantly increased. In 2010 there were a total of 131 confirmed, full-time BI/BA university degree programs, including 47 undergraduate-level programs. Today, that number has nearly tripled and continues to rise with new and improved programs at the undergraduate, graduate, and certificate levels—both on and off campus—springing up at accredited institutions across the country (see Figure 1.5). So, while we might not have access to all this new data talent yet, if academia has anything to say about it, help is on the way.

note

This dataset is regularly updated and maintained by Ryan Swanstrom, and is available via Github at https://github.com/ryanswanstrom/awesome-datascience-colleges.

Figure 1.5 Business analytics degree programs in the United States.

Summary

This chapter focused on providing an introductory discussion on data visualization and visual data storytelling by taking a look at how these concepts are similar and different, and how both have been transformed in the digital era. The next chapter takes a closer look at the power of visual data stories to help us understand what makes them so powerful and important in today's data deluge.

CHAPTER 2

THE POWER OF VISUAL DATA STORIES

This chapter uses quintessential and real-life examples from the visual storytelling canon to display the powerful ability of data stories to communicate discoveries and insights hidden in data. We will ground these lessons by taking time to understand what makes data visualization and stories so influential to the human brain from both a cognitive and an anthropological perspective.

The Science of Storytelling

The world of data is changing. So is how we tell stories about it.

In a September 2016 interview with NPR Marketplace,[1] *National Geographic* editor-in-chief Susan Goldberg spoke to host Kai Ryssdal about the power of visual storytelling, which has provided a transformative conduit for the publication in the new digital era. Speaking to *National Geographic*'s conversion from traditional print magazine to social media heavyweight, Goldberg commented that "everything is visual today"—especially stories. It's worth noting that *National Geographic* is dominating visual storytelling online, using powerful imagery to captivate and educate 19 million Snapchat users, 60 million Instagram followers, and 50 million Facebook followers. The magazine is also throwing its hat in the ring with data visualization with its Data Points blog.

Media and journalists are not the only ones putting emphasis on data storytelling, although they arguably have been a particularly imaginative bunch of communicators. Today we've seen the power of storytelling used to color in conversations on just about every type of data imaginable—from challenging astronomical principles, to visualizing the tenure pipeline at Harvard Business School, to quantifying the fairytale of Little Red Riding Hood. In every organization and every industry, data stories are becoming the next script for how we share information.

For as diverse as data stories can be, they all have one thing in common: They give us something to connect to in a very literal sense. Let's delve into the power of stories, first by looking behind the curtain at the science of storytelling and then looking at some incredible data stories over time to see how they have capitalized on the secret sauce of storytelling.

The Brain on Stories

In Chapter 1 I mentioned that evidence exists of the cognitive effects of storytelling embedded within our neurology. Here's how: When we are presented with data, only two parts of our brain respond. These are Wernicke's area—responsible for language comprehension—and Broca's area—responsible, again, for language processing. For the very powerful human brain, data is easy. The brain's response to these stimuli is a relatively simple input-and-respond transaction that requires the utilization of these two basic areas. Because we're focused only on seeing and responding to information (agree/disagree), there's no great need to overexert our neuro-horsepower.

Unlike simple data, stories require a substantial cognitive boost. Here's an easy thought exercise. Imagine that tonight we have pasta on the menu. However, our pantry is empty, so

---

1. www.marketplace.org/2016/09/26/sustainability/corner-office-marketplace/dont-call-national-geographic-stodgy

to prepare this meal we need to go to the market. Let's make a quick mental list of our ingredients: pasta, some tomato sauce, perhaps some herbs, garlic, and Parmesan cheese—if we're feeling fancy we can grab a loaf of garlic bread, too. Now, let's pretend we get to the market, only to discover it's closed. So, instead of cooking we decide instead to go to our favorite Italian restaurant (it's okay if yours is Olive Garden—mine is, too) and order something from the menu. Suddenly the image changes: We're no longer looking at a bunch of individual items on a grocery list; we're imagining a waiter setting down a big, beautiful dish of flavorful and delicious spaghetti in front of us. Perhaps we also hear the buzzing backdrop of restaurant sounds—water glasses, clinking silverware, and so on. If we think about it long enough—or if we're hungry enough—we can almost *taste* the food.

This is the difference between visualizing data, and presenting a story: rather than itemizing a list of ingredients (data points) we are presenting a full, sensory-engaging dining experience (see Figure 2.1).

Visualizing   Presenting

Figure 2.1 Visualizing versus presenting.

You can think of this storytelling experience in a more traditional way, too, by considering the difference in reading a novel and watching a film. When reading, you are tasked with using your imagination—you're reading the raw data of words and building the story in your own mind. Conversely, when watching a film, your imagination is off the hook. Images of characters and settings, costumes, spoken dialogue, music, and so on are displayed for you on the screen. When you watch a live presentation, like a play or a 4D movie, you also get a few extra pieces of sensory information, like the smell of a smoke machine or carefully chosen scents to accompany the story pumping through the air.

These extra storytelling details have a profound effect on the brain (see Figure 2.2). Beyond the two areas of the brain that activate when presented with data, when presented with a story, five additional areas respond. These are

- The visual cortex (colors and shapes)
- The olfactory cortex (scents)
- The auditory cortex (sounds)
- The motor cortex (movement)
- The sensory cortex/cerebellum (language comprehension)

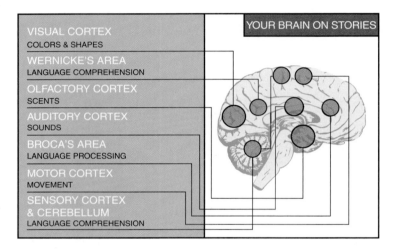

Figure 2.2 The brain on stories.

The Human on Stories

Beyond the sciences, there's also a lot of truth to the old saying "everyone loves a good story."

Storytelling has been an integral part of human expression and culture throughout time. All human cultures tell stories, and most people derive a great deal of pleasure from them—even if they are untrue (think of fantastical stories or fables). Beyond entertainment, stories teach us important lessons; we learn from them. In many cases they are how we transmit information—whether through metaphoric tales, instructions, or legends. Stories also have the ability to transport us; we give the author license to stretch the truth—although, in data storytelling, this license extends only as far as it can before the data loses its elasticity and begins to break down. Data stories, above all, must be true. They are works of narration, but of the non-fiction variety.

Okay, so we love stories—but why? There's no easy answer to this question, and frankly from academe to industry, the research is crowded with books and articles attempting to explain the cognitive basis of all storytelling and literature under the heading of storytelling psychology. That said, we can distill all of these dialogues into two primary possible contenders for *why* we tell stories: the need to survive (fitness) and the need to know (closure).

Fitness

As much as we might try to argue it, human beings did not evolve to find truth. We evolved to defend positions and obtain resources—oftentimes regardless of the cost—to survive. These concepts are at the heart of Darwinian theory of natural selection: survival of the fittest as the mechanism, and our ability to overcome (or, biologically, to reproduce), fitness.

Human biology aside to survive in competitive and often unstable environments—whether wilderness or business—one thing we've always had to do is understand other people. In fact, one of our most expensive cognitive tasks where we exert an impressive amount of energy is in trying to figure out other people: predict what they're going to do, understand motivations, assess relationships, and so forth. Beyond people, we are also driven to understand how things work. If we know how they work, we can conquer, fix, or control. All of these lead to winning, which equates to survival and continuation. Stories act as guides to give us the information and confidence we need to harness this knowledge. They increase our fitness.

Closure

Aside from being bent on survival, humans also tend to require closure. The few philosophical exceptions notwithstanding, in general we don't enjoy ongoing questions and curiosities with no resolution—we *need* endings, even unhappy ones. We simply can't abide cliffhangers; they're sticky in the worst of ways, bouncing around in our brains until we can finally "finish" them and put them to rest. There's actually a term for this phenomenon called the *Zeigarnik effect*. It was named for Soviet psychologist Bluma Zeigarnik who demonstrated that people have a better memory for unfinished tasks that they do for finished ones. Today, the Zeigarnik effect is known formally as a "psychological device that creates dissonance and uneasiness in the target audience."

In essence, the Zeigarnik effect speaks to our human need for endings. No matter the story's goal—to focus, align, teach, or inspire—we build narratives to foster imagination, excitement, even speculation. Successful narratives are those that are able to grab the audience's attention, work through a message, and then resolve our anxiety with a satisfactory ending. Thus, stories are therapeutic—they give us closure.

The Power of Stories

We've established that data stories are powerful, and that they are powerful because of their ability to communicate information, generate understanding and knowledge, and stick in our brains. However, as information assets, visual data stories have a few other noteworthy qualities.

But first, let's set the record straight. There is much to be said about how visual data stories creating meaning in a time of digital data deluge, but it would be careless to relegate data storytelling to the role of "a fun new way to talk about data." In fact, it has *radically changed* the way we talk about data (though certainly not invented the concept). The traditional charts and graphs we've always used to represent data are still helpful because they help us to better visually organize and understand information. They've just become a little static. With today's technology, fueled by today's innovation, we've moved beyond the mentality of gathering, analyzing, and reporting data to collecting, exploring, and sharing information—rather than simply rendering data visually we are focused on using these mechanisms to engage, communicate, inspire, and make data memorable. No longer resigned to the tasks of beautifying reports or dashboards, data visualizations are lifting out of paper, coming out of the screen, and moving into our hearts, minds, and emotions. The ability to stir emotion is the secret ingredient of visual data storytelling, and what sets it apart from the aforementioned static visual data renderings.

As we'll explore in later chapters, emotional appeal isn't enough to complete a meaningful visual data story. Like any good tale, a data story requires an anchor, or a goal—be it a reveal, a call to action, or an underlying message—to pass to its audience. This idea isn't unique to data storytelling by any means, but a construct applied to all varieties of stories. When a story imprints on our memory, it requires emotion plus a willingness to act on that emotion.

Instead of talking about the power of visual data stories, let's see them in action. As we do, we'll be looking for the following key takeaways:

- Sometimes the only way to see the story in data is visually.
- A good story should meet its goals—and it should be actionable.
- A story should change, challenge, or confirm the way you think.
- Storytelling evolves—don't be afraid to try something new.

The Classic Visualization Example

One of the core tenants of a visual data story is that it uses different forms of data visualization—charts, graphs, infographics, and so on—to bring data to life. Perhaps one of the most archetypal examples of the power of data visualization to help people see and understand data in ways they never would by looking at rows and columns of raw black and white data comes from Anscombe's Quartet (see Figure 2.3). Constructed in 1973 by statistician Francis Anscombe, these four datasets appear identical when compared by their summary statistics. If you review the table, you will notice that each dataset has the same mean of both X and Y, the same standard deviation, the same correlation, and the same linear regression equation.

	I		II		III		IV	
	X	Y	X	Y	X	Y	X	Y
	10	8.04	10	9.14	10	7.46	8	6.58
	8	6.95	8	8.14	8	6.77	8	5.76
	13	7.58	13	8.74	13	12.74	8	7.71
	9	8.81	9	8.77	9	7.11	8	8.84
	11	8.33	11	9.26	11	7.81	8	8.47
	14	9.96	14	8.1	14	8.84	8	7.04
	6	7.24	6	6.13	6	6.08	8	5.25
	4	4.26	4	3.1	4	5.38	10	12.5
	12	10.84	12	9.13	12	8.15	8	5.56
	7	4.82	7	7.26	7	6.42	8	7.91
	5	5.68	5	4.74	5	5.73	8	6.88
MEAN	9.00	7.5	9.00	7.5	9.00	7.5	9.00	7.5
STD	3.32	2.03	3.32	2.03	3.32	2.03	3.32	2.03
CORR	0.82		0.82		0.82		0.82	
LIN REG	$y = 3.00 + 0.500x$		$y = 3.00 + 0.500x$		$y = 3.00 + 0.500x$		$y = 3.00 + 0.500x$	

Figure 2.3 Four seemingly identical datasets known as Anscombe's Quartet.

Even though the individual variables are different, if the statistical outputs are the same, we would expect these, when graphed, to *look* the same. The "story" for each of these datasets should be the same—right? Wrong.

When graphed (see Figure 2.4), we can see beyond the limitations of basic statistical properties for describing data, and can tell a bigger picture of the datasets and the relationships therein.

Anscombe's example might be classic in terms of putting some support behind visual horsepower, but it only brushes the tip of the iceberg in terms of visual data storytelling. Although we might not yet have everything we need to tell a story, we can start to see that the sets are not so similar as they might appear, and there is *something* worth talking about in these datasets. We know there is a story there, and we know we need to visualize it to see it, but we are still left wanting. This isn't quite a visual data story, but it's definitely a first step.

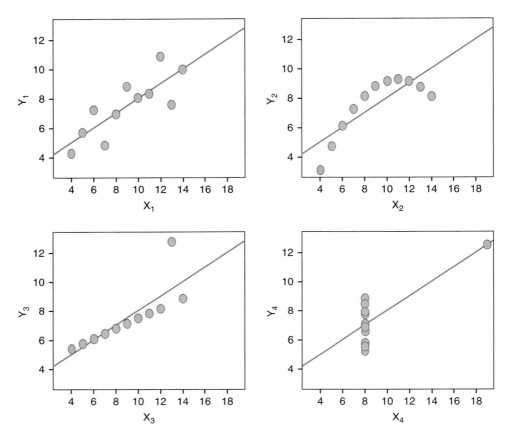

Figure 2.4 Anscombe's Quartet, visualized.

Story Takeaway

Sometimes the only way to see the story in data is visually.

Using Small Personal Data for Big Stories

When it comes to telling a story, no one knows how to do it better than Hollywood—except maybe networks like Netflix and AMC that are using massive amounts of consumer-generated data as recipes to create new content.

Graphic designer Chelsea Carlson decided to take this approach to a personal level. In a 2016 experiment, Chelsea focused on analyzing her personal Netflix viewing habits to see what story her own data might tell about her television binging habits, tastes and preferences, and—perhaps more important in a streaming TV market saturated with more new shows every day—possibly even help her predict a new favorite by telling her exactly what to look for (this, by the way, is not too unlike how Netflix is using its user viewing data to curate new shows).

Like many analysts, Chelsea began her experiment by collecting and organizing her Netflix viewing data in spreadsheets organized in Microsoft Excel. She tracked several variables on her top 27 favorite shows, including things like genre, language, main character gender, episode length, IMDB rating, and more (see Figure 2.5). As a tool, a color-coded spreadsheet helped Chelsea get a bird's eye view of some of the interesting patterns and trends in her data (like whether she seemed to prefer multi-season shows or if her favor aligned with award winners) as well as areas where her tastes were less predictable (no preference for age and race of the lead character or the show's setting or length). However, this was the extent of meaningful analysis that Chelsea could achieve when limited to scouring rows and columns of information—even colored ones (see the upcoming sidebar "Color Cues").

Like Anscombe's Quartet, when Chelsea plotted her data it transformed beyond its meager Excel boundaries and moved into the realm of visual storytelling, this time showing a much richer tale (see Figure 2.6).

ow name	time period	main character	character length	costume drama	# of seasons	years on the	IMDB us	IMDB # of users	golden	show creator
d Men	mid 20th	man	45	yes	7	2007-2015	8.7	131,187	4	Mathew Weiner
lvet	mid 20th	ensemble	60	yes	4+	2013-	7.9	879	0	Ramón Campos, Gema R. ...
andal	present	woman	45	yes	5+	2012-	7.9	45,209	0	Shonda Rhimes
REAL	present	woman	45	no	2+	2015-	7.8	3,732	0	Marti Noxon, Sarah Gert...
e Office	present	ensemble	20	no	9	2005-2013	8.8	179,606	1	Greg Daniels, Ricky Gerv...
rks & Recreation	present	woman	20	no	7	2009-2015	8.6	103,152	1	Greg Daniels, Michael Sc...
wnton Abbey	early 20th	ensemble	60	yes	6	2010-2015	8.7	98,003	3	Julian Fellowes
erlock	present	man	45	no	4+	2010-	9.3	430,133	0	Mark Gatiss, Steven Moff...
pire	present	ensemble	45	yes	2+	2015-	8	20,544	0	Lee Daniels, Danny Stro...
efly	future (2517)	man	45	yes	1	2002-2003	9.1	171,351	1	Joss Whedon
ested Development	present	man	20	no	5	2003-2013	9	195,532	0	Mitchell Hurwitz
tes Motel	retro present	woman	45	yes	3+	2013-	8.1	49,820	0	Anthony Cipriano, Carlto...
eaks & Geeks	1980s	woman	45	no	1	1999-2000	8.9	82,813	1	Paul Feig
ilight Zone	assorted	ensemble	20	no	5	1959-1964	9	39,253	1	Rod Serling
ad City	present	woman	20	no	3+	2014-	8.5	10,154	0	Ilana Glazer, Abbi Jacob...
shing Daisies	retro present	couple	45	yes	2	2007-2009	8.4	42,479	0	Bryan Fuller
-So-Called Life	present	woman	45	no	1	1994-1995	8.4	14,541	1	Winnie Holzman
ange Is the New Black	present	women ensemb...	45	no	4	2013-	8.4	159,370	1	Jenji Kohan
erican Horror Story	assorted	ensemble	45	yes	5	2011-	8.3	173,899	1	Brad Falchuk, Ryan Murp...
ad Like Me	present	woman	45	no	2	2003-2004	8.2	33,669	0	Bryan Fuller
e Riches	present	couple	45	no	1.5	2007-2008	8	7,004	0	Dmitry Lipkin
e Tudors	17th century	man	45	yes	4	2007-2010	8.1	47,512	0	Michael Hirst
ffy the Vampire Slayer	present	woman	45	no	7	1997-2003	8.2	96,018	0	Joss Whedon
llhouse	present	woman	45	no	2	2009-2010	7.8	38,314	0	Joss Whedon
oject Runway	present	ensemble	45	yes	14+	2004-	7.3	7,881	2	n/a
e Grand Hotel	early 20th	ensemble	60	yes	3	2011-2013	8.5	2,079	0	n/a

Figure 2.5 Chelsea Carson's Netflix data spreadsheet, in table form.

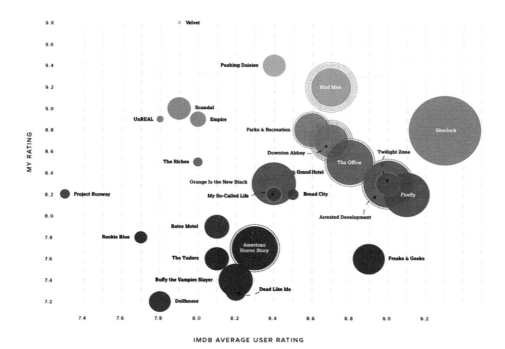

Figure 2.6 Chelsea Carlson's Netflix data visualized.

note

See more of Chelsea's Netflix data story at https://www.umbel.com/blog/data-visualization/netflix-chill-little-data-experiment-understanding-my-own-taste-tv/.

As a visual storyteller, Chelsea worked through visual discovery and a variety of graph types that included scatter plots, packed bubble charts, timelines, and even pie charts to build her data story. She also integrated expressive visual elements—particularly size and color—to provide visual cues to assign meaning to the visualization and highlight certain insights. As a result, Chelsea was able to come away with a rich visual data story encapsulated within a series of very deliberately crafted visualizations. There are several interesting story points to pick out within this visualization—including a strong bias for costume dramas and shows cut short—and you can explore them for yourself in the URL included. However, perhaps the most salient point is that through this story Chelsea can take action on the goals she set for this visual story. She can clearly see her tastes and preferences, and when she goes scrolling through Netflix for her next binge-worthy show, she'll know to look for a female-led costume drama with a genre-bending storyline.

Story Takeaway

A good story should meet its goals—and it should be actionable.

COLOR CUES

The Netflix experiment brings to mind an important learning point in the power of data visualization. One of the most important lessons in learning how to build data visualization is learning how to leverage what are referred to as pre-attentive features—a limited set of visual properties that are detected very rapidly (around 200 to 250 milliseconds) and accurately by our visual system, and are not constrained by display size. A good visualization—the building blocks of a visual data story—reduces time to insight and leverages our brain's pre-attentive features to shave time as low as possible.

Let's take a look at the pre-attentive feature known as *perceptual pop-out*. *Perceptual pop-out* is the use of color as a beacon to pre-attentively detect items of importance within visualization. The shape, size, or color of the item here is less important than its ability to "pop out" of a display. Further, these should be used sparingly, and with intention. Too many of these features at once negates their impact, or—worse—can have a detrimental effect on your visual.

Consider a visit to the eye doctor, when your vision is tested by the ability to spot a flash of color in a sea of darkness, or take a look at Figure 2.7.

	2013	2014	2015	2016
Target	22.27B	21.44B	21.34B	21.79B
Disney	9.45B	22.39B	24.1B	25.64B
Starbucks	8.51B	9.59B	11.38B	12.8B

Figure 2.7 A table showing companies with respective annual gross profits, 2013–2016.
*All data gathered from www.amigobulls.com

This is a simple table with only three companies, but suppose I asked you to tell me, in each year, which company had the highest gross profit? You are tasked with analyzing each box of the table, line by line, to assess each year independently and select the highest number. You might even have to write it down or mark it in some way to help you remember the winner. Go ahead and give it a try. It should take you roughly one minute to complete the exercise.

Now, take a look at Figure 2.8 and try again.

	2013	2014	2015	2016
Target				
Disney				
Starbucks				

Figure 2.8 A table showing companies with respective annual gross profits, replaced by color, 2013–2016.

This time, we've replaced the numerical data with a visual cue. Rather than reading the table, perceptual pop-out makes completing this exercise near instant. We don't have to actually "look" for answers; we simply "see" them instead.

Because the sample we are looking at is so small, this is a good time to remark on the special partnership between color and counting. Essentially, the fewer things there are to count, the quicker we can count them—which makes sense. If I asked you which company outperformed the others, Disney would be an easy response as it has three out of four of the orange squares.

Our ability to "count" visually is called *numerosity*. It is a numerical intuition pattern that allows us to see an amount without actually counting it, and it varies among individuals although the typical counting amount ranges between two and ten items.

As you build visualizations as part of your storyboard framework, be sure to pay careful attention to color and counting to help your audience easily and intuitively experience your story.

The Two-or-Four Season Debate

In school, we're taught that a full year includes four distinct seasons—spring, summer, fall, and winter. Yet, some people argue that only two true seasons exist—summer and winter—and they're using a form of visual data storytelling (and a good heaping of rationality) to prove their point. My favorite of these comes from artificial intelligence researcher Nate Soares' blog, Minding Our Way.[2]

The item up for debate in this story is a simple one: Is it fair to qualify "waxing summer" (also known as spring) and "waning summer"" (also known as autumn) as full seasons? Sure, it's *familiar* and if you live in the northern hemisphere you can likely distinguish the seasons according to their observable natural phenomena—such as their colorful transitions—flowers

---

2. http://mindingourway.com/there-are-only-two-seasons/

blooming or leaves changing color—rather than their actual astronomical dates (and this doesn't even begin to open the conversation on astronomical versus meteorological dates of change[3]).

Let's begin to build a story around this and see where we end up. First let's agree on a foundation: The year follows a seasonal cycle that starts cold and gets progressively warmer until it peaks and begins to cool again. Repeat. Right? This is a pretty basic assumption. More importantly, it's one that we can successfully chart—loosely and without requiring any more specific data or numbers at all. Rather, we'll use points from the basic story premise we laid out earlier to graph a seasonal continuum for the year, using length of daylight as our curve (see Figure 2.9). From there, we can try to decide just how many seasons are really in a year.

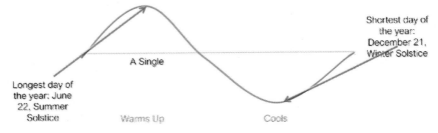

Figure 2.9 The seasonal cycle of a single year.

How many curves does the orange line trace? The answer, obviously, is two—hence the two-season viewpoint (see Figure 2.10).

Figure 2.10 Two seasons.

---

3. https://www.ncdc.noaa.gov/news/meteorological-versus-astronomical-seasons

Now, we could break this down further with more information. We could add in astronomical dates or mull over geographic differences in weather or meteorology. However, whether or not you agree with Nate and me (and others!) on the number of qualifying seasons that occur over the course of one year, the preceding two graphs represent a powerful data story—and they don't even require the type of "hard data" (rows and columns of numbers) that we would typically expect. This shows us—quite literally—that to tell a great story doesn't necessarily require a ton of data. It just requires a few points, a goal, and the creativity to visualize it for your audience in a way that affects their opinion.

Story Takeaway

A story should change, challenge, or confirm the way you think.

Napoleon's March

As I've mentioned, using visualizations to tell stories about data is not a new technique. French civil engineer Charles Joseph Minard has been credited for several significant contributions in the field of information graphics, among them his very unique visualizations of two military campaigns—Hannibal's march from Spain to Italy some 2,200 years ago and Napoleon's invasion of Russia in 1812. Both of these visualizations were published in 1869 when Minard was a spry 88 years old.

Minard's flow map of Napoleon's invasion of Russia (see Figure 2.11)—unofficially titled "Napoleon's March by Minard"—tells the story of Napoleon's army, particularly its size (by headcount) as it made its way from France to Russia and home again. As you read this visualization, moving left to right, the beige ribbon thins, signaling the waning of Napoleon's army from 422,000 to 100,000 as they marched east, during the winter, to Moscow. The army turned around and retreated, returning to France with a mere 10,000 men. We can move through the visualization, imagining the soldiers' journey and peril as they hiked through increasingly inhospitable and unfamiliar territory, turning around and coming home, losing more than 400,000 comrades on the way to war, cold, and disease.

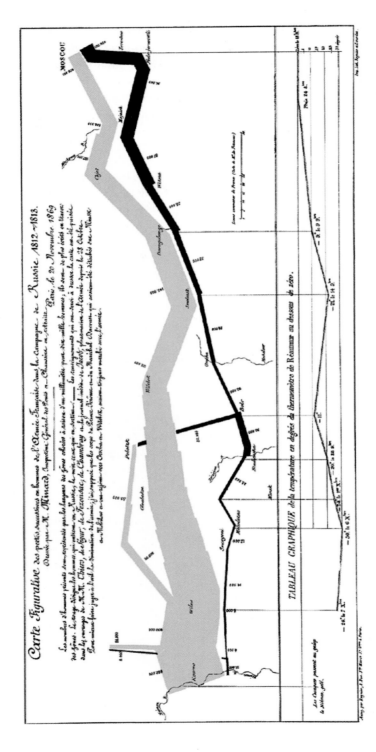

Figure 2.11 Napoleon's 1812 March by Minard, 1869.

Obviously, this was not a successful war, and as an analysis piece Minard's map is not a successful one analytically. However, as a visual story around human drama, it has earned the distinction of becoming known as one of the best storytelling examples in history. You would be hard pressed to take a data visualization class today and not experience Napoleon's march. It's fair to note, too, that several analysts have tried to recreate it, using more common statistical methods but all fall short of the original's storytelling appeal.

Minard's second military visualization, Hannibal's journey through the Alps (not pictured), is similar in concept to Napoleon's march, although it didn't quite pull off the same memorable story. Most stories have an inherent amount of entropy—we need to tell them quickly and succinctly, and many times this means we only get one chance. In fact, numerous examples of this "once and done" effect exist in more modern visual data stories, too. These one-hit wonders are an expected consequence of good stories. Sometimes we only need to tell them once—no sequels necessary.

> ## Story Takeaway
> Stories have an inherent amount of entropy, and some we tell only once.

Stories Outside of the Box

Thus far we've looked at some of the most classic examples of visual data stories to those more modern. We've even looked at visual data storytelling without data in the classic sense. Now, let's finish our tour of the power of visual data storytelling with one of the most quintessential instances on the books: Nigel Holmes' "Monstrous Costs" (see Figure 2.12).

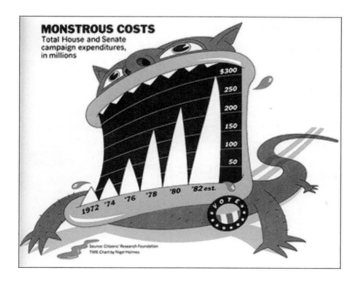

Figure 2.12 Nigel Holmes' Monstrous Costs.

This hand-drawn illustration does exactly what a visual data story is supposed to do: It transforms boring data into something alive. At its core, this data visualization is little more than a bar chart that shows rising costs on political campaign expenditures, but it's the storytelling detail that gives it the flair that has made it such a powerful example. It weaves a story around the data, anthropomorphizing these costs from dollars and cents to a ravenous beast, replete with jagged teeth and flying spittle. As with the Napoleon's March by Minard graph, we'll take a much closer and more critical look at this story in a later chapter, but for now the lesson is simply that visual stories come in all shapes and sizes, some more technical looking and some so unique and personalized that they are barely recognizable as visualizations.

What masterful storytellers can do is to straddle that balance, and capitalize on the best features to tell their story. In Monstrous Costs, these features allow the image to hook into memory, clearly telling the story of rising campaign costs with the intended emotion of the storyteller.

> ## Story Takeaway
> Don't be afraid to try something new.

Summary

In this chapter we discussed what makes stories so impactful on the human brain. We then looked at a few real-life examples of visual data storytelling in action. We could analyze many more examples for this purpose, and more are available online at the website companion to this book, www.visualdatastorytelling.com.

Now, let's get ready to put this information to work in Tableau. In the next chapter we'll begin exploring the Tableau ecosystem, and take a journey through its freshly redesigned user interface. This will form the basis for later hands-on practice in exploring and analyzing data visually as we work toward building complete visual data stories.

CHAPTER 3

GETTING STARTED WITH TABLEAU

The goal of this chapter is to help you get your footing with the Tableau product ecosystem and use the basic Tableau interface so that you are familiar enough with the tool to begin working hands-on with data. This chapter covers how to get started with Tableau, reviews the tool's basic functionality, discusses how to connect to data, and provides an overview of data types in Tableau. From here, you will be able to move on to the visual analysis process, curating visuals, and building stories. The version of Tableau available at the time of this writing is Tableau 10, and this chapter illustrates using the Mac version of the software (little to no difference exists between Mac and Windows versions, although some aesthetic differences might be apparent).

If you are already an intermediate Tableau user and familiar with the v10 interface and Tableau terminology, you might want to skip this chapter and move on to Chapter 4, "Importance of Context in Storytelling."

Using Tableau

Standing out against many other data visualization tools on the market, Tableau is an industry-leading, best-of-breed tool that delivers an approachable, intuitive environment for self-service users of all levels to help them prepare, analyze, and visualize their data. The software also provides delivery channels for the fruits of its user's visual analysis, including dashboards and native storytelling functionality, called "story points" in Tableau.

Tableau's stated mission is to help everyone "see and understand" their data, and to facilitate this the company offers a suite of software products, including a recently released free mobile app called Vizable, designed to suit the needs of a diverse group of clients from enterprise-level organizations to academic users and visualization hobbyists who want to visualize data in a mobile-first format. All the Tableau products excel at displaying data visually, using a drag-and-drop canvas on top of embedded analytics to help users explore their data. Tableau Desktop can connect to a wide variety of data, stored in a variety of places—from local spreadsheets, to multidimensional databases, and even some cloud database sources, like Google Analytics, Amazon Redshift, or Salesforce—and the number of connections is always increasing.[1] Although Tableau can mimic Excel by providing the capability to analyze rows and columns of numbers, its focus is on interactive, visual data exploration through its analytic capabilities as well as dashboarding and storytelling features, no programming required. For more advanced users, Tableau supports a complete formula language and robust data connections: Tableau's live query engine allows users to connect to more than forty different data sources; its in-memory data engine leverages the complete memory hierarchy from disk to L1 cache and shifts the curve between big data and fast analysis.

Why Tableau?

In his book, *Communicating Data with Tableau*, author Ben Jones included a personal note to his readers on why he chooses Tableau. I thought I might do something similar.

My reference for Tableau is part personal preference and part professional opinion. When I was an analyst in the data science community, I had the opportunity to work hands-on with many of the leading data visualization technologies on the market and get to know the vendors in the space. Being fluent on the tools available, their capabilities and limitations, and the viability of

---

1. http://onlinehelp.tableau.com/current/pro/desktop/en-us/basicconnectoverview.html

their provider was a required part of my job as clients, and the industry-at-large looks to trusted voices to help them navigate a sea of options. Many impressive data visualization and storytelling tools are available, but Tableau was—at least in my opinion—always at least one step ahead of the pack with its intuitive user interface, dynamic and ever-expanding off-the-shelf capabilities, and dedication to building and supporting an engaged community of visual analysts from the workplace to the classroom and everyone in between.

Today, much like Google has outgrown its noun-based role of search engine and data collection superpower and become a common use verb that encompasses all Internet searching, Tableau has expanded beyond the boundaries of a software package and become a required job skill—and one that is top of the list for employers. We searched Labor Insight, an analytics software company powered by the largest and most sophisticated database of labor market data (Burning Glass), to analyze data visualization–related IT job descriptions posted between the period of March 2017–February 2018 across the nation, and can you guess what popped up as the second most in demand skill of applicants—right behind data visualization and SQL itself? If you guessed Tableau, you are right (see Figure 3.1). The message that this look into the job market is sending is clear: If you're looking for a job as an analyst—which by the way is the number one job in this sector of IT—then employers expect you to have a working knowledge of Tableau.

Data Visualization Top Specialized Skills

Of ~31k visualization related jobs posted between March 2017 and February 2018, ~13k listed Tableau as a desired specialized skill. Above Excel (~11k) and SAS (~7k) it is the only software listed in the top specialized skill set.
Source: Labor Insight (Burning Glass Technologies)

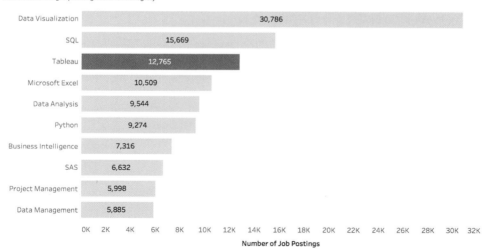

Figure 3.1 Out of a total 30,786 jobs that listed "data visualization" as a skill, roughly 13k (42%) listed Tableau as a critical specialized skill for applicants.

TABLEAU IN DEMAND

From my analysis of Labor Insight, approximately 30,786 jobs listed "Data Visualization" as a desirable skill—an increase of about 17.6% from the preceding annual period. Among the top job titles were Data Analyst (7%), Business Analyst (3%), and Data Scientist (3%). Interestingly, only 3.4% (1,050) of these jobs actually listed "Data Visualization" as the job title itself.

In addition to "Data Visualization," other high-ranking skills included SQL (50%) and Tableau (44%). Excel, Python, SAS, R, and Java also received mention. When pitted against the intersection of other required baseline "soft" skills, those listed were communication (47%), research (37%), writing (32%), teamwork (31%), problem solving (30%), and mathematics (28%). As a testament to visual data storytelling, data visualization and communication were the top skills in either category.

If you're wondering where these jobs are located, adjusted by population, "above average" job postings were found in the combined metropolitan areas of New York/New Jersey (13.7%), followed by Washington DC (8.45%), San Francisco (6.1%), Chicago (5.11%), Boston (5%), Santa Clara (4%), and Seattle (3.83%, and home to Tableau headquarters).

The Tableau Product Portfolio

Although Tableau Desktop is Tableau's cornerstone data visualization software product, and is the focus of the work in this book, Tableau also offers several other software products that incorporate essentially the same user interface and VizQL engine that makes it such a powerful tool. The primary differences between these core products is the different types of data sources users can connect to, how visualizations can be shared with others, and, in some cases, primary form factor intended for use.

note

VizQL is Tableau's proprietary analysis technology You can read more on VizQL at https://www.tableau.com/products/technology.

Tableau Server

As you might expect, Tableau Server is best suited for enterprise-wide deployments. It is intended to provide entire organizations with the ability to connect to any data source—on-premise or in the cloud—with centrally managed governance and granular security protocols to maintain balance between user flexibility and IT control. This product is used in conjunction with Tableau Desktop.

Tableau Desktop

Tableau's flagship product, Tableau Desktop is an application that can be used on either Windows or Mac machines. It allows connection to data on-premise or in the cloud, and facilitates the entire visual discovery and analytics process from connecting to data to sharing visualizations, dashboards, or interactive stories using Tableau Server or Tableau Online. The software also includes a device designer to help users design and publish dashboards optimized for various form factors.

Tableau Online

The online version of Tableau eliminates the need for a server and is a fully cloud-hosted platform that primarily works with cloud databases, but can also work with live on-premises queries or scheduled extract refreshes. It provides the ability for on-the-go users to build, explore, curate, and share visualizations and dashboards that are accessible from a browser or a Tableau Mobile app.

Tableau Public

One part data visualization hosting service, one part social networking, Tableau Public is a free service that allows users to publish interactive data visualizations online. These visualizations can be embedded into webpages and blogs, shared via social media or email, or made available for download to other users.

Getting Started

The first thing you need to do to get started with Tableau is to get your hands on a license. If you have not done so already, refer to the Introduction for guidance on how to get a free trial of Tableau Desktop. You can also visit the Tableau website to explore trial and purchase options.

Connecting to Data

When you first open Tableau Desktop, the Connect to Data screen appears (see Figure 3.2).

Figure 3.2 The Tableau Connect to Data screen.

There are several important elements to know on this screen:

- **Connect:** A long list of native connections to various data sources.
- **Open:** As you create your own workbooks, recently opened workbooks appear here for quick access.
- **Sample Workbooks:** These are default samples provided by Tableau.
- **Discover:** This pane connects you to various Tableau training, visualization, and other resources.

note

This book focuses on the art of visual data storytelling, and as such is not a user manual for Tableau. I recommend you review the Training videos provided by Tableau in the Discover pane.

Connecting to Tables

tip

I'm using the Global Superstore Excel training file provided by Tableau. This is a simple dataset of sales for a global retailer that sells furniture, office supplies, and technology goods. You can download this file from the Tableau Community to follow along.

For our purposes, connect to a very common file format—an Excel file. You can connect to any Excel file by clicking the Excel option under the Connect menu and navigating to the file's location on your machine. Once connected to your data file, Tableau opens the data connection window (see Figure 3.3).

Figure 3.3 The Data Connections screen.

The screen provides several options to help you prepare this file for analysis in Tableau.

- **Connections:** You can add additional data sources by clicking Add. You can also edit the name of the connection or remove it as desired by clicking the drop-down arrow to the right of the filename. (You can also rename the connection by clicking on its title on the canvas to the right.)

- **Sheets:** This pane displays all the sheets in the Excel file, corresponding to the names of individual worksheet tabs. Sheets in Excel are treated the same as tables in a database, and you can choose to connect to a single table or join multiple tables. To connect to a sheet, simply click and drag it into the data connection canvas to the right (you will notice a "Drag sheets here" prompt) or by double-clicking the sheet desired. After you connect to a sheet, three things happen (see Figure 3.4):

    - The sheet name appears in the data connection canvas.

    - The data displays in the preview pane below the data connection canvas.

    - A Go To Worksheet icon displays.

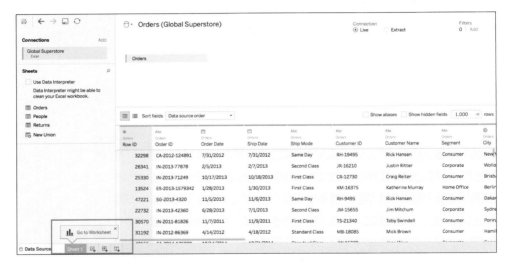

Figure 3.4 You have connected to the Orders sheet of the Excel file, populating the data preview pane. Tableau also provides the prompt to Go To Worksheet and begin visually exploring the data if you are ready.

Before moving on, there are a few more things to take note of on this screen.

First, if you aren't satisfied with any individual column name, you can click on the drop-down arrow to the right of the name and select Rename. Additionally, clicking on the data type icon allows you to change the default data type for that column (see Figure 3.5). You can also:

- Adjust the default data source sort order.
- Create calculated fields to populate in your worksheet.
- Hide or show hidden fields.
- Split fields by delimiter using an automatic or custom split.
- Pivot data fields as necessary.

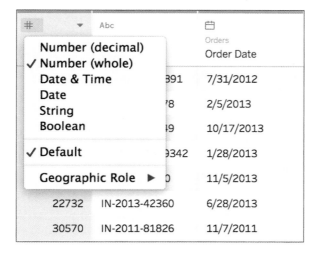

Figure 3.5 Clicking the data type icon allows you to change the default data type for that column. This determines how the fields are displayed on your worksheet in the next step.

Live Versus Extract

You might have noticed the option for a Live or Extract connection on the sheet canvas. The default is Live. However, before you begin analyzing data, this might be something you want to consider (see Table 3.1).

Table 3.1 Be sure to understand the benefits and drawbacks of Live versus Extract connection options.

Connection	Pros	Cons
Live	• Leverage a high-performance database's capabilities • See real-time changes in data	• Can result in a slower experience • Some cloud-based data sources must be extracted
Extract	• Can deter latency in a slow database • Could reduce query load on critical systems	• Most Online Analytical Processing (OLAP) data sources cannot be extracted

Connecting to Multiple Tables with Joins

Previously I mentioned that you can connect to multiple data sources in Tableau. You can also connect to multiple tables in the same data source.

To do this, drag and drop or double-click the second sheet you want to connect to (in Figure 3.6 I have selected the sheet named People). The join icon with the blue center indicates that Tableau has automatically joined these tables as an inner join, making it the default join clause. Clicking on the join icon displays the details as well as gives the option to edit the join clause, or even create a new one.

It's important to note that while Tableau will automatically join your tables, it does so by guessing what your matching ID is. You can change this by clicking on the fields, which shows a drop-down menu of all data fields available to join.

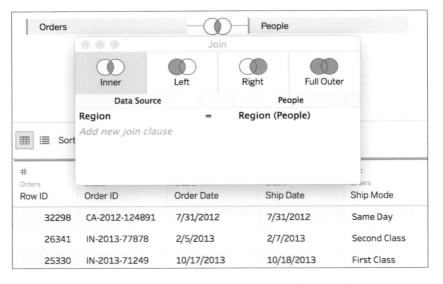

Figure 3.6 Tableau has automatically joined these tables by recognizing that Region is a common field between the two.

Overview of Join Types

As you prepare your data for analysis in Tableau, you might need to "join" data by connecting a collection of tables that are related by a specific field (or column). In a nutshell, joining is a method for combining the data located in those common fields into one virtual table for analysis.

Tableau provides four types of joins that you can use to combine your data: inner, left, right, and outer. Inner and left joins are the two most common types of joins.

- **Inner join:** Joins records where there is a matching field in both datasets. Using an inner join to combine tables produces a new virtual table that contains values that have matches in both tables.

- **Left join:** Joins records from the left and right sides of your equation when there is a match. Using a left join to combine tables produces a new virtual table that contains all values from the left table and corresponding matches from the right table. When there is no corresponding match from left to right, you will see a null value.

- **Right join:** Joins all the records from the data on the right side of your equation and any matching records from the left side. Opposite of a left join, using a right join to combine tables produces a table that contains all values from the right and corresponding matches from the left. Likewise, when a value in the right table doesn't have a corresponding match in the left table, you see a null value.

- **Outer join:** Joins all the records from each dataset together, even when there is no join—and rarely used. Using a full outer join to combine tables produces a table that contains all values from both tables. If a value from either table doesn't have a match with the other table, you see a null value.

WHAT ARE "NULLS"?

Occasionally as you work with data, you will discover a field name called null. What is that?

Null means that some empty cells are in your data and Tableau is, essentially, letting you know. Checking fields and formatting for extraneous information is always important when doing data analysis because you want to ensure these blank fields do not skew out results. A null field might indicate an error in the data, or some other inaccuracy.

In many cases, you don't want empty fields to show up in your data, and you'll want to exclude null fields. To do so, select the Null field and Ctrl-click (or right-click), and then select Exclude (see Figure 3.7). This excludes the null values from your analysis.

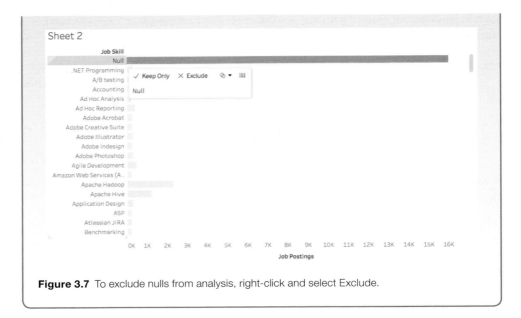

Figure 3.7 To exclude nulls from analysis, right-click and select Exclude.

Generally speaking, Tableau will do its best to automatically determine the best join. However, if you're unsure which type of joins your data supports, you can check the join dialog after you've connected your data. Additionally, you can adjust the join type by selecting a different join type in the Join dialog.

join errors!

Sometimes, an issue occurs in joins. Tableau notes these with a red exclamation point to the side of the join wherein the error occurs (see Figure 3.8).

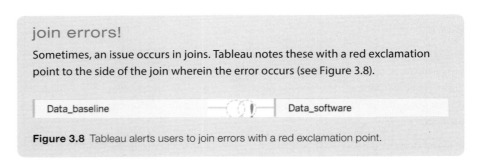

Figure 3.8 Tableau alerts users to join errors with a red exclamation point.

Basic Data Prep with Data Interpreter

The preceding example shows an Excel file that is already nicely formatted and ready to go for analysis in Tableau. However, in reality, data files are not always so analysis ready and might require extensive prep work before they are ready to be brought into Tableau for analysis and visualization work.

Tableau Desktop delivers some features to help automatically reshape files to get them ready for analysis in Tableau. Primary among them is Data Interpreter, Tableau's built-in tool for preparing data for analysis. When you connect to an Excel sheet in Tableau, the software can recognize issues such as missing column names, null values, and so on. To remedy these and clean the file for use in analysis, Tableau will suggest Data Interpreter (refer to Figure 3.4 to locate the Data Interpreter option on the Data Source screen). While this is a helpful feature, the tool is limited and somewhat superficial in its ability to prep data.

To use Data Interpreter, select the check box to turn on the tool. This executes a query to the Excel file and confirms its automated prep tasks with a revised data preview pane addressing the issues it has identified. To get more specifics on what Data Interpreter has adjusted in the file, including a before-and-after view and an explanation table, click the link that is provided following the Interpreter's action to "Review the results." This opens an Excel file describing the changes. You can also clear the check box to undo these changes and revert to your original sheet.

After verifying the data you'll be connecting to, you can go to your worksheet and begin exploring the Tableau interface and your data—you are ready to begin your analysis!

Navigating the Tableau Interface

Now that you have some data in Tableau, you can click the prompt to Go To Worksheet and start getting to know the Tableau user interface in a more meaningful way (see Figure 3.9). The Tableau UI is a drag-and-drop interface that fosters rich interactivity between sheets, dashboards, and stories, allowing for in-depth visual exploration and powerful visual communication. Tableau is similar to Excel in that its files are called workbooks and the sheets inside the workbook are called sheets. Every Tableau workbook contains three elements:

- **Sheets:** For creating individual visualizations. Each workbook can contain multiple sheets—one for each data visualization you create.
- **Dashboards:** For combining multiple sheets as well as other objects like images, text, and web pages, and adding interactions between them like filtering and highlighting. Dashboards are great for looking at the interactions between multiple visualizations.
- **Stories:** These frameworks can be based on visualizations or dashboards, or based on different views and explorations of a single visualization, seen at different stages, with different marks filtered and annotations added—however is best suited to narrate the story in your data.

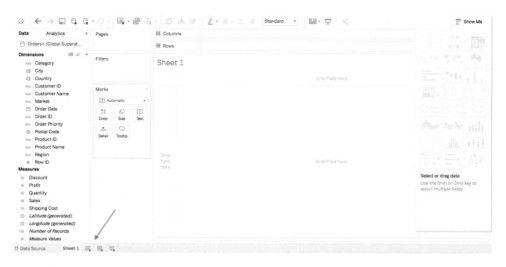

Figure 3.9 The Tableau user interface, a blank canvas.

Later chapters cover Dashboards and Stories in more depth. For now, let's focus on sheets and take a high-level view at the various areas of the screen. As you begin to work directly with data to build visualizations and stories, you will take a more detailed approach to each of these areas.

There are four basic elements to the Tableau interface:

- Menus and toolbar
- Data window
- Shelves and cards
- Legends

Menus and Toolbar

At the top of the screen are the menus that accompany Tableau Desktop. These contain many powerful controls.

Below, at the top of your Tableau sheet, is the toolbar. It is similar in concept to the ribbon in Microsoft Office products. Like the menu, this toolbar contains many powerful buttons that give you control over your Tableau experience and enable you to navigate from the data source all the way to story presentation mode. A few items of special consideration:

- **Logo:** The Tableau logo button brings you back to the original Connect to Data screen (clicking the icon from this screen returns you to your sheet).
- **Undo:** There is no limit to how much you can undo in Tableau, which is an important feature for exploration and discovery. The icon is grayed until there is an action to undo.
- **Save:** There is *no automatic save* in Tableau. Be sure to save your work incrementally.

Another menu appears along the bottom of the sheet. This menu, similar in concept to a Tableau workbook, enables you to return to the Data Source screen; create new sheets, Dashboards, or Stories; and do things like rename, rearrange, duplicate, delete various sheets, and so on.

Data Window

The pane on the left of the sheet is called the Data window and has two tabs: a Data tab and an Analytics tab.

Data

At the top of the Data tab is a list of all open data connections and the fields from that data source categorized as either dimensions or measures (discussed shortly).

Analytics

The Analytics tab enables you to bring out pieces of your analysis—summaries, models, and more—as drag-and-drop elements. We review these functions later.

Shelves and Cards

Shelves and cards are some of the most dynamic and useful features of the Tableau UI.

- **Columns and Rows shelves:** Control grouping headers (dimensions) and axes (measures)
- **Pages shelf:** Lets you break a view into a series of pages so you can better analyze how a specific field affects the rest of the data
- **Filters shelf:** Filters visualizations by dimensions or measures
- **Marks card:** Controls the visual characteristics of a visualization, including encoding of color, size, labels, tooltip text, and shape
- **"Show Me" card** (shown open): A collapsible card that shows application visualization types for a selected measure and dimension

Legends

Legends will be created and automatically appear when you place a field on the Color, Size, or Shape card. To change the order (or appearance) of fields in a visualization, drag them around in the legend. Hide legends by clicking on the menu and selecting Hide Card. Likewise, bring them back by selecting the Legend option on the appropriate space in the Marks card or by using the Analysis menu.

Understanding Dimensions and Measures

When you bring a data source into Tableau, Tableau automatically classifies each field as a dimension or a measure. The differences between these two are important, though they can be tricky to those new at analysis. Perhaps the best way to differentiate these two classifications is as this: dimensions are categories, whereas measures are fields you can do math with.

Dimensions

Dimensions are things that you can group data by or drill down by. They are usually—but not always—categories (such as City, Product Name, or Color), and they can be grouped into strings, dates, or geographic fields.

Measures

Measures are generally numerical data on which you want to perform calculations—summing, averaging, and so on.

Remember, setting a field as a measure or dimension can be adjusted in the Data Source screen by clicking on the data type icon. You can also change this directly in the sheet by either dragging and dropping a dimension to measure, or vice versa, or by clicking the drop-down menu by any field and selecting the Convert to Measure (or Dimension) option.

Continuous and Discrete

Generally, dimensions are discrete and measures are continuous. We could break this down a little more into four types or levels of measurement: nominal, ordinal, interval, and ratio.

- Nominal measures are discrete and categorical (for/against, true/false, yes/no)
- Ordinal measures have order but there are not distinct, equal values (for example, rankings)
- Interval measures have order and distinct, equal values (at least we assume they are equal; for example, Likert scales)
- Ratio measures have order, distinct/equal values, and a true zero point (length, weight, and so on)

In Tableau, continuous fields produce axes, whereas discrete fields create headers. Continuous means "forming an unbroken whole, without interruption." Discrete means "individually separate and distinct." Be sure you understand the difference between these mathematical terms. Text and categories (dimensions) are inherently discrete. Numbers can be discrete if they can only take one of a limited set of distinct, separate values (like, for example, a rating). Numbers, including dates, can be continuous if they can take on any value in a range.

COLORFUL PILLS

When a field is brought from the data window pane and dropped into the Rows and Columns shelves, Tableau creates a "pill." These pills are color coded: blue pills represent discrete variables whereas green pills are continuous. The data type icons also reflect these color codes (see Figure 3.10).

Figure 3.10 Color-coded pills reflect continuous (green) measures and discrete (blue) dimensions.

Summary

This chapter introduced the Tableau product ecosystem and then took a high-level view of the Tableau user interface, including connecting and preparing data and the core functionality of the Sheets canvas. In future chapters, you will put this knowledge into practice as you begin working hands-on with this functionality.

The next chapter addresses the importance of context in building a visual data story.

CHAPTER 4

IMPORTANCE OF CONTEXT IN STORYTELLING

This chapter describes the importance of understanding data's context and its role in helping data storytellers ask the right questions to build a story framework. You'll learn about exploratory and explanatory analysis and strategies for successful storytelling, including narrative flow, considerations for spoken versus written narratives that support visuals, and structures that can support your stories for maximum impact. You will also explore helpful techniques in Tableau that guide you to crafting effective data narrative structure.

More than twenty years ago, Bill Gates coined the iconic phrase, "Content is king." Gates was, of course, referring to the importance of content on demand in the early days (circa 1996) of the World Wide Web. His words were prophetic, however, and over the past two-plus decades this mantra has been applied to everything from Internet marketing to media to viral online content—suddenly *everybody* is a media company.

The never-ending quest for bigger, bolder, better online content has radically changed the way people acquire and share information and how we interact and communicate with others. However, although Gates might have been right then, his mantra is missing a critical ingredient: context.

If you type Gates' "content is king" into your Google search bar, you might notice that a "but" is coming right behind it (see Figure 4.1). Content is king—but context is god.

Figure 4.1 Sorry, Bill. Content might be king, but context is god.

Context is especially important in the field of analytics. Just as communication begins before you ever start building your first data visualization, like any good story, a visual data story requires context—a setting, a plot, a need—before you can begin to communicate. Discovering this context is part of the storytelling process.

This chapter focuses on helping you understand the importance of context in data visualization and visual storytelling, how to ask the right questions in analysis that will help you begin to build out your story framework, and how to let context drive the story as you share it with your audience. The context of a data story is made up of four ingredients:

Context of **data**

Context of **structure**

Context of **audience**

Context of **presentation**

Context in Action

To quote football consulting company 21st Club, without context [in analytics] data is "meaningless, irrelevant, and even dangerous."[1] This might sound aggressive, but in practice, it's an understatement. Without context we can't answer any of the pivotal journalistic questions—who, what, where, when, why, and how—that provide pertinent details to help us get to the bottom of any big question. In fact, we can't do much beyond just make good guesses. We have a whole lot of information, but it is incomplete and this can often cause us to miss out on major points that change the entire scope of our story. Beyond just bad storytelling, omitting critical context carries an even bigger risk. Ultimately, we use data stories to drive decision-making, and nothing paves the way for bad decisions like a lack of good information.

Rather than me just writing about the importance of context in data storytelling, let's take a quick look at a fun example of a story where context makes all the difference. I use this practice in the dissection of data stories throughout this book.

Harry Potter: Hero or Menace?

In June 2017, *Harry Potter* and JK Rowling's world of wizards celebrated its 20th anniversary.

By now, most of us are familiar with The Boy Who Lived. The *Harry Potter* series has been distributed in more than 200 territories, translated into 68 languages, and has sold more than 400 million copies worldwide.[2] However, although we are familiar with Harry's story in its novelized form, most of us haven't taken such a concentrated look on the data inside the story.

---

1. http://www.21stclub.com/2013/08/11/contextual-intelligence-a-definition/
2. http://harrypotter.scholastic.com/jk_rowling/

> **note**
>
> If you're a Potterhead, you're in luck! A later chapter explores several stories hidden within the wizarding world's data—working through the entire storytelling process from collecting and preparing data to presenting a complete data narrative.

Even if you don't know all the nuances of *Harry Potter*, you likely know that the story follows the journey of young wizard Harry Potter as he fights against the evil dark wizard, Lord Voldemort, and his minions. With that minimal amount of context, we can assume that Harry is the good guy and Voldemort the bad.

To aid in visualizing the story of good versus evil in *Harry Potter*, we can use a fantastic public dataset of all the instances where characters in each of the books acted aggressively. When we visualize this data at the most superficial level (see Figure 4.2)—aggressive acts enacted by Harry and Voldemort in each of the books—these "lightning bolts" seem to show that over the course of the series Harry committed significantly more aggressive behaviors than did his nemesis, Lord Voldemort. In this version of the story, our good wizard suddenly looks a little more sociopathic than we might have expected. Yikes!

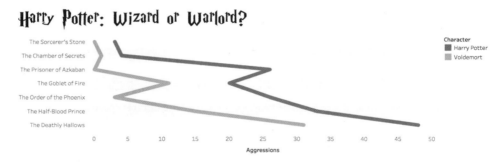

Figure 4.2 A modified bar chart of aggressive actions committed by Harry Potter and Lord Voldemort.

The good news to Potter fans is that if we look at the data like this we are overlooking critical context and showcasing a faulty story. Remember, the danger of a story told wrong is the prospect of making a bad decision based on inaccurate or otherwise incorrect information, and this logic applies to any story—even Harry's. If we had presented this visual to, for example, Rowling's publisher prior to the series being published, we might never have been introduced the wizarding world. Who would want to publish a children's book that condones violence? Who would want their kids to read about a malevolent hero? Thus, telling an incorrect story could have resulted in a wrong decision (no Potter), rather than introducing a pop culture phenomenon that swept the world. Fortunately, we can remedy this by putting context back into the narrative.

Ensuring Relevant Context

To make sure we're including context in a meaningful way, we need to revisit our initial assumptions of how we approached visualizing two key variables: the two characters and their aggressive acts.

In the previous attempt, we simply visualized a count of aggressive acts and neglected to consider the context in which the acts were committed (or the influence of the character on the narrative). Doing so puts an undue spotlight on Harry and presents an immediate contextual fallacy. This is Harry's story, and as the protagonist all of his actions, aggressive or not, are heavily documented. In contrast, Voldemort, while a main character, has a lesser presence in the story. This logic helps us see critical context we neglected in a simple counting exercise. Rather than how many aggressive acts were committed by each character, we need to look at how often each character appears *and* how often they commit aggressive acts when mentioned.

Out of Context: How *many times* Harry and Voldemort acted aggressively.

In Context: How *often* Harry and Voldemort acted aggressively *when mentioned*.

Putting the data back into a relevant context, when we visualize again we see something very different (see Figure 4.3).

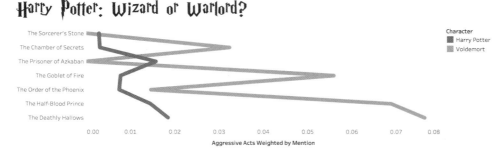

Figure 4.3 With a little bit of context added back into the data, we see a different story.

With more context added into the narrative, we see Voldemort's true colors emerge. While Harry *rarely* acts aggressively when mentioned, Voldemort *usually* acts aggressively when his name is spoken. This completely changes the story takeaway that we presented before.

Of course, there is much more exploration we could do with this data to dig deeper into the role of aggression in *Harry Potter* and craft a richer visual narrative. We could bring more characters into view to analyze whether Voldemort is the ultimate bad guy in the series. We could look at aggression by book rather than by character, or look at who committed aggressive acts against whom and how and when character relationships affect how these aggressions are brought into play. We could even break down aggressive acts into violent and non-violent categories, or rank aggressive acts by level of severity. In any case, it's unlikely the full context of this story could ever be told without knowledge of the series and its complicated plot, and both of these require support on the part of the presenter. This hints to the value of presentation in a visual data story. No matter how deep, data alone will never be able to tell a story as well as *you*.

> note
>
> Be especially careful with *counts* as these can influence your data and present a distorted version of the truth. To prevent this, "normalize" your data with a calculated field.

Exploratory versus Explanatory Analysis

Before moving on to looking at storytelling techniques and story structures, we need to draw a distinction between exploratory and explanatory analysis, and how these contribute to storytelling.

Exploration fuels discovery. It's the process we take to explore data and uncover its story. In my visual analytics classes, I use an image of Indiana Jones to illustrate the concept of exploratory analysis because, like Dr. Jones, this is where we go looking for a discovery to share and hope to find something. We take time to search, digging in and out of data iteratively and with curiosity as we work to build a story, or perhaps many stories, or perhaps even none at all. Exploration is a process of "look and see," and we must explore before we can explain.

Our job as analysts is to explore. Our job as data storytellers is to explain. Exploratory analysis might yield important story points, but they are not part of the storytelling process. As storytellers, we are focused on explanatory analysis and communicating our discoveries in the form of a story.

The distinction between explanatory and exploratory analysis has an important impact on context, particularly in how we present our results.

It is common for people to present exploratory graphics as part of their data story—after all, the discovery process can be an undertaking and we can be eager to show all of our hard work or display every detail we've found! However, the inevitable result is that this adds bulk to what should be a streamlined, focused story and muddies the message for the audience. In addition to telling a story, data storytellers must also act as their own editors. This requires trimming unnecessary content away so that the core of the data story remains unencumbered and intact. The following sections cover techniques to help achieve this.

> recommended reading
>
> For more on visual data discovery and working through exploratory analysis, read my book, *The Visual Imperative*. Additional resources are provided in Chapter 10 as well as on the website www.visualdatastorytelling.com.

EXPAND THE SHOW ME CARD!

You met the Show Me card in Chapter 3. The Show Me card (see Figure 4.4) can help guide you to building visualizations that best represent your data. As you choose measures and dimensions and bring them to the shelves, the Show Me card will display what chart types are available based on the fields you've selected. Likewise, if you're unsure of which data to bring over to the shelves, you can use the Show Me card as a tool to select the right measures and dimensions.

Figure 4.4 The Tableau Show Me card, opened on symbol maps.

FILTERING OUT, ZEROING IN

Filters are a great way to help cut out the noise and let your data's story shine (see Figure 4.5). You can strip out unnecessary information, or, likewise, focus on specific fields or elements critical to your data story. Like many things in Tableau, filtering can be done in several ways and several places. You explore some of these when working with real data sets later in this book.

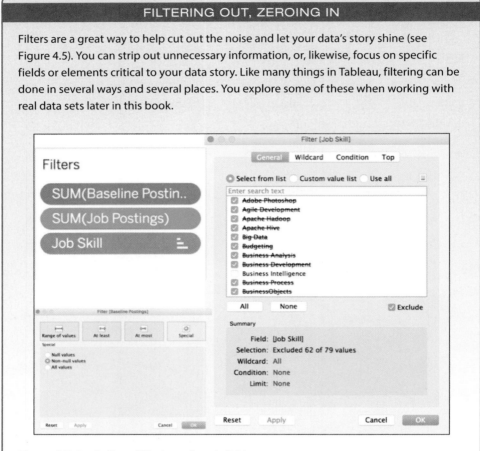

Figure 4.5 A selection of filtering options in Tableau.

Structuring Stories

Like traditional stories, data stories have shape—and not just bars and bubbles!—or "structure." Story structure plays an important role in developing a story's context, and can be broken down into two parts:

- **Part One:** Story Plot
- **Part Two:** Story Genre

Story Plot

The events of a story (or the main part of a story) are its plot (this is also called its storyline). These events generally relate to each other in a pattern or a sequence, and the storyteller (or author) is responsible for arranging these actions in a meaningful way to shape the story.

Like other forms of storytelling, the plot of a data story can be organized into a linear sequence (see Figure 4.6) or not—not all data stories are told in order; however, they all have one thing in common: They must be true. Data stories are not the place to practice fiction.

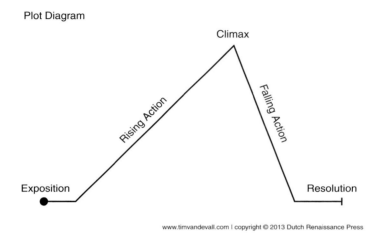

Plot Diagram

www.timvandevall.com | copyright © 2013 Dutch Renaissance Press

Figure 4.6 The basic plot diagram.

> note
>
> The plot diagram is an organizational tool to help map events in a story. Its familiar triangle shape (representing the beginning, middle, and end of a story) was described by Aristotle and later modified by Gustav Freytag who added rising and falling action. Though designed for traditional stories, data stories can be built using this same framework.

For the purposes of data storytelling, there are eight basic "plots" to help shape your visual data story (see Figure 4.7). Can you identify the plot used in the *Harry Potter* example (Hint: We were telling a story of aggressive acts *over* the series)?

Change over time—See a visual history as told through a simple metric or trend

Drill down—Start big, and get more and more granular to find meaning

Zoom out—Reverse the particular, from the individual to a larger group

Contrast—The "this" or "that"

Spread—Help people see the light and the dark, or reach of data (disbursement)

Intersections—Things that cross over, or progress ("less than" to "more than")

Factors—Things that work together to build up to a higher-level effect

Outliers—Powerful way to show something outside the realm of normal

Story Genre

The other half of story structure is its genre. Like the diversity in plot, there is more than one genre to choose from. In fact, there are seven genres of narrative visualization. Developed by Segel and Heel,[3] they vary primarily in the number of frames and the ordering of visual elements and include the magazine style, the annotated chart, the partitioned poster, the flow chart, the comic strip, the slide short, and finally, the conglomerate film/video/animation (see Figure 4.7).

Figure 4.7 Genres of Narrative Visualization by Segel and Heer.

In Tableau, you can use dashboards and story points to each of these genres, and Chapter 7, "Preparing Data for Storytelling," explores how to build them. For now, keep in mind that data stories are most effective when they have constrained interaction at various checkpoints and allow the user to explore and engage with the story without veering too far away from the intended narrative. Stories unfold, and each visualization should highlight one story point at a time (whether within the same visualizations or within multiple) as storytellers layer points to build a complete data narrative.

3. Segel, E. and Heer, J. (2010). Narrative visualization: Telling stories with data. *IEEE Transactions on Visualization and Computer Graphics, 16*(6), 1139–1148. https://doi.org/10.1109/TVCG.2010.179

Audience Analysis for Storytelling

A successful data storyteller has to be a master of their craft, able to meld the worlds of data visualization and storytelling together into a cohesive whole. However, the story is only half of the equation. A story is a piece of communication, and like every communication, stories are part of a two-way dialogue between the sender (you) and the receiver (your audience). If the story gets interrupted or otherwise lost in translation, you've lost the ability to communicate and will likely fail. Therefore, storytellers need to be clear on exactly who is on the receiving end of their story, and have confidence that they have the information they need to build the right story for their audience.

Many visualization instructors might phrase this step of the story-building process in terms of asking the "right" questions, though a lot of ambiguity exists that surrounds just what these questions are. Just like in any type of analysis, there is no silver bullet approach for gathering audience expectations or stakeholder requirements. Questions, like stories, have entropy: They change based on everything from the nature of the relationship of the storyteller to the audience, to the action the audience would like to take, to the mechanism in which the story is presented. So, a good storyteller knows that the trick isn't asking the *right* questions, but in asking *many*. It's okay to be really, really curious, even insatiable in your desire to really understand your audience and every situation you encounter. It's iterative, and a process of compromise between what you want to say and what the audience needs to hear. Ultimately you need to be able to learn as much as you can about your audience and what they need to know, and then build a story that anticipates and delivers on audience needs.

Curiosity is a learned skill. It takes time to develop a palate for asking the right research questions and plucking out the relevant details from the noise. Remember, visual data storytelling is fact, not fiction, and as such involves a requisite degree of research as you move through visual analysis. As you practice molding yourself into a thoughtful questioner, however, you can use the some of the same journalistic questions that help to parse out the correct context for a story—particularly who, what, why, and how—to make sure you build a presentation that's going to resonate with your audience and give them the information they need to take action. Let's look more closely at these.

Who

Be specific about your audience. Avoid generalizations and assumptions. Taking a broad view of your audiences has the consequence of overlooking nuances and specific needs that help you zero in on what your audience needs and wants to hear, as well as how you might be best able to communicate with them to capture their interest. Also, narrowing in on your audience will show you who the decision makers and key influencers are, who needs and wants to hear your story, and those whose buy-in you really need to earn. Remember, engaging with your audience is a critical part of successful storytelling.

It's also important to consider the affect of your relationship with the audience. Do they know you? Do they trust you? Do they believe that you are a credible and reliable source of information and insight? The answers to these questions are important because they might influence how you structure your presentation as well as any pre- or post-presentation communication. Your audience must believe in you as an analyst *and* a storyteller before they will listen to your story and be open to taking any actions you might suggest.

What

Analytics begins with understanding data—what you have, what you need, its capabilities and its limitations. Additionally, you should have a realistic view of its quality and validity, and thus its ability to answer business questions or explore a hypothesis—as well as if you should seek additional or external data to complete your dataset for analysis. Understanding your data also requires you to have a good grasp on how to visually represent this data compellingly and accurately, so that you are practicing "no harm" data visualization as you design your narrative.

In addition to knowing the ins and outs of your data, be sure you've asked enough questions to work out what your audience is asking of you, or what story they are asking you to tell with the information you have at your disposal. Be sure to have a solid alignment of ideas between what questions can be answered with your data and what insight or information your audience needs or wants; otherwise, your data story will fall flat, unable to satisfy audience expectations.

Why

Every good story should prompt an action, whether you are building a story intended to help your audience to make a decision; to cause them to change their opinion; or otherwise to convince, persuade, or educate. Ultimately, you should be crystal clear on what your goal is with the story, and why your audience should care about what you are saying. This helps to both ensure your story is meaningful and necessary, and to give you a clear target of how to build logical arguments toward a salient end goal.

To help crystalize the answers to the "why" part of the equation, be able to articulate an answer to clearly and concisely answer the following questions:

- Who is your audience? (They might not be as homogenous as you think.)
- What do they want?
- What do they need?
- How might they be feeling?
- What action do they need to take?
- What type of communication do they prefer?
- How well do they know the data?
- What beliefs or bias might they have that you need to reinforce or challenge?
- What, specifically, are you sharing with your audience?
- What, specifically, do you want them to do with this information?

If you cannot readily answer most (if not all) of these questions, you might need to revisit your purpose.

How

Finally, the communication medium and channel you use to present your story matter. In fact, it has a number of implications for how you deliver your story, as well as how much influence you have as a storyteller and how interactive your audience can be with you as well as with the story itself. Although there are many facets to explore in this step, one of the most constructive is to understand the differences between data stories delivered as narrated, live versions or those that are non-narrated or otherwise "static" presentations.

Narrated

Narrated storytelling presentations are those that are delivered live—whether in person or virtually—where the storyteller has the ability to narrate the presentation and guide the experience. In this mode, the storyteller has full control of the narrative and is able to direct the audience's attention to points of interest and facilitate transitions between story points, explaining any potential areas of ambiguity, or likewise, emphasize or soften points as needed.

In addition to the ability to direct the audience, live presenters also have an obligation to be sensitive to the audience and respond to their needs. As a presenter, you have a front row seat to your audience, and remember: You are not a TV screen—you can react and respond to visual cues to determine whether you need to speed up or slow down or go into more or less detail as you move through your presentation. One tip I give to students learning to present is to always have more pieces of the story than you are planning to share stored in your back pocket. That way, if you need to dive into detail or add an embellishing point to your story, you can introduce it without adding junk into your presentation and interfering with the flow of your data story.

Non-Narrated

On the other hand, non-narrated storytelling presentations are those that are delivered without the benefit of a storyteller to guide the experience, such as reports or emails or even dashboards. In any of these instances, the storyteller relinquishes control of the audience's experience and relies on the puts it in the hands of the tool used to distribute the information.

To ensure the integrity of the visuals and the story, a highly curated and detailed view of the information is necessary. In the case of Tableau, dashboards or story points, this translates into not just well-crafted visualizations, but cohesive, logical storylines and appropriate filters, highlights, and other venues to let the audience explore visuals without degrading the story or the underlying data's integrity. Pay attention to device form factor here, too, as you will need to be aware of how your story presents across multiple devices (laptop screens, tablets, smartphones, and so on).

TIPS FOR SUCCESS IN PRESENTATIONS

Telling data stories through a live presentation is as much an art as building the story itself. This means that storytellers must, in addition to their skills in data analysis and visualization, be skilled presenters, equipped with the capability to guide the audience through the story and facilitate a shared experience.

It's a known fact that public speaking in any form isn't a concept that excites many people. In fact, in a statistic made humorous by comedian Jerry Seinfeld, according to most studies, people's *number one* fear is of public speaking. Number two is death. Thus, Seinfeld's joke is that the average person at a funeral would rather be the one in the casket than the one conducting the eulogy.

The secret to overcoming presentation anxiety and polishing up your skills as a speaker is this: practice. Practice gives you opportunities to learn your own strengths as well as identify areas to improve, helps you discover and fine-tune your speaking style, and—perhaps most important—it is the one and only venue to building confidence earned from experience.

Here are a few tips to help you become more comfortable to go "on stage":

- There's wisdom in the mantra "practice makes perfect." Rehearse, revise, rehearse.

- Write out speaking points, not speaking paragraphs. Document three to four important points you want to make for each slide to be your compass.

- Design presentations to support your story, not presentations to tell your story. Your audience should be listening to you, not reading slides. Just like in a chart or graph, maximize the data-to-ink ratio and keep visuals clean and minimal.

Summary

This chapter looked closely at the importance of understanding data's context and its role in helping data storytellers ask the right questions to build a story framework. You learned about exploratory and explanatory analysis and strategies for successful storytelling, including narrative flow, considerations for spoken versus written narratives that support visuals, and structures that can support stories for maximum impact.

The next chapter looks at the importance of choosing the right visual—or combinations of visuals—to support your data story, as well as how to build basic visualizations in Tableau.

CHAPTER 5

CHOOSING THE RIGHT VISUAL

This chapter introduces the common types of visuals used to communicate data in a business setting, discusses appropriate use cases for each, and highlights their use through examples built from the catalog of charts available in Tableau. You will also learn techniques to help you assess when to use these graphs, when to avoid certain types of charts, and how to generate them according to best practices, along with some of the special features in Tableau designed to help you get the most from your visual.

When it comes to visualizing data, there is no shortage of charts and graphs to choose from. From traditional graphs to innovative hand-coded visualizations, there is a continuum of visualizations ready to translate data from numbers into meaning using shapes, color, and other visual cues. However, each visualization type is intended to represent different types of data in specific ways to best represent its insight. Let's look at seven of the most common visualization types to help you choose the right chart for your data.

The Bar Chart

A traditional favorite, the bar chart is one of the most common ways to visualize data. It is best suited for numerical data that can be divided into distinct categories to compare information and reveal trends at a glance (see Figure 5.1).

An old classic, there are a few ways to spice up a bar chart.

- Bars can be oriented on the vertical or horizontal axis, which can be helpful for spotting trends.
- Additional layers of information can be added using clustered bars or by stacking related data.
- Color can be added for more impact or to overlay for immediate insight.
- Trend lines and other annotations can be added to highlight important data points.
- Use side-by-side or stacked bars (see Figure 5.2) to give depth to your analysis and answer multiple questions at once.
- Bar charts can be combined with maps or line charts to act as filters that correspond to different data points as they are selected.
- Finally, multiple bar charts could be set on a dashboard to help viewers quickly compare information without navigating several charts.

Sussex County Year End Fund Balance Record
Fund Balance as of 12/31

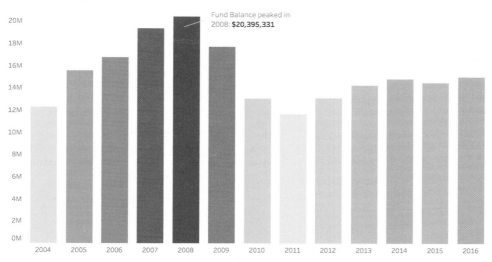

Figure 5.1 This simple, classic bar chart with color gradient shading and a point annotation compares the year end balance for Sussex County, NJ over a period of 13 years.

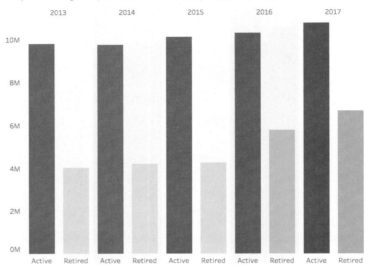

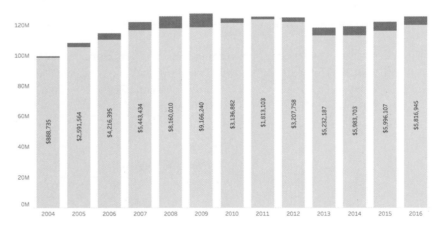

Figure 5.2 Alternative bar charts: a side-by-side bar chart with color gradient shading and a stacked bar chart with labeled and banded columns.

Tableau How-To: Bar Chart

To begin a vertical bar chart in Tableau, place a dimension on the rows shelf and a measure on the columns shelf (or vice versa to create a horizontal bar chart—place a measure on the rows shelf and a dimension on the columns shelf as in Figure 5.3). You will notice that the Bar mark type is already selected on the Mark card. Tableau automatically selects this mark type when the data view matches one of the two field arrangements mentioned previously. From here, you can add additional fields to these shelves and further modify your bar chart as desired.

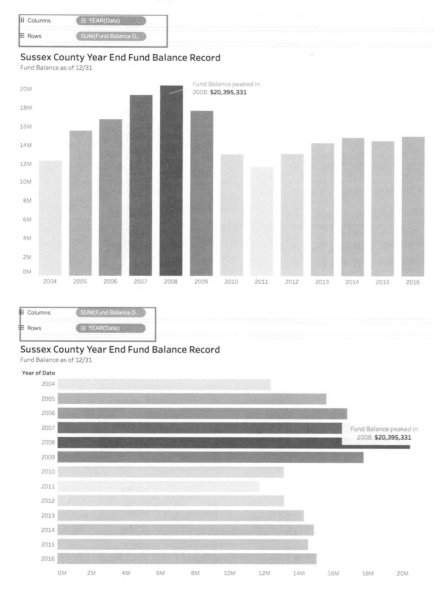

Figure 5.3 You can create vertical or horizontal bar charts by rearranging measures and dimensions on the rows and columns shelves. However, pay attention to how many bars you have on a horizontal bar chart to avoid the Moire effect (see Chapter 6).

> **tip**
> Instead of manually rearranging pills on the shelves, you can also use the Swap
> Rows and Columns button on the toolbar to rearrange rows and columns and
> toggle between views (see Figure 5.4).
>
>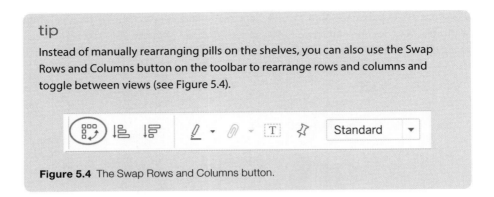
>
> **Figure 5.4** The Swap Rows and Columns button.

The Line Chart

Like the bar chart, the line chart is another of the most frequently used chart types. These
charts connect individual numeric data points to visualize a sequence of values. As such, they
are most commonly used when an element of time is present. In fact, the best use case for line
charts involves displaying trends over a period of time (see Figure 5.5), when your data are
ordered, or when interpolation makes sense.

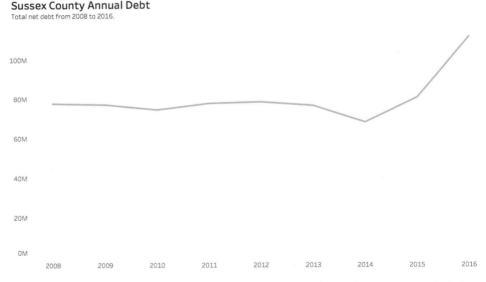

Figure 5.5 This line chart shows the audited annual net debt for Sussex County over a period of
nearly ten years.

Dual-axis line charts can be created by bringing two measures to the rows shelf, and then right-clicking on the second measure and selecting Dual-axis from the drop-down menu (see Figure 5.6).

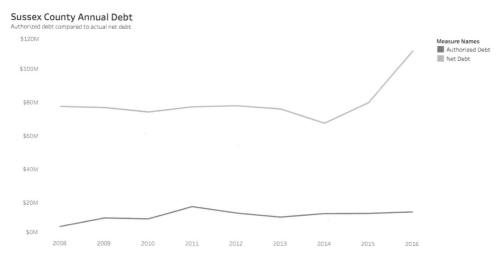

Figure 5.6 Create a dual-axis line chart by combining two measures. This produces a line chart with multiple lines.

Additionally, when two or more lines are present, you can transform line charts by adding additional chart types to deepen insight. For example, a line chart can be combined with a bar chart (see Figure 5.7) to provide visual cues for further investigation. Or, the area under lines can be shaded into an area chart by filling the space under each respective line to extend the analysis and illuminate the relative contribution that a line contributes to the whole.

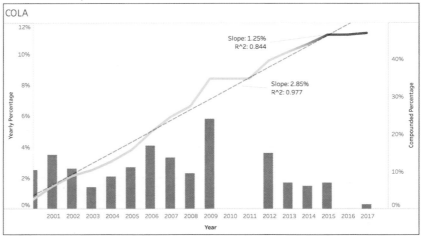

Figure 5.7 Adjust the Marks card to help you combine chart types. This work-in-progress line chart has been combined with a bar chart. It also includes annotations, trend lines, and a color gradient shade element on the line to enhance insight.

Tableau How-To: Line Chart

You create a line chart in Tableau by placing one or more measures on either the columns shelf or the rows shelf, and then plotting the measures against either a date or continuous dimension (see Figure 5.8). Additionally, the Automatic Marks card drop-down menu will select Line as the mark type. You can further expand line charts by including additional summary analytics, like forecasting. Be sure to synchronize or adjust axes to keep numbers in context.

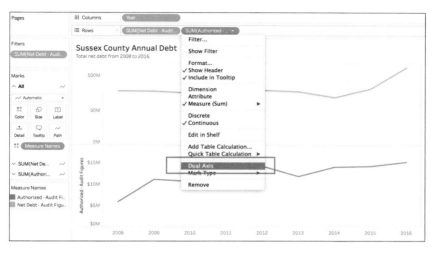

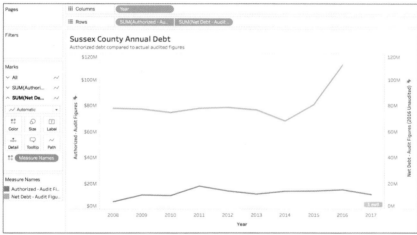

Figure 5.8 Create a dual-axis line chart to show two pieces of data on the same chart.

The Pie and Donut Charts

We all love to hate the pie chart and its cousin the donut chart. This hatred for "dessert charts" is prolific with a lot of opinions thrown in the mix, but a substantial amount of empirical research explores many good reasons not to use these charts. Among these, known problems exist with how we read and understand angles and the many distortion effects caused by too many slices (which apply to both pie and donut charts). Even so, these charts are still among the most misused and overused of chart types. Nevertheless, with a few tweaks there are ways that both of these notorious chart types can be used—with discretion—as viable options to visualize parts of a whole, or percentages (see Figure 5.9), particularly for use as storyteller, rather than analytical, visualizations.

In both charts the circle represents the 100% whole, and the size of each wedge (the largest of which should start on the upper right and move clockwise) represents a percentage. The trick to properly reading pie or donut charts is to not rely on the angle, but to look at area or arc length. To avoid a bad pie chart, focus on comparing only a few values (less than six is preferable, two if possible) and use distinct color separation for maximum readability. Donut charts can help clarify your data story by including a key takeaway in the center white space (see Figure 5.9).

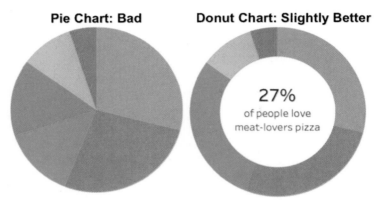

Figure 5.9 A side-by-side comparison of an unlabeled pie chart and a donut chart displaying percentages of America's favorite pizza toppings.

Tableau How-To: Pie and Donut Charts

To begin either a pie or donut chart, you start by building a basic bar chart and then use the Show Me card to select the pie chart option (see Figure 5.10). You could also create a pie chart directly in the Marks card. This will produce a rather small pie chart.

> tip
>
> You can increase the size by holding down Ctrl+Shift (or holding down Command+Shift on a Mac) and pressing B several times.

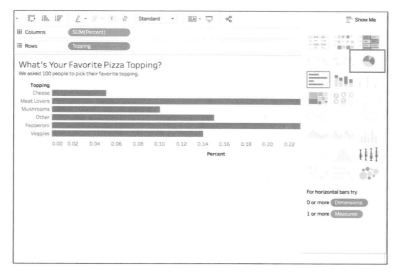

Figure 5.10 Create a bar chart, and then select the pie chart from the Show Me card.

While there is not a one-click or Show Me option to change a pie chart into a donut chart, a few additional steps will transform your chart:

1. Beginning with a pie chart, drag your measure to the Rows shelf again. Right-click both instances and select Measure (Sum) > Minimum (see Figure 5.11).

2. Right-click the second instance of Number of Records and select Dual Axis.

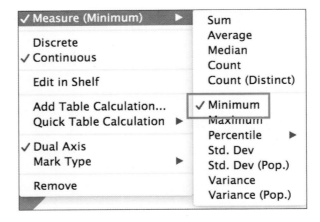

Figure 5.11 Transform a pie chart into a donut chart by creating a dual-axis chart.

3. Now to combine two pie charts into one, transforming the second into what will become the center of your donut: Move to your Marks card, click the second instance of your measure and click MIN(Number of Records) (2).

4. Remove any pills from the Color and Size marks.

5. Click Color and choose the same color as the background (in this example, white).

6. At this point, your pie chart will appear to disappear; however, select Size and drag the slider to the left to make the circle smaller. As the white circle decreases, the center of your donut "hollows" out (see Figure 5.12).

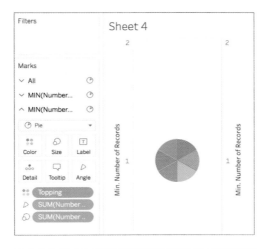

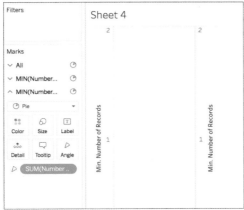

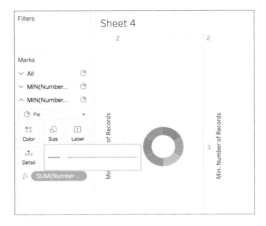

Figure 5.12 These visuals reflect the steps to transform your pie chart into a donut chart.

From this point, you can finalize your donut chart by removing headers, showing labels, and so on.

SKETCHING YOUR STORY

Sketching out ideas for your graphics can aid with the artistic process as you work to frame your story (see Figure 5.13). If you can create a vision of your story, you can use this as a guide to curate meaningful charts and graphs. Of course, Tableau doesn't support sketching; however, these guides can be helpful as you work to curate your visual in Tableau to tell its best story.

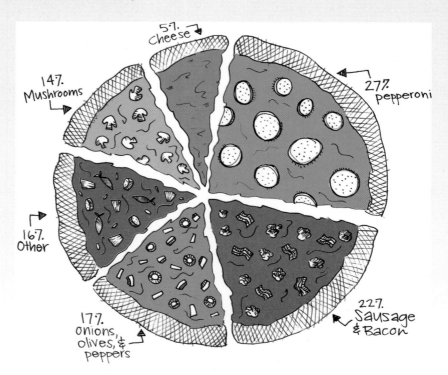

Figure 5.13 Sketching out stories can facilitate the artistic process of visualization and help you see your end goal as you work to curate it in Tableau.

The Scatter Plot

Scatter plots are an effective way to visualize numerical variables to compare measures and quickly identify patterns, trends, concentrations (clusters), and outliers. These charts can give viewers a sense of where to focus discovery efforts further and are best used to investigate relationships between variables. Scatter plots are particularly useful when exploring statistical relationships such as linear regression. Figure 5.14 illustrates an example of the scatter plot.

What Effect Does Mileage of a Used Car Have On Price?
A regression scatterplot of used coupes, SUVs, sedans, and trucks.

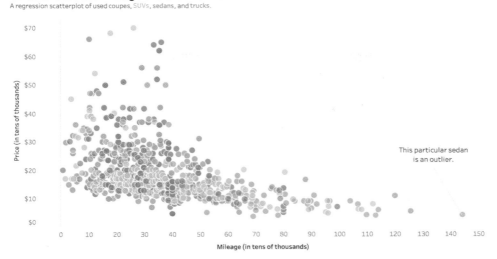

Figure 5.14 Scatter plot example.

Tableau How-To: Scatter Plots

You can create a scatter plot in Tableau in two ways: as a **simple scatter plot** or a **matrix scatter plot**.

You create simple scatter plots by dragging a measure to the Columns shelf and a measure to the Rows shelf. When you plot one number against another, the result is a Cartesian chart—a one-mark scatter plot with a single x and y coordinate (see Figure 5.15).

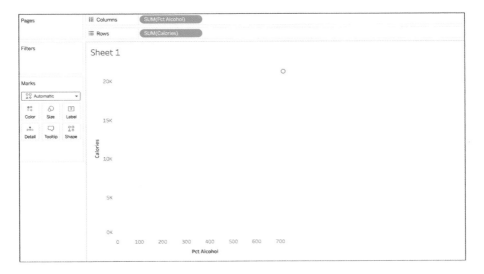

Figure 5.15 Simple scatter plots begin with aggregated measures, showing only one mark.

To view all of your measures, deselect the Aggregate Measures option from the Analysis menu (see Figure 5.16).

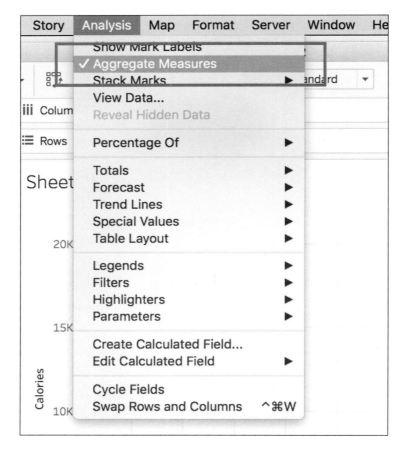

Figure 5.16 Deselect Aggregate Measures to view all of your data points on a scatter plot.

Doing so generates a simple scatter plot, as shown in Figure 5.17.

Do Calories Affect Alcohol Content in Beer?
This simple scatterplot shows the linear relationship between calories and percent of alcohol.

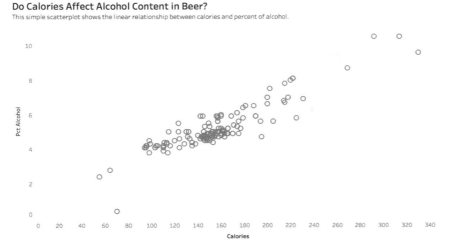

Figure 5.17 A simple scatter plot.

You can add depth and visual richness to a scatterplot by:

- Bringing over dimensions and using them to add color or additional shapes onto the scatter plot.
- Changing the shape of the data via the Marks card to provide additional relevance and visual cues. You can choose these shapes from a set of sample default shapes as well as a selection of shape palettes included in Tableau (see Figure 5.18).

Figure 5.18 Choose shapes from the Marks card to add depth to your scatter plot.

- Incorporating filters can reduce noise and help limit investigation to the factors that matter most to your analysis.

- Scatter plots are excellent candidates to include statistical information to review trends and other analytics. Via Tableau's Analytics pane, you can add a variety of analytic models to highlight the statistics in your data. Hover the cursor over the trend lines to display statistical information used to create the line(s), as shown in Figure 5.19.

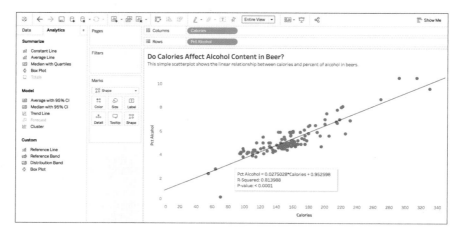

Figure 5.19 A scatter plot with a trend line and summary statistics.

If these shelves contain both dimensions and measures, Tableau will create a **Matrix of Scatter Plots** and place the measures as the innermost fields, which means that measures are always to the right of any dimensions that you have also placed on these shelves. The word *innermost* in this case refers to the table structure (see Figure 5.20).

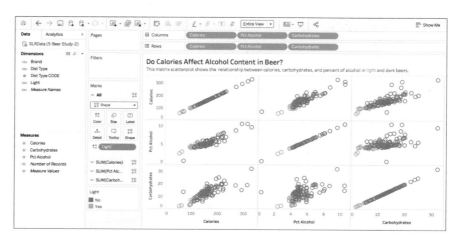

Figure 5.20 A matrix scatter plot.

The Packed Bubble Chart

The bubble chart is a variation of the scatter plot that replaces data points with a cluster of circles (or bubbles), a technique that further emphasizes data that would be rendered on a pie chart, scatter plot, or map. This method shows relational values without regard to axes and is used to display three dimensions of data: two through the bubble's location and another through size.

These charts allow for the comparison of entities in terms of their relative positions with respect to each numeric axis and size. The sizes of the bubbles provide details about the data, and colors can be used as an additional encoding cue to answer many questions about the data at once (see Figure 5.21). As a technique for adding richness to bubble charts, consider overlaying them on a map to put geographic data quickly in context.

America's Favorite Pie Flavor
Year over year, apple takes the cake..erm, pie.

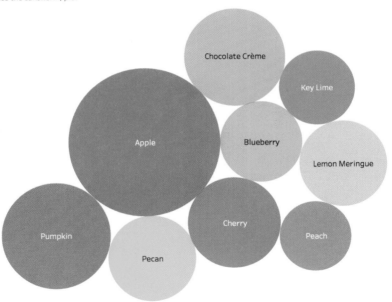

Figure 5.21 A packed bubble chart displays data in a cluster of circles, using size and color to encode the bubbles with meaning.

Tableau How-To: Packed Bubble Charts

To create a basic packed bubble chart, drag a dimension to the Columns shelf and a measure to the Rows shelf. Tableau will aggregate the measure as a sum and create a vertical axis to display a bar chart. This is the default functionality when you select one measure and dimension in this manner. Next, use the Show Me card to select the Packed Bubble chart from the list of options (see Figure 5.22).

In this example, the size of the bubble represents the number of survey responses whereas the color of the bubble represents the flavor or pie chosen. The circle is also labeled with the flavor.

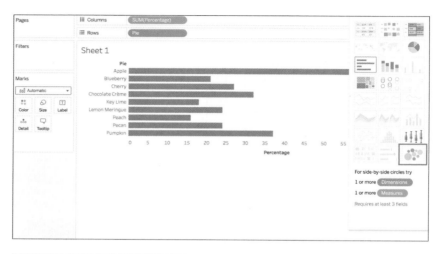

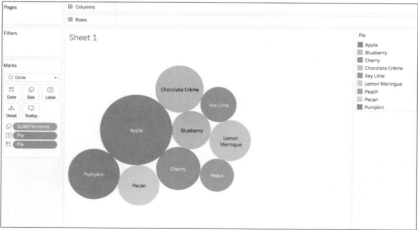

Figure 5.22 Building a packed bubble chart in Tableau begins with building a bar chart and changing the chart type.

Like most chart types, there are ways to add more insight into a packed bubble chart or embellish the chart with storytelling techniques. For example, use different dimensions to encode color, or adjust labels to add additional information. (Chapter 9 covers formatting Mark labels.)

Shapes, especially circles, also provide an interesting opportunity to move beyond data visualization tools to bring your story to life in creative ways (assuming, of course, this works for your audience and your story). In Figure 5.23, images of the pie flavors overlay the bubbles, presenting the same data in a more visual way. Because we are interested in the story here more than the analytics, this works.

Figure 5.23 A more artistic storytelling approach to this same data story.

> **note**
>
> You might recognize this image from Wake's Pis: A Kid's Guide to Delicious Data Stories. For more of Wake's work, check out www.wakespis.com.

The Treemap

One of the two more advanced visualizations covered in this chapter, the treemap uses a series of rectangles of various sizes to show relative proportions (see Figure 5.24). It works especially well if the data being visualized has a hierarchical structure (with parent nodes, children, and so on) or when analyzing a parts-to-whole relationship. As its name suggests, a treemap divides and subdivides based on parts of a whole by breaking down into smaller rectangles nested within a larger rectangle, often of a different color or different color gradient, to emphasize its relationship to the larger whole.

The treemap also provides a much more efficient way to see this relationship when working with large amounts of data by making efficient use of space. It is ideal for legibly showing hundreds (or perhaps even thousands) of items simultaneously within a single visualization.

How Would Students Fight Back?
Students recognize that schools have a responsibility to educate and support students who experience cyberbullying.

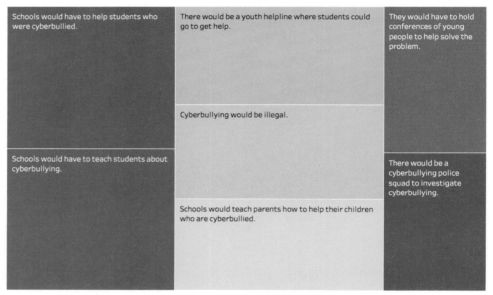

Figure 5.24 This treemap shows the rate of student survey responses on how they perceive schools should fight back against cyberbullying. The sizes and shapes of the rectangles give further detail on their relationship within the hierarchy of total answers.

Tableau How-To: Treemaps

Use dimensions to define the structure of a treemap, and measures to define the size (or color) of the rectangles.

Again, drag a dimension to the Columns shelf and a measure to the Rows shelf. Tableau will aggregate the measure as a sum and create a vertical axis to display a bar chart (see Figure 5.25). From here, use the Show Me card to select a treemap from the list of available chart types.

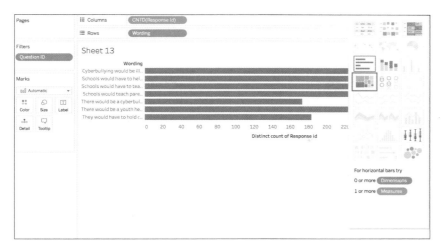

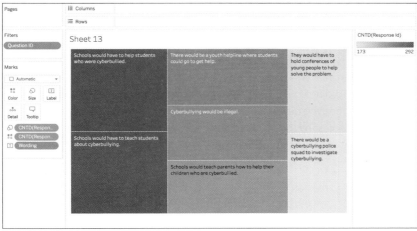

Figure 5.25 Building a treemap in Tableau begins with building a bar chart and changing the chart type.

In this example, we are using survey data to create the treemap and looking at how many respondents selected each of the options presented. Both the size of the rectangles and their color are determined by the value of Response ID—the greater the sum of unique responses for each category, the darker and larger its box (this is further clarified by the color legend at right).

Size and Color are crucial elements in treemaps. You can modify a treemap by adjusting how color is utilized. For example, in Figure 5.26 I have removed count of Response ID from Color and replaced it with Grade. Now, Grade determines the color of the rectangles and the count of Responses still determines the size of rectangles, allowing us to see top responses per grade.

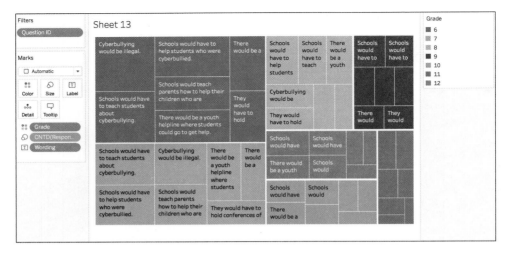

Figure 5.26 Modify elements on the Marks card to adjust the elements of color and shape in a treemap.

The Heat Map

A heat map graph is a great way to compare categorical data using color (see Figure 5.27). Similar to the tree map, a heat map represents the values by a variable in a hierarchy. They are similar in concept to the type of complex visual data representation that you might see used on your local weather forecast by the meteorologist to illustrate rainfall patterns across a region. However, they are not limited to use with maps.

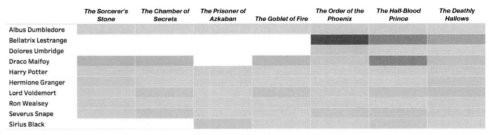

Figure 5.27 A heat map of frequency of aggressive acts committed in *Harry Potter*.

Tip for navigating this type of visualization include:

- Adding a size variation for squares to show the concentration of intersecting factors while adding a third element.

- Using a shape other than a square to convey meaning in a more impactful way.

Tableau How-To: Heat Maps

Building a heat map in Tableau takes a few more clicks than with some of the other charts discussed.

To begin, place one (or more) dimensions onto the Columns shelf *and* one (or more) dimensions on the Rows shelf. Select Square as the mark type and place a measure on the Color shelf (see Figure 5.28).

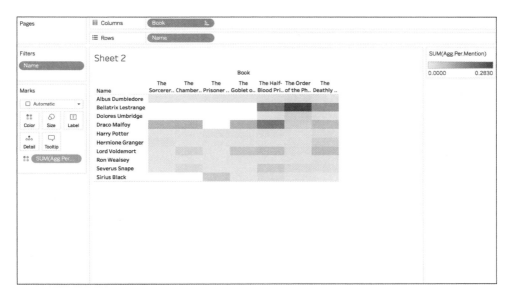

Figure 5.28 Building a heat map.

> **note**
>
> In Figure 5.28 I have already manually sorted the order of books (you can see the sort icon on the Book pill) and filtered the number of characters down (you can see the Name pill in on the Filters shelf).

There are a few more steps to curate this heat map. The preceding example uses an automatic blue gradient color palette. There might be more appropriate color palettes depending on the data you are looking at. For example, Figure 5.27 shows the use of a red-gold gradient scheme to progressively darken the cell color in line with characters' aggressive action counts. You can enter the Colors box in the Marks card, and then select Edit Colors to open the Edit Colors dialog box (see Figure 5.29). From here you can select another color palette from the drop-down menu. This can be either a gradient palette or a diverging palette.

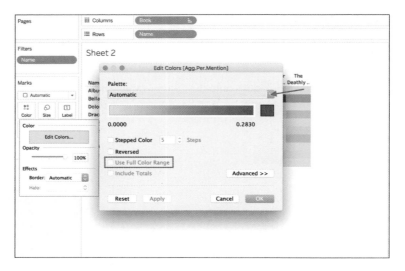

Figure 5.29 Use the Edit Colors dialog box to select an appropriate color scheme for a heat map.

- If you **select** the Use Full Color Range check box for a diverging option, Tableau will assign the starting number a full intensity and the ending number a full intensity.

- If you **don't select** Use Full Color Range, Tableau will automatically assign the color intensity as if the range were from –100 to 100, maximizing the color contrast as much as possible.

Additional visual cues, like lines, are also important contributors to curating heat maps. You can add borders to each colored cell in the view by revisiting the Color Editor box and selecting an appropriate border color from the Effects portion of the border dialog (see Figure 5.30).

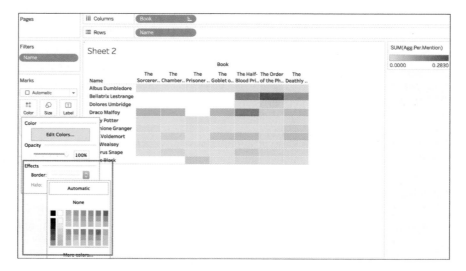

Figure 5.30 Adding borders to colored cells helps to distinguish individual cells in the view.

RECOMMENDED READING

Check out the Tableau white paper: *Which Chart or Graph* for additional information: https://www.tableau.com/learn/whitepapers/which-chart-or-graph-is-right-for-you.

Maps

If you want to analyze or present your data geographically, Tableau has several native mapping capabilities. Maps can be used to display geographic data or as a way to communicate answers to spatial questions, like "Which states offer the most analytics education programs" or "Which regions in the U.S. have the most incidents of Lyme disease?"

While maps can be a great way to tell a story about your data, remember that they are a type of visualization and do have an appropriate use case. Depending on the question you are trying to answer or the insight you are trying to communicate, another chart type might be a more appropriate fit. Before you begin building a map, be sure to take a careful look at your data, your analysis, and your story. Maps, as Tableau explains, should answer questions that have both *"appropriate* data representation and *attractive* data representation. As a storytelling device, maps can be particularly tricky in their tendency to mislead or inadvertently cause people to misinterpret the data, or to dictate a not-quite-true story.

Tableau can be customized to create several types of maps; however, this section covers the two most common: proportional symbol maps and choropleth (or filled) maps.

note

Tableau capabilities include many advanced map types and customization functions that are not covered in this text. Tutorials and use case information for more advanced maps, such as point distribution maps, which help you look for visual clusters of data; flow (or path) maps that connect paths to see where something went (for example, storms or product sales) over time; and spider (or origin-destination) maps that show how an origin location and one or more destination locations interact can be found online. For more info, visit Tableau Help > Maps.

WHAT GEODATA DOES TABLEAU SUPPORT?

Tableau recognizes a set of geographic roles defined by a geocoding database that uses latitude and longitude coordinates. By default, Tableau supports geodata including:

- Worldwide airport codes

- Cities

- Countries/regions/territories

- States/provinces

- Some postcodes and second-level administrative districts (county-equivalents).

- U.S. area codes

- Core-Based Statistical Areas (CBSA)

- Metropolitan Statistical Areas (MSA)

- Congressional districts

- Zip codes

Additionally, Tableau organizes geographic roles within a hierarchical order. The order is City > County > Zip Code > CBSA/MSA > Area Code > State > Country/Region. When you place multiple geographic fields on Detail on the Marks card, Tableau plots the data points in the field with the highest geographic role on this list.

Connecting to Geographic Data

Although you are already familiar with connecting to data in Tableau at this point, geographic data comes in many shapes and formats so it is useful to walk through this step of the process again within the context of mapping to discuss where geodata nuances might affect the process as you prepare to work with geographic data.

note

Newer visions of Tableau Desktop can connect directly to spatial files (like shapefiles or geoJSON files); however, following the precedent established in this book these examples demonstrate connecting to data in Excel.

In this exercise, I connect to a dataset of incidents of Lyme disease. This dataset provides a count of Lyme disease cases by state and county from 2000 to 2015 (see Figure 5.31).

> note
>
> This Lyme disease dataset is publically available from the Center for Disease Control. You can download the data at https://www.cdc.gov/lyme/stats/index.html.

Figure 5.31 This dataset, available from the CDC, contains the number of incidents of Lyme disease over a 15-year period.

Assigning Geographic Roles

After connecting to your data source, you might need to take a few more steps before your geographic data is fully prepared for analysis in Tableau. These steps will not always be necessary to create a map, and might differ depending on your data and the type of map you intend to create. Regardless, all geographic fields should have a data type of string, a data role of dimension, and be assigned the appropriate geographic roles. (The exception is latitude/longitude, which should have a data type of number (decimal), a data role of measure, and be assigned the Latitude and Longitude geographic roles.)

Let's practice adjusting data types for geographic data in the CDC dataset.

This simple dataset has two geographic fields: State and County. Tableau has correctly identified these data types as string; however, clicking on the field and looking at geographic roles reveals that none have been assigned (see Figure 5.32). You might need to assign or edit the geographic role assigned by Tableau. In this example, two things must be done:

- Adjust the State field to the Geographic Role of State
- Adjust the County field to the Geographic Role of County

Figure 5.32 Geographic roles can be assigned, or changed directly from the data source screen. They can also be changed in a worksheet.

With this adjustment you will see the data type icon change to a globe, representing that the field now has a geographic role assigned (see Figure 5.33). Further, the icon designated in blue indicates that Tableau has assigned this field as a dimension. This is correct.

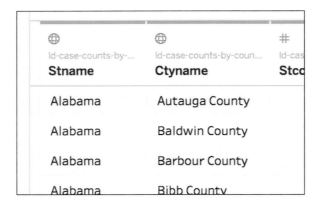

Figure 5.33 The globe icon reflects the geodata field assignment in Tableau.

When you assign the correct geographic role to a field in Tableau, the software will also assign a latitude and longitude to each location. It does this by finding a match that is already built into the geocoding database that is installed with Tableau Desktop. These latitude and longitude fields will display on the Data pane as measures, and are how Tableau knows where to plot your data locations as you begin building a map (see Figure 5.34). (Note: In some advanced maps, you might elect to have your latitude and longitude coordinates as dimensions. These should be considered special uses and are not covered here.)

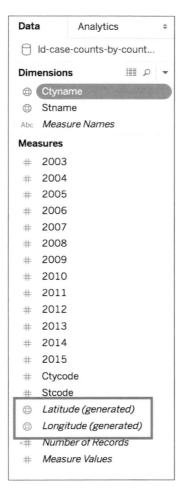

Figure 5.34 When Tableau recognizes geodata, latitude and longitude fields are automatically displayed as measures on the Data pane.

Creating Geographic Hierarchies

In the Tableau worksheet space, if you have more than one level of geographic data in your dataset you can create geographic hierarchies. While these are not critical to creating a map, geographic hierarchies will allow you to quickly drill into the levels of detail your data contains. Because this dataset has both State and County, you can create a hierarchy using these two fields. As State is the larger field in the hierarchy, let's begin there.

To create a geographic hierarchy, right-click the field that represents the highest level of geographic data in the Data pane. Select Hierarchy > Create Hierarchy (see Figure 5.35).

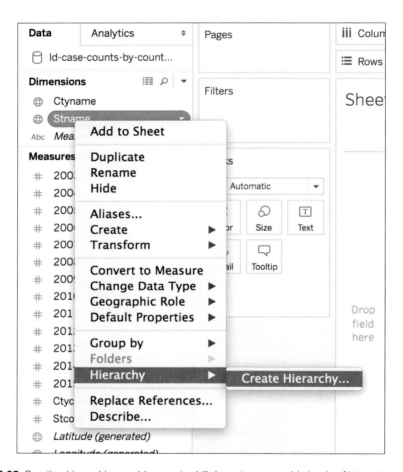

Figure 5.35 Creating hierarchies enables you to drill down to geographic levels of interest.

A dialog box appears that prompts you to name the hierarchy schema, such as Location Data. Enter a name and click OK.

A new field now appears in the Dimensions pane with the name of the hierarchy just created. The highest level geographic data used to create the hierarchy, in this example, state, appears as the first rung in the hierarchy. To add additional fields, simply drag and drop into the hierarchy, placing them in correct order. Repeat as necessary until all geographic fields are included in the hierarchy. Figure 5.36 shows county has been added into the hierarchy below state.

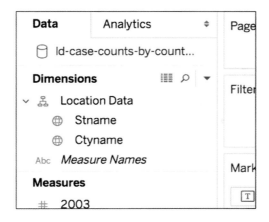

Figure 5.36 Example of geographic hierarchy.

Proportional Symbol Maps

Proportional symbol maps are useful ways to show quantitative values for individual locations. They can show one or two quantitative values per location, and can be encoded with visual cues like size and color. The proportional symbol map displayed in Figure 5.37 shows the number and level of analytic academic programs across the U.S. plotted using the open dataset used in Chapter 1.

> note
>
> You can download this public, and constantly updating, dataset from https:// github.com/ryanswanstrom/awesome-datascience-colleges.

Figure 5.37 This symbol map shows the number and type of academic analytics programs available in the U.S. with legends.

The first step to building a map is to give Tableau geographical coordinates to work with to lay the foundation of the map. Double-click the Latitude and Longitude generated fields under Measures. Latitude is added to the Rows shelf, and Longitude to the Columns shelf. Initially, a blank map view is created (see Figure 5.38).

Figure 5.38 The first step in building a map visualization is to display the Latitude and Longitude coordinates to generate a blank map.

Next, drag out the dimension that represents the location you want to plot your map by and drop it on the Details card. From the hierarchy group in this dataset, I've brought over City to look at programs offered at specific universities. A lower level of detail is added to the view.

note

In this dataset, several international locations now show as Unknown. I've filtered these out to focus only on U.S.–based programs. I have further limited the view to the contiguous 48 states (see Figure 5.39).

Figure 5.39 Add dimensions to the Detail Marks card to begin populating the data displayed on the map.

With a level of detail now on the map, the next step is to bring over the Measure to encode size. In this example I am interested in seeing the number of programs per location, so I can simply bring the Number of Records Dimension to the Size Marks card. With the size of the bubbles representing the number of programs at each location, we can visualize the range of values more clearly (see Figure 5.40).

Figure 5.40 Adding detail to the Size Marks card can enhance the ways symbols appear on the map and encode additional data.

This is the basis of a proportional symbol map. The larger data points represent the locations with the larger total number of programs, and the smaller data points represent the locations with few analytics program options.

Although this shows a good picture of program availability, there is more to do to encode this map with more data and tell a better story. To get a better of idea of which programs are offered at various locations, by degree level, we can bring over Degree dimension to the Color Marks card. (Note: Although this dataset includes everything from Associate Degrees through Doctoral Degrees, I have excluded Associates.)

The proportional symbol map is now complete (see Figure 5.41).

Figure 5.41 Together, color and size can add significant layers of detail to a map.

At this point, your map should look similar to the one displayed previously in Figure 5.37. However, a few more tweaks can help to make the data in your map shine. Try the following:

- **Sort** your categories in an order that makes logical sense. This map has degrees sorted by highest level (Doctoral) to lowest (Bachelor).
- **Color** as usual; I've used the colorblind palette to manually select appropriate colors for each degree in the hierarchy, on a makeshift blue-orange color scale. Additionally, adjust the opacity so that no points are lost behind colors of larger value/darker color. You can also add borders around circles to separate marks.

Choropleth Map

A choropleth (or filled) map is a great tool for showing ratio or aggregated data. These maps use shading and coloring within geographic areas to encode value to a quantity in those areas.

A dataset for choropleth maps should include both quantitative and qualitative values, along with location information recognizable by Tableau.

This example returns to the CDC Lyme disease dataset.

To begin building the map, double-click State. Longitude and Latitude are moved to the Columns and Rows shelves, and a map view with one data point for each state in the data source appears. To look at only the contiguous 48 states, select the Alaska and Hawaii data points, and click Exclude to remove them from view (see Figure 5.42).

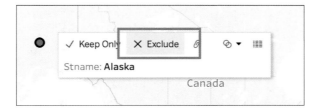

Figure 5.42 You can exclude data by hovering over the data point and clicking Exclude.

Now, let's drill down to a better level of detail. On the Marks card, click the plus icon to drill town to County. This results in a data point for every county within the data source (see Figure 5.43). (If necessary, you can filter any nulls at this point.)

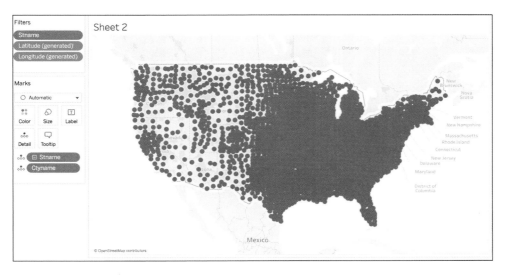

Figure 5.43 This is a nice example of why a choropleth can be a better alternative than a symbol map. There is simply too much data to show in individual points, but all is necessary for analysis.

From here, to transform the symbol map to a filled map, bring a measure to Color on the Marks card. This example uses 2015, the most recent date for the data. The map changes to a filled map mark type and the polygons are colored blue by default (see Figure 5.44). Notice that the default aggregation type for the 2015 measure is SUM by default; however, this might not be the best fit depending on your data. Take a moment to verify that the field should be aggregated as a sum (because this is a count of incidents reported, a sum is appropriate).

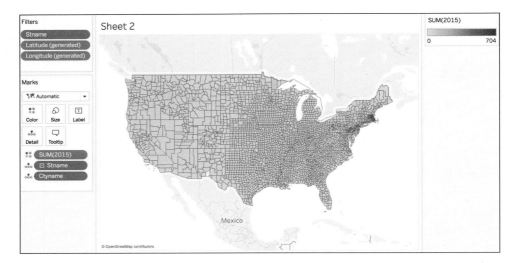

Figure 5.44 Choropleth maps use sequential coloring to embed values in map regions.

Now, let's improve this visualization to tell a better story about the data and complete this choropleth map.

1. On the Marks card, click Color and Edit Colors. Because these are disease incidents, choose a more alerting color, perhaps Orange.

2. Click again on the Marks card and under Effects, remove the Border option by clicking None.

3. Edit the color filter so that it applies colors only to counties that have had at least one incident of Lyme disease. This is an important step in ensuring that the map tells an accurate story, while drawing attention to areas in which Lyme disease is prevalent.

The choropleth map displaying 2015 incidents of Lyme disease within the contiguous states is complete, and paints a grim picture for New England (see Figure 5.45).

Figure 5.45 Color choice on a choropleth map is important and should follow the color practices described earlier in this text.

note

The level of detail specified in the map as well as the color distribution specified for the polygons affects how the data is represented, and how people will interpret the data. In some cases, stepped color might be more appropriate.

note

Again, as discussed in the previous chapter, context is everything. With maps, keeping population sizes in context is especially important. You might need to "normalize" your data with a calculated field to ensure you are looking at populations in context of their geographic regions.

MAP LAYERS

Of the many customization features for maps in Tableau, one of the most interesting is choosing between the built-in map background styles to adjust the background of your map. The three background options offered in Tableau are Normal, Light (the default), or Dark. Figure 5.46 shows each background option.

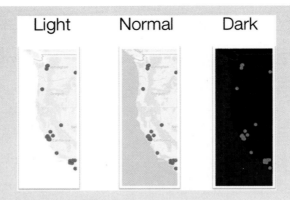

Figure 5.46 Three standard map backgrounds available in Tableau.

To select a Tableau map background style choose Map>Map Layers and adjust the Style in the Map Layers box (see Figure 5.47).

Figure 5.47 You can adjust map backgrounds and other formatting stylistics in the Map Layers pane.

You can also experiment with importing your own background map, adding a static background map image, and adding or subtracting map layers by data layers. Learn more at http://onlinehelp.tableau.com/current/pro/desktop/en-us/maps_options.html.

KEEPING MAPS NEUTRAL

Visualizations are not neutral and maps, like any storytelling device, can be used to mislead audiences if not designed correctly and honestly—and customized for the audience. Google Maps does this with lines and how it adjusts views for disputed territories. For example, Russian users see Crimea marked off with a solid line indicated that the area belongs to Russia, but for Ukrainian users the solid line is replaced with a dashed stroke indicating that the peninsula belongs to the Ukraine. Everyone else, like us in the U.S., see a hybrid line that reflects Crimea's disputed status (see Figure 5.48).

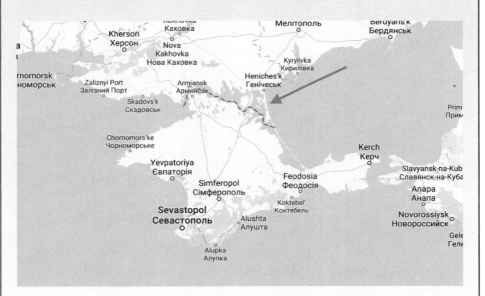

Figure 5.48 This Google Maps version of the Crimea border is intended for a U.S.–based audience and shows a hybrid line that reflects the border's disputed status.

Additionally, the manner in which we use shapes and colors to encode data that represents humans can be tricky on a map. One Minnesota poverty map recently changed from representing humans as red dots—which results in a map full of red swarm—to a gradient purple to look less aggressive (see Figure 5.49).

Figure 5.49 This unfortunate design choice to represent population was later adjusted to a more neutral, and less offensive, approach.

These examples, and many more, speak to the importance of paying special attention to how our assumptions, intuitions, and biases—or even the things we might not consider—affect how we build visualizations to tell stories about people and places. Check out this article for more: https://source.opennews.org/articles/when-designer-shows-design/.

Summary

This chapter explored how to create basic charts and maps displayed on the Show Me card in Tableau. The following chapter presents a pragmatic look at how to curate meaningful visualizations that take advantage of the visual processing horsepower of the human brain.

CHAPTER 6

CURATING VISUALS FOR YOUR AUDIENCE

This chapter dives into human cognition and visual perception to frame the contribution of pre-attentive attributes like size, color, and position and how important they are to the storytelling process. It explores how these can be used strategically to help direct an audience's attention and create a visual hierarchy of components to communicate effectively. This chapter provides the framework for curating story arcs and layouts with visualizations in Tableau that the following chapters explore in-depth.

It's been said—by Tableau, actually—that data visualization is one of the most significant technologies of the 21st century. Of course, the act of visually representing data is not limited to the 21st century. Chapter 2 looked at Minard's flow map of Napoleon's invasion of Russia, published in 1869. In addition to Minard, many other quintessential examples exist of peoples' attempts to visually explore, explain, and communicate data throughout the last several centuries. Many of these have had significant influence on modern data visualization—from Ptolemy's earliest preserved use of a data table to display astronomical information in 150 BCE; to Descartes' 17th century introduction of the Cartesian coordinate system; to Playfair's invention of the time-series line graph, bar chart, and pie chart in the 19th century, Nightingale's 1858 Coxcomb plot, Snow's map of the 1854 London cholera outbreak, and Tukey's box plot just a few decades ago (see Figure 6.1). As far back as we can look, we seem to have always looked for visual ways to see and understand data more clearly.

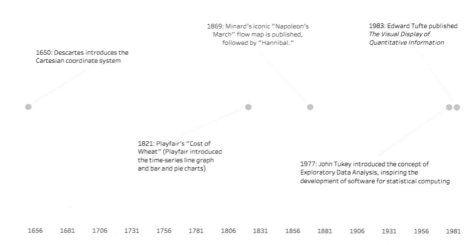

Figure 6.1 Noteworthy names in data viz through time.

Why? Humans are intrinsically visual creatures. In fact, of all the powerful processing systems hardwired into the human brain, none are more powerful than our visual system. Our brains are literally designed with cognitive and perceptual abilities to visually process complex information. We've been learning, remembering, and even writing (our earliest forms of written languages were cuneiform) using the power of pictures for nearly all of recorded human history, so it makes sense that we would apply this same cognitive horsepower to how we interact with data, too.

note

John Medina, a developmental molecular biologist who studies how the mind reacts to and organizes information, developed the concept of the picture superiority effect, which recognizes that information learned by viewing pictures is more easily and more frequently recalled than that learned purely by textural or other word-form equivalents, including audio (see Figure 6.2).

Picture Superiority Effect, Visualized
Memory Retention After 3 Days

65%
Text & Picture

10%
Text or Audio Only

Figure 6.2 John Medina's picture superiority effect, visualized.

note

Read more on our shared visual human history, including a study of visual communication from cave drawings through advance visualizations, in *The Visual Imperative*.

The power of pictures isn't only limited to helping us transform data into meaning. Visuals also act as memory magnets in our brains: We embed and retain memories in visual form. We're extremely good at this visual memorization, too: Research into our visual retention systems dating back as early as the 1970s has measured our visual memory capacity to be somewhere in the vicinity of 10,000 images with a recognition rate of approximately 83%.

With that kind of retention power, one can easily understand how our visual capacity demands careful attention when working with data. We want to make sure that we are visualizing data both efficiently to leverage our cognitive abilities, and accurately to ensure that we are representing information correctly.

Visual Design Building Blocks

Chapter 2, "The Power of Visual Data Stories," briefly covered perceptual pop-out and some of the cognitive aspects that make data visualization and visual data stories so powerful. We must discuss many important elements as we dissect the visual properties of visualization and the best ways to capitalize on them. The steps you take to format your analysis and presentation are critically important as they can make or break the visual appeal and effectiveness of any visualization.

As you might have noticed in our previous work in building basic charts and graphs in Tableau, you can format just about every visual element you see on a worksheet, from titles and subtitles; to typeface fonts; to color use, shape and size of symbols; and shading, borders, and lines. Further, you can specify format settings for a specific field within an individual worksheet, entire workbooks, or within dashboards and stories. This chapter provides a closer look at a few of the most important visual design building blocks, and how you can use Tableau functionality to embed these visual cues purposefully and intuitively as you format your visualizations.

In particular, this chapter covers:

- Color
- Lines
- Shapes

Chapter 8, "Storyboarding Frame by Frame," covers additional formatting for dashboards and stories.

> **note**
>
> Before curating your visualization, you must first understand and explore the data, and represent it using the chart or graph best suited for your data's story. From there you can apply visual cues that enable you to intuitively and meaningfully communicate to audiences. Chapters 5, "Choosing the Right Visual," and 9, "Advanced Storytelling Charts," cover selecting and building the best charts.

Color

Color is one of the most important, most complicated, and most frequently misused elements of data visualization. Used well, colors can enhance and clarify a visualization, but used poorly color can confuse, misrepresent, or obstruct clear communication. Color is such a critical element in representing data visually that Tableau employs color scientists to help design the best color palettes as well as provide deep education on the appropriate use of color. This section covers how to properly apply color to a visual that aligns to its data and your story; however, this is an area in which you should invest more time learning.

All marks in Tableau have a default color, even no fields are placed on the Color Marks card. For most marks, blue is the default color. For text, gray is the default color. We'll explore how to use the Color Marks card when looking at how it is used in different types of visualization.

> **note**
>
> The visuals in this section use the Global Superstore dataset available from Tableau.

Tableau applies color depending on the field's values. For discrete values, or dimensions, Tableau typically uses a categorical palette, whereas for continuous, or measures, Tableau assigns a quantitative palette. These translate into the three primary ways to encode data with color in data visualization:

- Sequential
- Diverging for continuous, quantitative values
- Categorical for discrete values.

Sequential color encodes a quantitative value from low to high using gradients of a single color and is usable when all values are positive or all values are negative. A great example of this is Sales, which goes from zero to infinity. The map in Figure 6.3 uses a sequential color scale to encode positive sales amounts into each U.S. state.

Figure 6.3 This map uses sequential color to show the sum of sales from least to greatest—the darker the blue, the higher the sales.

The automatic sequential color palette used in Tableau is blue. In addition to being able to change the palette itself, you can also adjust the distribution of color by clicking the Color Marks card, which opens the Edit Colors dialog box (see Figure 6.4).

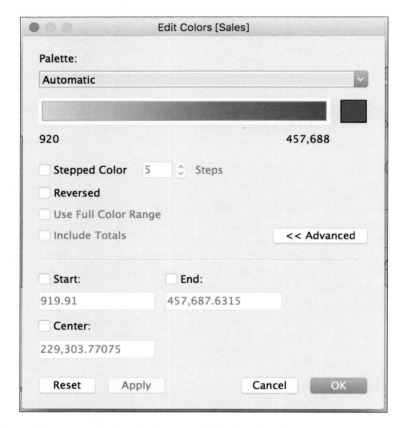

Figure 6.4 Select and adjust color palettes in the Edit Colors dialog box.

Diverging color encodes a quantitative value but has a midpoint—for example, zero—and numbers on either side of this midpoint—positive and negative—are displayed in a different color with each having its own sequential palette.

Figure 6.5 uses a diverging color palette to display profit by state (top) and profit by product category and subcategory (bottom). Positive profit is colored blue with darker blue reflecting higher profit. Profit could also be negative, and in this visual negative values are encoded in orange with the darker orange reflecting a bigger loss.

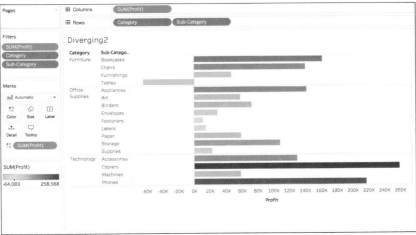

Figure 6.5 Diverging color palettes display positive and negative values using gradient shading of two contrasting colors to encode values.

Similarly to the sequential color palette, Tableau automatically assigns a color palette for diverging values. The default is an orange-blue diverging color palette (we discuss why *not* to use a red-green diverging color palette and instead use better palettes to avoid issues of color vision deficiency later in this chapter). As with any color palette, you can adjust the diverging one (see Figure 6.6).

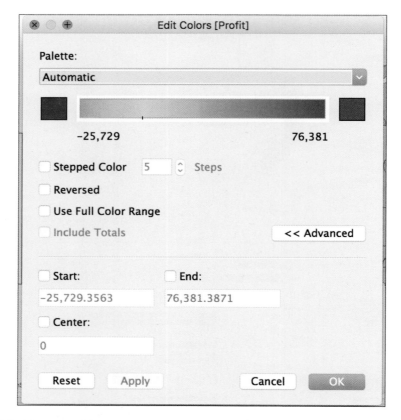

Figure 6.6 Using the new Tableau automatic diverging color palette, orange-blue, is the best practice; it replaces the red-green color palette.

Diverging color palettes are clearly designated in the Tableau color library. Beyond changing the colors themselves, you can also adjust the midpoint. Midpoints are not exclusively zero. They could be the average, such as above or below average, or target, whether exceeding or below.

Stepped Color

In addition to changing the range of colors, you can also group values into color-coded bins using stepped colors. Use the up and down arrows to specify how many bins to create (see Figure 6.7).

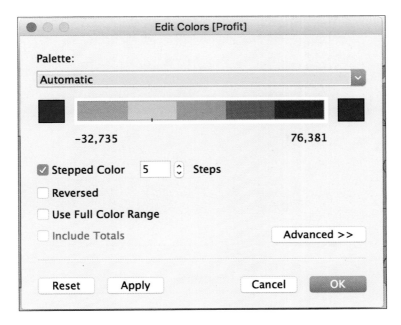

Figure 6.7 Rather than use gradient shading, you can also use stepped color palettes to distinguish colors.

Reversed Color

If it makes sense to do so, you can select the Reversed option to reverse the order of colors in the range. For sequential colors, this means darkening the intensity in the lower values rather than the higher. Likewise, for diverging colors, this means swapping the two colors in the palette in addition to reversing the shades within each range.

Finally, *categorical* colors encode categories—apples, bananas, and oranges; shoes, socks, and shirts; or in the case of Figure 6.8, furniture, office supplies, and technology—using distinct colors appropriate for fields that have no inherent quantitative order.

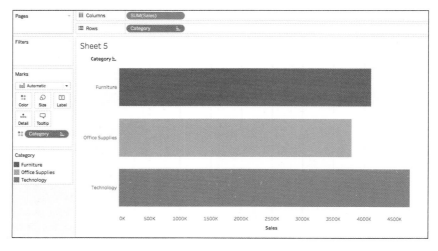

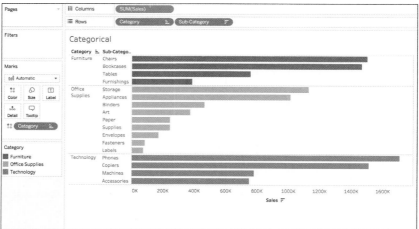

Figure 6.8 These examples use the Tableau automatic palette for categorical color coding.

By default, Tableau assigns categorical color using the automatic Tableau color palette. As you might expect, you can adjust this to use a color palette of your choosing (see Figure 6.9). To change color values, click the Color Marks card and select Edit. A dialog box opens that allows you to select from the color palettes in Tableau. You can assign an entirely new palette to every item in the field, or you can manually assign a color to each field by selecting and assigning a color swatch to individual items. If you need to manually add a specific color shade to comply with company branding guidelines, you can do that, too.

Figure 6.9 The Tableau color library includes a wide variety of pre-programmed color palettes to choose from. You can also program your own.

Color Effects

Beyond advanced color options, additional configuration options not related to the actual colors shown are available in Tableau. These include adjusting opacity, mark borders, and mark halos (see Figure 6.10). The preceding chapter explored some of these functions briefly within the context of curating maps.

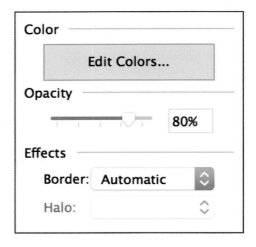

Figure 6.10 The Color Marks card offers additional options for color formatting.

Opacity

Adjusting the opacity can be helpful for looking at dense scatter plots or in maps overlaying a background image. Moving the slider left makes the marks become more transparent. Consider the before and after in Figure 6.11: The map on the top has opacity at 100% whereas the opacity in the map on the bottom is at 50%.

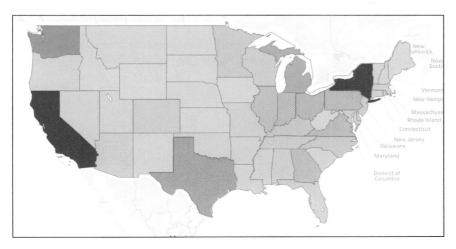

Figure 6.11 Adjusting the opacity in color can be a helpful way to show layers without obscuring marks in the visualization. This is especially helpful in maps and scatter plots, which might have many layers of data or overlapping marks in one viz.

Mark Borders

Tableau automatically displays all marks without borders; however, you can turn these on for all mark types except text, line, and shapes.

Borders can be helpful in distinguishing closely spaced marks. However, they can also make distinguishing color-encoded dimensions (as they make marks narrower) more difficult (like in a stacked bar chart). Adjust your visualization with and without borders to see whether they add or reduce clarity.

Mark Halos

Lastly, mark halos can assist in making marks more visible, particularly on maps, by surrounding each mark with a ring of contrasting color (see Figure 6.12).

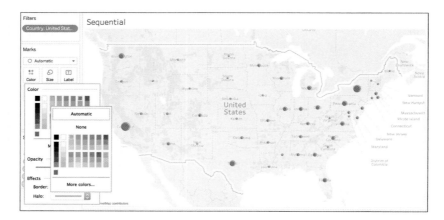

Figure 6.12 You can choose mark halos from the color palette to "ring" a data point and increase its visibility and separation from other marks on the viz.

We can also use color to highlight data or alert audiences to important insights.

You use a *highlight* color to highlight one data point or category. For example, if you are tracking profits of product categories over time with a separate line representing each category and you want to highlight the consistent high profits in a certain category, perhaps technology, you can highlight one state by coloring only this line and using gray for the other categories (see Figure 6.13). This allows the audience to clearly see how well this category is doing in comparison to others on the chart.

Earth-tone colors, like blue, are great colors for highlighting.

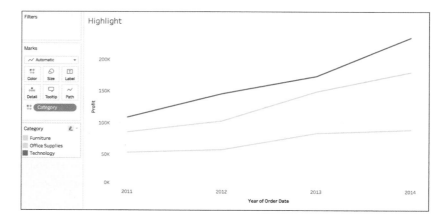

Figure 6.13 Using a highlighting color, like blue, drives attention to one mark on a viz without the need for additional labeling.

Similarly to highlighting, you can use *alerting* colors to draw the audience's attention to a particular data point. Using the same line chart as in Figure 6.13, rather than highlighting the high profits of technology maybe the goal is to instead alert the audience of the low profits in furniture (see Figure 6.14). In this use case, alerting is done with an alarming or alerting color—like red—to indicate to the audience that something is wrong.

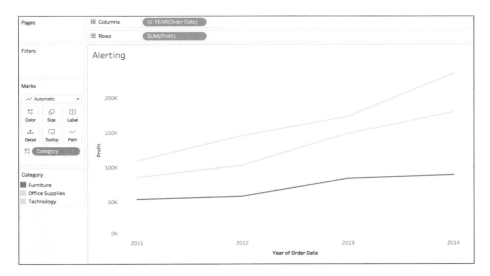

Figure 6.14 Using an alerting color, like red, drives attention to one mark on a viz without the need for additional labeling.

It's important to note that in Western culture red is often associated with negative values or associations; however, this is not always consistent with color culture in other countries, like China. Bright alerting colors could be red, orange, or yellow.

The Truth about Red and Green

This note about the cautious use of red in visualization brings us to an important conversation regarding the use of red/green color palettes in visualization. Most of us are familiar with the traffic light palette, where red is stop, green is go or positive, and yellow or orange (or white as a midpoint) means to proceed with caution.

Although this option is available in Tableau, there is very rarely—if ever—a valid and compelling reason to use it. Instead, a very compelling reason exists *not* to use it: color vision deficiency (CVD). For the most part, we all share a common color vision sensory experience. However, as many as 8% of men and 0.5% of women suffer from some kind of color vision deficiency. Most prolific among these is red-green, or deuteranope, making this palette particularly troublesome. (Even if the red/green palette *must* be used, there are techniques to make this color palette appropriate for circumventing color vision deficiency issues, such as using a blue-green rather than a pure green, which will help make the colors distinct enough that they can be recognized by someone with CVD.)

Take a look at Figure 6.15. The highlight table on the left will appear commonly red-green to someone without color deficiency, but to someone with deuteranope, the colors appear as the image on the right. As you can tell, the colors to someone with red-green color vision deficiency are much less distinguished, which reduces the potency of the visualization.

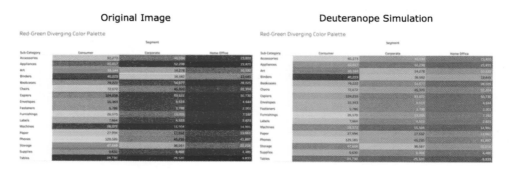

Figure 6.15 A red-green image is virtually unreadable to someone with deuteranope color deficiency.

To provide an easy solution for navigating complexity of color vision deficiencies, Tableau has both an orange-blue diverging color palette (for quantitative values) and a color-blind palette (for categorical values); see Figure 6.16.

> tip
>
> To experiment with how your own visuals might appear to someone with various types of color vision deficiencies, visit http://www.vischeck.com.

Orange-Blue Diverging (Color blind, quantitative)

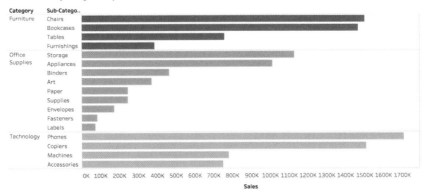

Color Blind (Categorical)

Figure 6.16 An orange-blue color palette is best suited to mitigate any color deficiency issues.

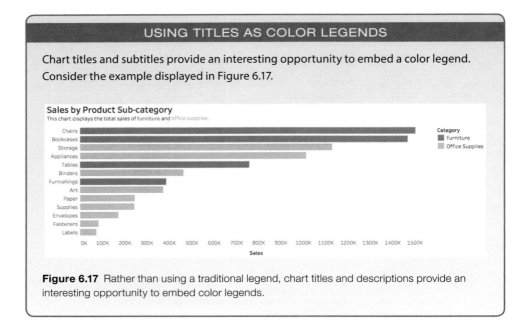

USING TITLES AS COLOR LEGENDS

Chart titles and subtitles provide an interesting opportunity to embed a color legend. Consider the example displayed in Figure 6.17.

Figure 6.17 Rather than using a traditional legend, chart titles and descriptions provide an interesting opportunity to embed color legends.

Lines

Lines facilitate several purposes in data visualization. They act as guides, they reinforce patterns, they provide direction, and they create shapes. Like any visual element, too many lines—or lines given too much emphasis—can cause distraction or confusion in data visualization. However, used wisely, they can be transformative. Like color, lines should be used sparingly to reduce the amount of ink onscreen so that the data can lead the story.

This section covers how to format lines within individual visualizations in Tableau and make effective use of them as view lines (axis lines, reference lines, and so on), borders, and shaded bands. It also looks at how lines can affect visualizations in the form of gridlines, axis rulers, and panes in Tableau.

To format lines in Tableau worksheets, select the Format menu, then the part of the view that you want to format (see Figure 6.18).

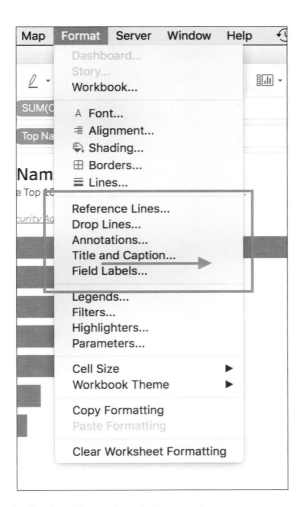

Figure 6.18 Access the line formatting options via the Format menu.

You can also right-click on your sheet and select Format (see Figure 6.19).

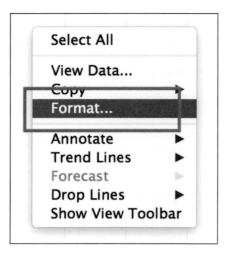

Figure 6.19 You can also granted right-click the worksheet and select the Format option to access the line formatting options.

Either of these methods opens the Format pane as a new tab in place of the Data pane with icons to help direct formatting of individual elements in the worksheet (see Figure 6.20).

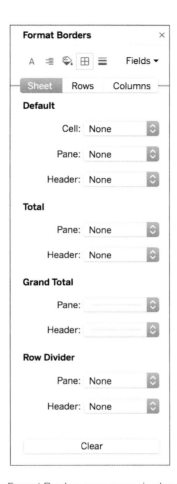

Figure 6.20 Once activated, the Format Borders pane opens in place of the Data pane.

note

In this section, I create visualizations using a Tableau-provided dataset of the most popular male and female baby names in each state for each year from 1910–2012. This data is collected from the Social Security Administration.

By default, most chart types in Tableau include gray axis lines, zero lines, drop lines, and borders. If added, reference lines that help you analyze statistical information in the data are also gray by default.

In general, a best practice is to remove as many of these as possible, keeping only what are necessary to guide audiences through the visualization or highlight important aspects of the data.

Let's walk through the steps of formatting lines together using a series of simple visualizations.

Formatting Grid Lines, Zero Lines, and Drop Lines

Grid lines, zero lines, and drop lines connect marks to the axis. You format them using the lines icon on the Format pane and you can adjust them by sheet, row, or column (see Figure 6.21).

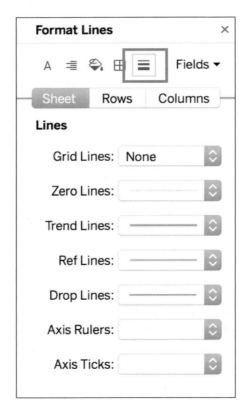

Figure 6.21 Format grid lines, zero lines, and other reference lines using the Lines icon on the Format pane.

Figure 6.22 is the default view of a sorted bar chart reflecting the Top 10 Girls' Baby Names in the U.S. from 1910–2012. (Titles/subtitles have been formatted by double-clicking on the default title line.) We will use this visualization to experiment with formatting lines.

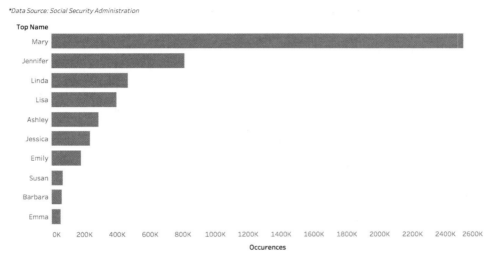

Figure 6.22 A simple bar chart of top baby names, without line formatting.

To create this chart and follow along, follow these steps:

1. Filter the data by Gender, selecting Female.
2. Drag Occurrences (SUM) to Columns, and Top Name to Rows.
3. Sort Top Name descending by Occurrence.
4. Select all names after the first ten, right-click, and select Hide.
5. You might also adjust the view to Entire View.

Selecting which lines to remove is a matter of judgment. Typically, I remove all grid lines. You can turn off zero lines, too, but whether or not you choose to remove this line should depend on how important being above or below zero is in your data.

In this example, I remove all grid lines, zero lines, reference, and drop lines. I also remove axis ticks and row axis rulers, but keep column axis rulers for reference and reformat them as dotted lines (see Figure 6.23).

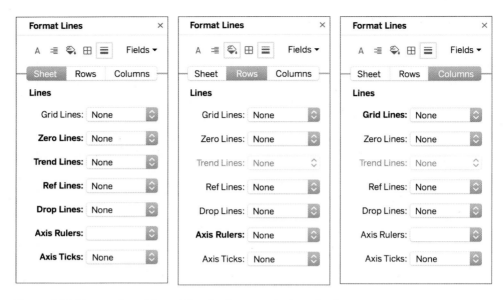

Figure 6.23 You can format lines at the sheet, row, and column levels.

The resulting visualization is much cleaner, with only one line at the bottom of the x-axis, as shown in Figure 6.24.

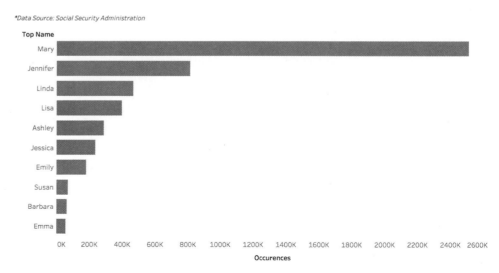

Figure 6.24 A simple bar chart of top baby names, with line formatting.

Formatting Borders

Borders are the lines that surround visualizations, demarking the table, pane, cells, and headers. You can specify the border style, width, and color for the cell, pane, and header areas. You format these using the grid icon on the Format pane (see Figure 6.25).

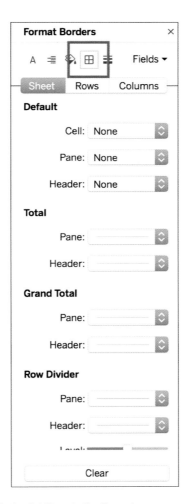

Figure 6.25 Format borders via the Grid icon in the Format pane.

Returning to the bar chart, I have added orange row dividers as borders to show how they appear when formatted (see Figure 6.26). Notice that because I changed the format of the axis line to a dotted line, it now appears as colored dots.

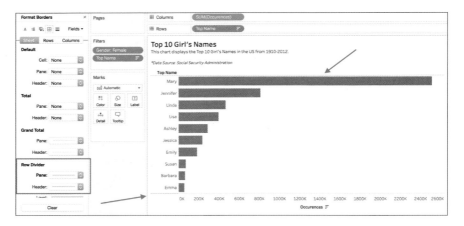

Figure 6.26 This figure shows an example of border formatting for row dividers.

Row and column dividers are most commonly used in nested tables, because they serve to visually break up a view and separate data fields, especially when several levels of data exist. Figure 6.27 is the default view of a nested table bar reflecting the Top 10 girls and boys baby names from 1910–2012. (Titles/subtitles have been formatted by double-clicking on the default title line.)

Top Baby Names 1910-2012
Data Source: Social Security Administration

Gender	Top Name	
Female	Mary	2,510,913
	Jennifer	811,054
	Linda	465,969
	Lisa	396,100
	Ashley	287,670
	Jessica	233,289
	Emily	181,136
	Susan	69,966
	Barbara	62,384
	Emma	55,096
Male	Michael	2,274,105
	James	1,566,897
	Robert	1,213,750
	John	756,249
	David	291,260
	Jacob	201,448
	Christopher	192,699
	William	111,884
	Daniel	69,552
	Jason	63,069

Figure 6.27 A basic nested table, without additional formatting.

To create this table and follow along, follow these steps:

1. Drag Gender and Top Name to Rows.
2. Drag Occurrences (SUM) to the Text Marks card.
3. Sort Top Name descending by Occurrence.
4. Scroll through the table and select all names after the first ten for each gender, right-click, and select Hide.

Using the Format Borders function, you can modify the style, width, color, and level of the borders that divide each row or each column by using the row and column divider drop-down menus. The level refers to the header level you want to divide by; at the highest level, all fields are divided (as shown earlier in Figure 6.27, which at the highest level is divided by Top Name).

This many lines are unnecessary, even in a table. Thus, at the sheet level, I've reformatted the row dividers to a Level 2 heading so that I can differentiate between genders rather than separating each name. At the column level, I've also removed the column divider on the right to simplify the table's appearance (see Figure 6.28).

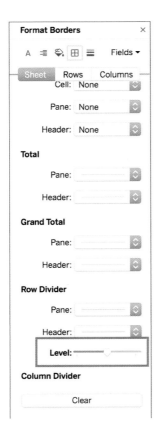 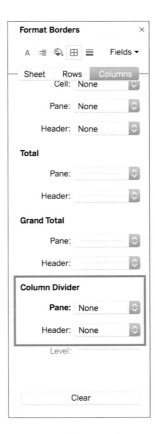

Figure 6.28 Formatting lines at several levels requires individual attention to each.

The resulting table shown in Figure 6.29 is a cleaner, easier-to-read table.

Top Baby Names 1910-2012		
Data Source: Social Security Administration		
Gender	Top Name	
Female	Mary	2,510,913
	Jennifer	811,054
	Linda	465,969
	Lisa	396,100
	Ashley	287,670
	Jessica	233,289
	Emily	181,136
	Susan	69,966
	Barbara	62,384
	Emma	55,096
Male	Michael	2,274,105
	James	1,566,897
	Robert	1,213,750
	John	756,249
	David	291,260
	Jacob	201,448
	Christopher	192,699
	William	111,884
	Daniel	69,552
	Jason	63,069

Figure 6.29 A simple table, with some considerate line formatting.

Formatting, Shading, and Banding

Finally, at the intersection of lines and color, you can use shading to set a background color to the entire visualization or to various areas of importance, like headers, panes, or totals.

Commonly, shaded areas are a technique used for banding, where the background color alternates from row-to-row or column-to-column. This technique is useful for tables, as shown earlier in Figure 6.29, because it helps the eye distinguish rows or columns more intuitively than added superfluous lines. To format shading and banding you use the paint can icon on the Format pane (see Figure 6.30).

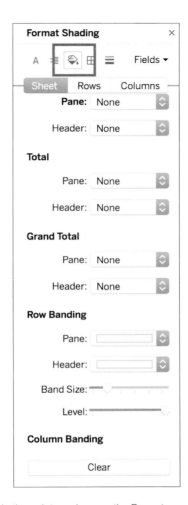

Figure 6.30 Format shading via the paint can icon on the Format pane.

The nested table in Figure 6.29 has row banding by default. If desired, you could change this by sliding the band size to zero (see Figure 6.31).

Figure 6.31 You can adjust row banding manually on the Format pane.

Explore additional banding options by interacting with the various settings on the Format pane. As a guide, practice with the following:

- **Pane and header:** This affects the color of the bands.
- **Band size:** This affects the thickness of the bands.
- **Level:** As described earlier, if you have nested tables or multiple dimensions, this option allows you to add and format banding at specific levels.

REMOVING FIELD LABELS AND UNNECESSARY HEADERS

By default, when you create a visualization, Tableau provides both field labels and headers for each axis. Often, this is redundant, especially when you add a title to your chart. Removing unnecessary elements streamlines the visualization for your audience.

As an example, reconsider Figure 6.24. You can see the field labels for Top Name rows, as well as the axis header for Occurrences directly below the count. Does your audience need this duplicated information, or can we trust them to infer the fields without an additional header? If the latter is true, consider right-clicking the field label for Top Name and removing it. Next, to remove the axis header, right-click to Edit Axis and remove the title by erasing text in the field. The resulting visualization is much simpler (see Figure 6.32).

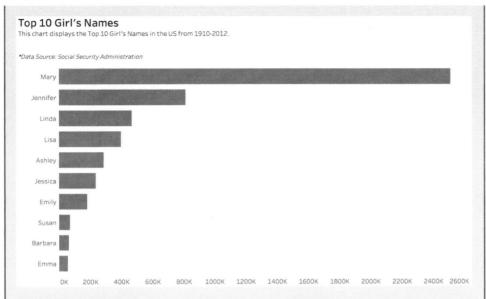

Figure 6.32 A modified view of a simple bar chart after eliminating redundant headers.

For additional simplification, you can remove the x axis entirely, and label individual bars instead (see Figure 6.33).

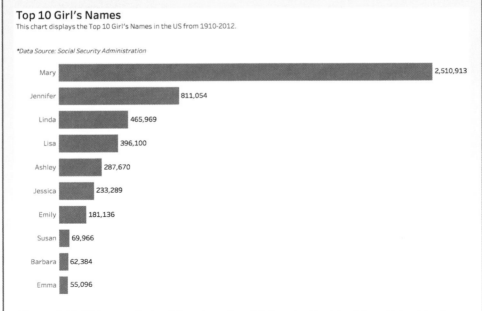

Figure 6.33 With some final polish and curation, this bar chart is data-rich and ink-minimal.

Figure 6.34 shows a before and after view of the original and finished versions of this chart

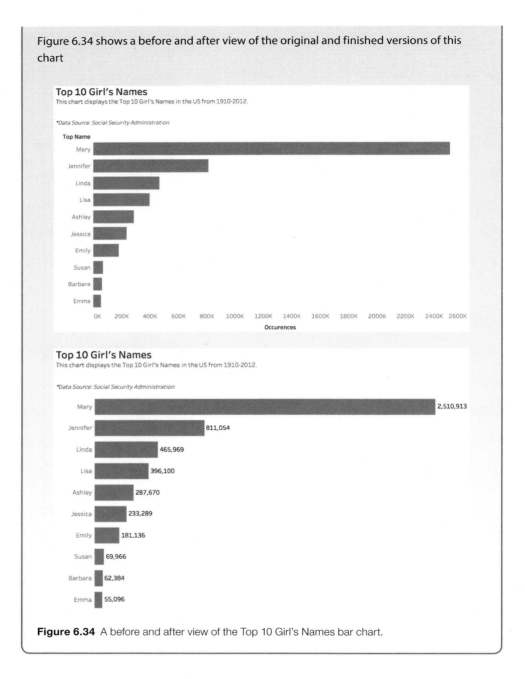

Figure 6.34 A before and after view of the Top 10 Girl's Names bar chart.

> **tip**
>
> Adding back a previously removed header can be a bit of a trick in Tableau. To
> unhide a header, go through Analysis > Table Layout. You can also unhide any
> header from the rows or columns by simply right-clicking on the pill. Use the
> header's check box to toggle the header's display on or off for each pill.

Shapes

As a time-saving technique, shapes are one of the ways that our brains recognize patterns. We
immediately group similar objects and separate them from those that look different. Some
chart types, like packed bubble charts, use shapes (along with size and color) to encode meaning. Additionally, we can use shapes in interesting ways to personalize data stories in Tableau.
The two ways to use shapes in Tableau are with the Shape Marks card and custom shapes.

Shape Marks Card

The Shape Marks card feature allows you to assign different shapes to data marks. Dropping a
dimension on the Shape Marks card prompts Tableau to assign a unique shape to each member
in the field, as well as display a shape legend (see Figure 6.35). Using the Size Marks card allows
you to enlarge or reduce the size of each shapes mark.

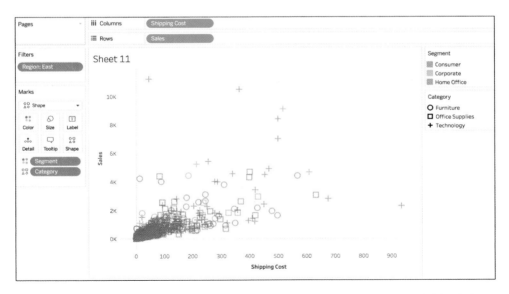

Figure 6.35 The Size Marks card allows you to use shapes to encode categories, a helpful technique
on a crowded scatter plot.

As displayed in Figure 6.35, default shapes in Tableau are unfilled symbols. This palette contains ten unique shapes. If your data has more than ten members, the shapes will repeat.

You can edit this default palette and assign a different palette from the library of shape options within Tableau. Choices include a variety of shape palettes, arrows, weather symbols, and KPI metrics. To edit the shapes palette assigned to your data, click the Shape Marks card and select Edit Shape. A dialog box, similar to the Color dialog box, appears that allows you to select a new palette as well as manually assign shapes to each data item (see Figure 6.36).

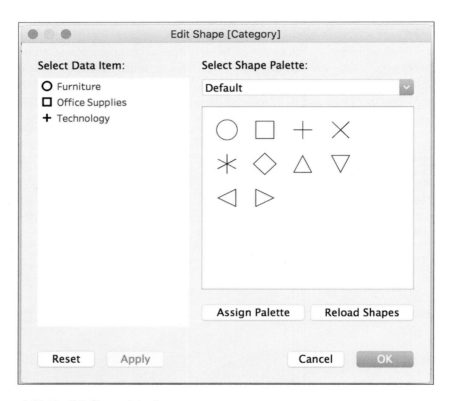

Figure 6.36 The Edit Shape dialog box.

Custom Shapes

If none of the palettes in the Tableau library appeal to you or are suitable for your dataset, you can also add custom shapes into your Tableau environment for use in your workbooks. Custom shapes can add a nice design touch to your visualization, particularly when you are building a narrative or working to create engagement or visual appeal.

This function requires accessing your Tableau Repository on your machine. To add custom shape palettes into the Tableau library, follow these steps:

1. Create your image files. Each shape should be its own file, and most image formats (including .png, .gif, .jpg, .bmp, and .tiff) are acceptable. (Tableau does not support symbols in .emf format.)

2. Copy the shape files to a new folder in the My Tableau Repository>Shapes folder on your computer. The name of the folder will be the name of the new palette in Tableau.

> **note**
>
> If you plan to use color to encode shapes, use a transparent background in your image file (PNG). Otherwise, the entire square of the symbol thumbnail will be colored, rather than just the symbol itself.

Figure 6.37 shows that I have added two new palettes, Harry Potter and Hogwarts House Crests, to my shapes library.

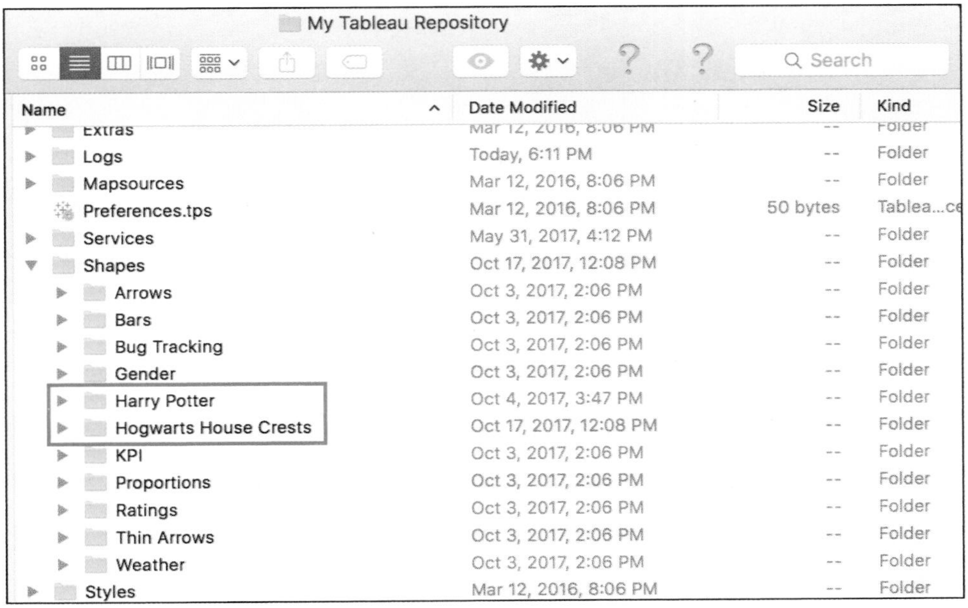

Figure 6.37 You can manually add shape palettes to Tableau's shape library by dropping them into the Shapes file of your Tableau Repository.

When you return to Tableau, you will see the new palettes included in the Shape Palette library in the Edit Shape dialog box. If you modified the shapes while Tableau was running, you might need to click Reload Shapes (see Figure 6.38).

You can assign these new shapes in the same manner as you do any shape palette within Tableau.

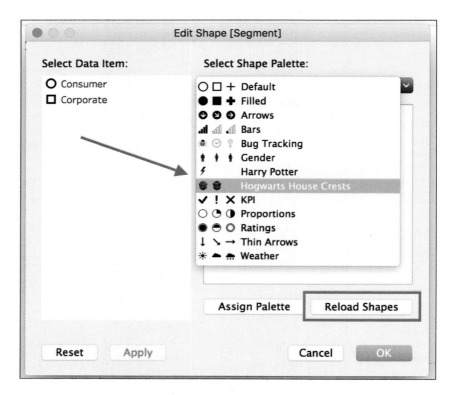

Figure 6.38 Manually added shapes now appear in the Edit Shape dialog box.

> **tip**
>
> For tips on creating custom shapes best suited for use in Tableau, see the help article at https://www.tableau.com/drive/custom-shapes.

Summary

This chapter looked at how to format important visual cues in data visualization that can enhance your data's story if used wisely. The next chapter covers preparing data for visual analysis and storytelling in Tableau. Chapter 8 reviews how to use additional formatting options in Tableau to build visualizations, dashboards, and story points to present a complete and compelling visual data story.

CHAPTER 7

PREPARING DATA FOR STORYTELLING

This chapter covers the very beginning of the data storytelling process, providing the processing steps necessary to ready messy data for visual analysis and storytelling in Tableau. You will leverage the lessons learned thus far in the text as you work through preparing data for analysis, connecting to data, and beginning to visually explore it in Tableau. This chapter walks you through this process, from exporting raw data from survey platforms in order to discuss some important data preparation steps that matter in Tableau, through manually preparing it in Excel and using Tableau 10 and to get data just where it needs to begin building a compelling visual data story.

Knowing the basics of visual data storytelling from context, to charts, to curation, better prepares you to begin crafting a compelling data narrative to deliver to your intended audience and make an impact. However, before you can start working with real data in Tableau, you need to be sure it is in the right shape for analysis. Most, if not all, data needs a little bit of work before it's ready to become a story. We'll work through this process using messy survey data, a common experience for data storytellers.

> note
>
> Follow along with these steps by downloading the raw survey data exports from www.visualdatastorytelling.com.

Basic Data Prep in Tableau: Data Interpreter

Like its predecessor versions, Tableau 10.X includes built-in data prepping capabilities that help make reshaping data a smoother and less labor-intensive experience than doing it by hand (or using the no-longer-supported Tableau Excel add-in, which only worked for Windows-based licenses).

Before getting into a specific data prep exercise using survey data, let's review some of the basic data preparation tools included in Tableau with Data Interpreter. Chapter 3, "Getting Started with Tableau," covered this function superficially; however, this section takes a closer look at how it can be used with a real dataset.

 This exercise uses a dataset titled "Significant Volcanic Eruptions." This sampled dataset is available from the Tableau website and contains a global listing of more than 600 volcanic eruptions from 4360 BC to the present via the Significant Volcanic Eruptions Database. Within this data, a significant eruption is classified as one that meets at least one of the following criteria: caused fatalities, caused moderate damage (approximately $1 million or more), Volcanic Explosivity Index (VEI) of 6 or greater, generated a tsunami, or was associated with a significant earthquake.

> note
>
> While the Significant Volcanic Eruptions dataset is a relatively clean dataset, I have made some additions to it for the sake of exploring preparation tasks. You can download the modified version from visualdatastorytelling.com

Data Interpreter in Action

Although Tableau can easily connect to the sheet, you can see in the preview shown in Figure 7.1 that some issues exist. There are no column names, the headers from Excel have a lot of nulls, and so forth. Tableau has recognized these issues and suggests Data Interpreter to help prepare this data.

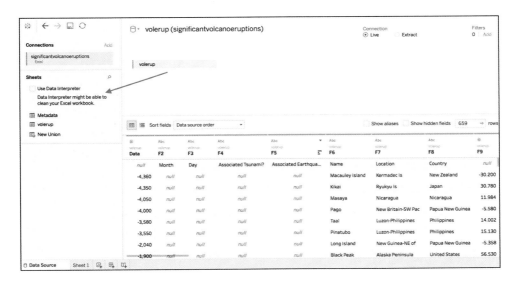

Figure 7.1 Although Tableau can connect to this messy data, some cleanup is still needed.

To "turn on" Data Interpreter, you need simply to click the check box. Tableau will run the interpreter tool and update the contents of the preview pane accordingly (see Figure 7.2). You can see that those headers have been stripped out, and the columns are now properly identified.

Figure 7.2 With one click, Data Interpreter has helped prepare data for analysis.

If you want to explore more specifics on what Data Interpreter did, you can click the Review the Results hyperlink. This opens an Excel file that describes the changes (see Figure 7.3).

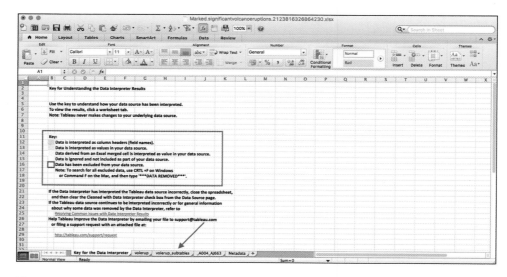

Figure 7.3 Data Interpreter provides a "marked" Excel worksheet that details the changes made in the data.

If you click through the sheets, you can see which fields are being used as headers, in orange, and which are considered data, in green (see Figure 7.4).

> **note**
>
> Data Interpreter is not available if the data contains more than 2000 columns or more than 3000 rows *and* 150 columns.

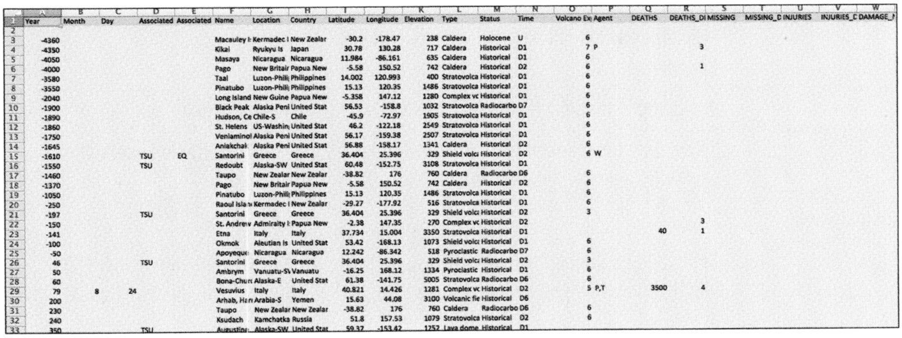

	A	B	C	D	E	F	G	H	I	J	K	L	M	N	O	P	Q	R	S	T	U	V	W
1	Year	Month	Day	Associated	Associated	Name	Location	Country	Latitude	Longitude	Elevation	Type	Status	Time	Volcano Ex	Agent	DEATHS	DEATHS_DI	MISSING	MISSING_C	INJURIES	INJURIES_C	DAMAGE_
2																							
3	-4360					Macauley I	Kermadec I	New Zealar	-30.2	-178.47	238	Caldera	Holocene	U	6								
4	-4350					Kikai	Ryukyu Is	Japan	30.78	130.28	717	Caldera	Historical	D1	7	P		3					
5	-4050					Masaya	Nicaragua	Nicaragua	11.984	-86.161	635	Caldera	Historical	D1	6								
6	-4000					Pago	New Britair	Papua New	-5.58	150.52	742	Caldera	Historical	D2	6			1					
7	-3580					Taal	Luzon-Phili	Philippines	14.002	120.993	400	Stratovolca	Historical	D1	6								
8	-3550					Pinatubo	Luzon-Phili	Philippines	15.13	120.35	1486	Stratovolca	Historical	D1	6								
9	-2040					Long Island	New Guine	Papua New	-5.358	147.12	1280	Complex vc	Historical	D1	6								
10	-1900					Black Peak	Alaska Peni	United Stat	56.53	-158.8	1032	Stratovolca	Radiocarbo	D7	6								
11	-1890					Hudson, Ce	Chile-S	Chile	-45.9	-72.97	1905	Stratovolca	Historical	D1	6								
12	-1860					St. Helens	US-Washin	United Stat	46.2	-122.18	2549	Stratovolca	Historical	D1	6								
13	-1750					Veniaminol	Alaska Peni	United Stat	56.17	-159.38	2507	Stratovolca	Historical	D1	6								
14	-1645					Aniakchak	Alaska Peni	United Stat	56.88	-158.17	1341	Caldera	Historical	D2	6								
15	-1610			TSU	EQ	Santorini	Greece	Greece	36.404	25.396	329	Shield volc	Historical	D2	6	W							
16	-1550			TSU		Redoubt	Alaska-SW	United Stat	60.48	-152.75	3108	Stratovolca	Historical	D1									
17	-1460					Taupo	New Zealar	New Zealar	-38.82	176	760	Caldera	Radiocarbo	D6	6								
18	-1370					Pago	New Britair	Papua New	-5.58	150.52	742	Caldera	Historical	D2	6								
19	-1050					Pinatubo	Luzon-Phili	Philippines	15.13	120.35	1486	Stratovolca	Historical	D1	6								
20	-250					Raoul Isla	Kermadec I	New Zealar	-29.27	-177.92	516	Stratovolca	Historical	D1	6								
21	-197			TSU		Santorini	Greece	Greece	36.404	25.396	329	Shield volc	Historical	D2	3								
22	-150					St. Andrew	Admiralty I	Papua New	-2.38	147.35	270	Complex vc	Historical	D2				3					
23	-141					Etna	Italy	Italy	37.734	15.004	3350	Stratovolca	Historical	D1			40	1					
24	-100					Okmok	Aleutian Is	United Stat	53.42	-168.13	1073	Shield volc	Historical	D1	6								
25	-50					Apoyeque	Nicaragua	Nicaragua	12.242	-86.342	518	Pyroclastic	Radiocarbo	D7	6								
26	46			TSU		Santorini	Greece	Greece	36.404	25.396	329	Shield volc	Historical	D2	3								
27	50					Ambrym	Vanuatu-S\	Vanuatu	-16.25	168.12	1334	Pyroclastic	Historical	D1	6								
28	60					Bona-Chur	Alaska-E	United Stat	61.38	-141.75	5005	Stratovolca	Radiocarbo	D6	6								
29	79	8	24			Vesuvius	Italy	Italy	40.821	14.426	1281	Complex vc	Historical	D2	5	P,T	3500	4					
30	200					Arhab, Har	Arabia-S	Yemen	15.63	44.08	3100	Volcanic fie	Historical	D6									
31	230					Taupo	New Zealar	New Zealar	-38.82	176	760	Caldera	Radiocarbo	D6	6								
32	240					Ksudach	Kamchatka	Russia	51.8	157.53	1079	Stratovolca	Historical	D2	6								
33	350			TSU		Augustin	Alaska-SW	United Stat	59.37	-153.42	1252	Lava dome	Historical	D1									

Figure 7.4 The data is color coded in the marked file.

Handling Nulls in Tableau

Before moving forward with this dataset, it is important to mention that the handling of nulls in Tableau is a dynamic and important step in the analysis process, because null values and how they are used or not used can have a significant effect on the quality of your analytical work and visual outputs.

When a measure contains null values, they are usually plotted as zero. However, sometimes that changes the view and you would rather just suppress null values altogether. A variety of functions in Tableau work with null values:

- **IFNULL functions:** Perform a true/false test on whether the value in the tested field is null. The first value in the function is used if the value is not null, and the second is used if it is null.
- **ISNULL functions:** Tests whether an expression is null (TRUE) or not (FALSE).
- **IIF functions:** Creates a shorthand function for an IF-THEN-ELSE statement with the added benefit of defining a value if the test yields an unknown result.
- **ZN function:** A variation on the ISNULL and IFNULL function, ZN tests to see whether a function is null, and if it is, returns a value of zero.

Table 7.1 displays some of the different ways you can handle null values in Tableau. More training on handling nulls is available on the Tableau website.

Table 7.1   Key of Tableau functions for handling nulls.

Function	Explanation	Formula
Numeric Values		
ISNULL	Tests the numerical columns, and then gives output as "True" or "False"	IF ISNULL ([Measure]) THEN 0 ELSE [Measure] END
IFNULL	Tests the data, and then if a value is null, it is replaced by the desired value (in this example by 0)	IFNULL ([Measure], 0)
ZN	Tests the data and replaces nulls with 0	ZN([Measure])
IIF	Tests the data, and if null is found, it is replaced by the desired value (0).	(IIF(IS NULL([Measure]), 0, [Measure]))
String Data		
ISNULL	Tests the data, and if nulls are found they are replaced by the desired string value.	IF ISNULL([Dimension]) THEN "This is desired string value" ELSE [Dimension]
IFNULL	Test the data, and if nulls are found they are replaced by the desired string value.	IFNULL([Dimension], "This record is null")
IIF	Tests the data, and if nulls are found they are replaced by the desired string value.	IIF(ISNULL([Dimension]), "This record is Null," [Dimension])

Cleaning Messy Survey Data in Excel

Working with survey data is a common task in analytics, and it provides an opportunity to explore a more robust data preparation process as well as some additional data-shaping capabilities within Tableau to prepare data for analysis and visualization, like pivots and joins. This is because survey data is inherently messy and requires a bit more TLC than your average dataset, and this preparation extends beyond what Data Interpreter can handle on its own. Without some extensive cleanup, analyzing raw survey data exported from tools like SurveyMonkey or Qualtrics can be near impossible, both because of the usual formatting issues as well as the need to translate textual data to a format usable in analysis while preserving its metadata.

There are four elements of survey data you need to organize and fit together:

- Demographic information
- Responses in text form
- Responses in numeric form
- A "meta file" that acts as a legend to describe the survey

The goal is to combine all of these elements to see a comprehensive view of the data (see Figure 7.5). Another task is to reshape the data from "wide" to "tall" data, a concept explored further in a later section.

> ## note
>
> A word of caution is necessary here. There is truth to the old adage "garbage in, garbage out." Before you begin preparing your data for analysis, you should spend time reviewing your data, even in its messiest raw form and tidy up errors or issues you see before you take further steps. In particular, look over and confirm date and geographic data formats, remove duplicate records, and change or correct any identifiers to a format that you need (like capitalization). Fields that allow for manual text entry are especially prone to these latter issues that might require your attention before you begin working with your data. This is also a perfect time to assess the presence of nulls in your data, and determining when a field should be a null or a zero.

ResponseId	Gender	Age	Zipcode	QuestionID	TextValue	NumericValue	Wording	Question	Code
R_0TmzS5YcOfEwABH	Woman	38	91010	Q11_1	Non-Aggressive	2	On a scale of 1 t	Likert	Extremely Non-Aggressive = 1, Non-Aggressive = 2, Neither Non-Aggress
R_10HsSNZHkBWTO29	Woman	31	1238	Q11_1	Aggressive	4	On a scale of 1 t	Likert	Extremely Non-Aggressive = 1, Non-Aggressive = 2, Neither Non-Aggress
R_10uCOapl3xSOTIM	Woman	41	2478	Q11_1	Aggressive	4	On a scale of 1 t	Likert	Extremely Non-Aggressive = 1, Non-Aggressive = 2, Neither Non-Aggress
R_1170yWGLUoS5QMM	Woman	11	Hong Kong	Q11_1	Aggressive	4	On a scale of 1 t	Likert	Extremely Non-Aggressive = 1, Non-Aggressive = 2, Neither Non-Aggress
R_124LeNMDuAOVh2O	Woman	26	4218	Q11_1	Neither Non-Aggressive Nor Aggressive	3	On a scale of 1 t	Likert	Extremely Non-Aggressive = 1, Non-Aggressive = 2, Neither Non-Aggress
R_12JRz7Az6SREyro	Woman	33	623	Q11_1	Non-Aggressive	2	On a scale of 1 t	Likert	Extremely Non-Aggressive = 1, Non-Aggressive = 2, Neither Non-Aggress
R_12Jh6uxNmERzSbG	Woman	23	45331	Q11_1	Aggressive	4	On a scale of 1 t	Likert	Extremely Non-Aggressive = 1, Non-Aggressive = 2, Neither Non-Aggress
R_12Shw1knPpTLu2q	Woman	34	55809	Q11_1	Aggressive	4	On a scale of 1 t	Likert	Extremely Non-Aggressive = 1, Non-Aggressive = 2, Neither Non-Aggress
R_12m3uPd22Z6LQj0	Woman	17	1920	Q11_1	Aggressive	4	On a scale of 1 t	Likert	Extremely Non-Aggressive = 1, Non-Aggressive = 2, Neither Non-Aggress
R_12nGucKwhb9SXF8	Woman	35	Uk	Q11_1	Neither Non-Aggressive Nor Aggressive	3	On a scale of 1 t	Likert	Extremely Non-Aggressive = 1, Non-Aggressive = 2, Neither Non-Aggress
R_12yI57YXwDnFwT0	Woman	28	Dubai UAE	Q11_1	Neither Non-Aggressive Nor Aggressive	3	On a scale of 1 t	Likert	Extremely Non-Aggressive = 1, Non-Aggressive = 2, Neither Non-Aggress
R_18SjvdgE2Nvgx8I	Woman	12	92284	Q11_1	Neither Non-Aggressive Nor Aggressive	3	On a scale of 1 t	Likert	Extremely Non-Aggressive = 1, Non-Aggressive = 2, Neither Non-Aggress
R_1C8yEUyvSIyK6IJ	Woman	24	98311	Q11_1	Neither Non-Aggressive Nor Aggressive	3	On a scale of 1 t	Likert	Extremely Non-Aggressive = 1, Non-Aggressive = 2, Neither Non-Aggress
R_1DBDRy7MB1CW5Yc	Woman	34	74063	Q11_1	Aggressive	4	On a scale of 1 t	Likert	Extremely Non-Aggressive = 1, Non-Aggressive = 2, Neither Non-Aggress
R_1DTpCtST1ueziLa	Woman	24	49534	Q11_1	Aggressive	4	On a scale of 1 t	Likert	Extremely Non-Aggressive = 1, Non-Aggressive = 2, Neither Non-Aggress
R_1DTpX1kDqtiAauK	Woman	33	54703	Q11_1	Aggressive	4	On a scale of 1 t	Likert	Extremely Non-Aggressive = 1, Non-Aggressive = 2, Neither Non-Aggress
R_1EdiNtVOUELf2CI	Woman	35	24101	Q11_1	Non-Aggressive	2	On a scale of 1 t	Likert	Extremely Non-Aggressive = 1, Non-Aggressive = 2, Neither Non-Aggress
R_1FOE3zP5DA7hQc8	Woman	38	76710	Q11_1	Aggressive	4	On a scale of 1 t	Likert	Extremely Non-Aggressive = 1, Non-Aggressive = 2, Neither Non-Aggress
R_1Ffxnwsa3yegvdo	Woman	22	78666	Q11_1	Aggressive	4	On a scale of 1 t	Likert	Extremely Non-Aggressive = 1, Non-Aggressive = 2, Neither Non-Aggress
R_1GC7PQrtMXVUY5F	Woman	21	834009	Q11_1	Neither Non-Aggressive Nor Aggressive	3	On a scale of 1 t	Likert	Extremely Non-Aggressive = 1, Non-Aggressive = 2, Neither Non-Aggress
R_1GHNdQzIkBNoAKp	Woman	29	48185	Q11_1	Aggressive	4	On a scale of 1 t	Likert	Extremely Non-Aggressive = 1, Non-Aggressive = 2, Neither Non-Aggress
R_1Gwst7yu0fQXdeU	Woman	33	19701	Q11_1	Neither Non-Aggressive Nor Aggressive	3	On a scale of 1 t	Likert	Extremely Non-Aggressive = 1, Non-Aggressive = 2, Neither Non-Aggress
R_1H8mUlss84A9Wa7	Woman	38	82070	Q11_1	Neither Non-Aggressive Nor Aggressive	3	On a scale of 1 t	Likert	Extremely Non-Aggressive = 1, Non-Aggressive = 2, Neither Non-Aggress
R_1HhKIO1fUjJ5VsK	Woman	46	45702	Q11_1	Aggressive	4	On a scale of 1 t	Likert	Extremely Non-Aggressive = 1, Non-Aggressive = 2, Neither Non-Aggress
R_1I9IbvFomOXLs6k	Woman	19	84005	Q11_1	Non-Aggressive	2	On a scale of 1 t	Likert	Extremely Non-Aggressive = 1, Non-Aggressive = 2, Neither Non-Aggress
R_1IL8Qx9rOieJAZk	Woman	47	1020	Q11_1	Extremely Non-Aggressive	1	On a scale of 1 t	Likert	Extremely Non-Aggressive = 1, Non-Aggressive = 2, Neither Non-Aggress
R_1IQlLfSsbNzc3lg	Woman	35	47404	Q11_1	Aggressive	4	On a scale of 1 t	Likert	Extremely Non-Aggressive = 1, Non-Aggressive = 2, Neither Non-Aggress
R_1Io1LxfzoSuBLy9	Man	22	7644	Q11_1	Aggressive	4	On a scale of 1 t	Likert	Extremely Non-Aggressive = 1, Non-Aggressive = 2, Neither Non-Aggress
R_1JDsiYv6idSn0sN	Woman	13	2645	Q11_1	Neither Non-Aggressive Nor Aggressive	3	On a scale of 1 t	Likert	Extremely Non-Aggressive = 1, Non-Aggressive = 2, Neither Non-Aggress
R_1JWIHUUn2rm3vpv	Woman	35	95407	Q11_1	Aggressive	4	On a scale of 1 t	Likert	Extremely Non-Aggressive = 1, Non-Aggressive = 2, Neither Non-Aggress
R_1LTlfAUvJdrq4hh	Man	15	1760	Q11_1	Aggressive	4	On a scale of 1 t	Likert	Extremely Non-Aggressive = 1, Non-Aggressive = 2, Neither Non-Aggress
R_1LYaWcmMZQ2pz5q	Woman	27	64836	Q11_1	Non-Aggressive	2	On a scale of 1 t	Likert	Extremely Non-Aggressive = 1, Non-Aggressive = 2, Neither Non-Aggress

Figure 7.5 After preparing the survey data, it looks like this.

> ## note
>
> Some survey platforms, like Qualtrics, provide the option to export raw data in many formats (including SPSS) and avoid some of the steps taken in the following sections. However, the assumption for this example is that the data has messy CSV files. This allows explanation through the entire process with as much detail as possible.

The first step in preparing data is to tackle some basic clean-up tasks. Let's walk through a real dataset. This dataset includes 341 responses to a survey on perceptions of violence and aggression in the *Harry Potter* series.

> **note**
>
> This data was collected for a presentation at the 6th Annual *Harry Potter* Conference hosted by Chestnut Hill College in Philadelphia. You can view the presentation or learn more at HarryPotterConference.com.

Figure 7.6 shows a file of raw data export from Qualtrics

IP Address	Progress	Duration (in	Finished	Response ID	Location Lati	Location Lon	Distribution	User Langua	I am a....	How old ar
184.5.229.85	100	795	TRUE	R_27EiPVX0lxyV9dw	36.9497986	-81.128899	anonymous	EN		5
72.20.135.16	100	1116	TRUE	R_1jwdjyt2QisuZdh	29.7346039	-95.416	anonymous	EN	Man	3
45.3.85.131	100	489	TRUE	R_AhcPM3cygTSwPsZ	37.1790924	-80.351501	anonymous	EN	Woman	2
162.234.139.	100	1598	TRUE	R_1poEcTA7a9MKk2Z	39.6869049	-84.164101	anonymous	EN	Woman	3
76.177.47.44	100	1343	TRUE	R_2f1yptBdNLCngoq	38.2532043	-84.552399	anonymous	EN	Woman	4
172.90.214.5	100	1427	TRUE	R_rkFuvMEmZWacSlz	33.9163971	-118.4041	anonymous	EN	Woman	4
69.136.85.32	100	1634	TRUE	R_3m7CjmtausuGqlP	39.9983978	-75.271202	anonymous	EN	Woman	4
107.77.209.5	100	1057	TRUE	R_2SXfr8vF9OTpf7V	41.8482971	-87.651703	anonymous	EN	Woman	4
174.199.20.2	100	858	TRUE	R_3nTbhI6PHTfH4RD	41.9756012	-71.544899	anonymous	EN	Woman	2
107.77.225.2	100	451	TRUE	R_3iwCLmUkxPEGa7z	40.7357025	-74.172401	anonymous	EN	Woman	4
64.147.48.86	100	868	TRUE	R_3oEDOoVvtMCYR2H	44.3760986	-68.275703	anonymous	EN	Woman	4
24.27.2.199	100	505	TRUE	R_2ayOQdtLepFZaru	29.9893036	-97.857201	anonymous	EN	Woman	3
40.136.63.18	100	821	TRUE	R_1dcZ3w15Njeizhv	39.740097	-90.2388	anonymous	EN	Woman	5
71.197.0.185	100	310	TRUE	R_2aailQoezsj0itu	37.2669067	-80.432503	anonymous	EN	Woman	3
67.161.139.2	100	522	TRUE	R_3PFQg8zAvGS6zLB	40.0496063	-105.2769	anonymous	EN	Woman	3
134.129.113.	100	878	TRUE	R_3ez7GBEXfOWLvZU	46.8771973	-96.789803	anonymous	EN	Woman	3
174.30.58.14	100	1464	TRUE	R_3oENhIZxhY7ehZ	43.7162933	-123.0374	anonymous	EN	Woman	3
107.77.195.1	100	2223	TRUE	R_3JLvivuwCawIVCd	39.9611969	-82.998802	anonymous	EN		3
192.104.181.	100	983	TRUE	R_1rillKYZdco5fjJJ	40.6152039	-75.543701	anonymous	EN	Woman	3
105.184.202.	100	1781	TRUE	R_30jmYdh7XFsKKSi	-33.916702	18.4167023	anonymous	EN	Woman	3
8.14.172.48	100	870	TRUE	R_27QCOxhHqGrntJs	40.5677948	-75.482803	anonymous	EN	Man	3
107.77.224.2	100	670	TRUE	R_2UabFFZYG2Za2x5	40.7142944	-74.005997	anonymous	EN	Woman	3
73.6.206.21;	100	702	TRUE	R_3iQrc3IRLR7s6qD	29.8262024	-95.426399	anonymous	EN	Woman	3
184.99.149.3	100	1505	TRUE	R_21ApF4BBgKMESNG	32.1784973	-110.7897	anonymous	EN	Woman	3
128.135.100.	100	768	TRUE	R_ptmWSld1YZ4qBPj	41.7803955	-87.602699	anonymous	EN	Woman	3
81.103.32.24	100	752	TRUE	R_3QQ84QvEkTFig4g	52.1999969	0.11669922	anonymous	EN	Woman	4
66.69.207.16	100	662	TRUE	R_3f8kWZ6zvyw12Er	29.9893036	-97.857201	anonymous	EN	Woman	4
73.66.141.26	100	551	TRUE	R_3PY49Zoh8BRpNkq	38.5856018	-121.3777	anonymous	EN	Woman	4
104.38.146.6	100	2066	TRUE	R_2riYcshFanROIVH	40.802002	-77.8564	anonymous	EN	Woman	4
174.223.128.	100	458	TRUE	R_2wKvydC6vgCkfWb	32.4813995	-84.903297	anonymous	EN	Woman	3

Figure 7.6 This Excel worksheet contains a dump of exported data.

Step 1: Surface Cleaning

This initial data export contains all survey data, including responses as well as data provided by the survey platform. It also includes respondent survey responses in their original text form (Step 2 is when you code these numerically).

The immediate first action to take to get this data in a usable format is to do some basic tidying up. Start by removing unnecessary columns (such as columns A–H, which do not contain usable information) and data not relevant to the analysis (such as rows 2–3). This step is an opportunity to make sure your column headers are in the first row of your spreadsheet and that no wacky formatting exists that would cause issues when bringing your data into Tableau. You also need to clearly identify your demographic data fields and make sure those immediately follow the ResponseID fields.

> **note**
>
> This section covers many survey data cleanup tasks; however, these tasks might differ depending on the survey platform (Qualtrics, SurveyMonkey, and so on) you are using. The ResponseID field is a critical field, because you will use it as a join in later steps. Any demographic questions should be noted as such in the column headers for use as pivot fields later.

After removing extraneous information and cleaning up headers, leave the remaining data as is. This now becomes worksheet 1 in your Excel workbook: Text (see Figure 7.7).

	A	B	C	AD	AE	AF	AG	AH	AI	AJ	AK	AL	AM	AN	AO	AP	AQ	AR
1	ResponseId	Gender	Age	Q11_1	Q11_2	Q11_3	Q11_4	Q11_5	Q11_6	Q11_7	Q11_8	Q11_9	Q11_10	Q11_11	Q11_12	Q11_13	Q11_15	Q11_16
2	R_27EiPVX0lxyV9dw	Woman	51	Aggressive	Extremely Ag	Extremely Ag	Extremely Ag	Extremely Ag	Neither Non-	Aggressive	Non-Aggress	Aggressive	Aggressive	Aggressive	Non-Aggress	Non-Aggress	Non-Aggress	Neither
3	R_1jwdJyt2QisuZdh	Man	33	Aggressive	Extremely Ag	Aggressive	Aggressive	Aggressive	Neither Non-	Aggressive	Extremely Ag	Aggressive	Aggressive	Aggressive	Non-Aggress	Extremely Nc	Aggressive	Extreme
4	R_AhcPM3cygTSwPsZ	Woman	25	Aggressive	Extremely Ag	Aggressive	Aggressive	Extremely Ag	Non-Aggress	Aggressive	Aggressive	Aggressive	Extremely Ag	Non-Aggress	Non-Aggress	Extremely Nc	Neither Non-	Aggressi
5	R_1poEcTA7a9MKk2Z	Woman	39	Aggressive	Extremely Ag	Aggressive	Extremely Ag	Extremely Ag	Non-Aggress	Aggressive	Aggressive	Aggressive	Aggressive	Non-Aggress	Neither Non-	Neither Non-	Non-Aggress	Aggressi
6	R_2f1yptBdNLCngoq	Woman	41	Extremely Ag	Extremely Ag	Extremely Ag	Aggressive	Extremely Ag	Aggressive	Aggressive	Neither Non-	Non-Aggress	Extremely Ag	Neither Non-	Aggressive	Extremely Nc	Aggressive	Non-Agg
7	R_rkFuvMEmZWacSlz	Woman	45	Neither Non-	Extremely Ag	Extremely Ag	Aggressive	Extremely Ag	Neither Non-	Neither Non-	Neither Non-	Extremely Ag	Extremely Ag	Aggressive	Non-Aggress	Extremely Nc	Extremely Nc	Neither
8	R_3m7CjmtausuGqlP	Woman	33	Aggressive	Extremely Ag	Aggressive	Aggressive	Extremely Ag	Aggressive	Aggressive	Neither Non-	Extremely Ag	Extremely Ag	Non-Aggress	Non-Aggress	Extremely Nc	Non-Aggress	Neither
9	R_25Xfr8vF9OTpf7V	Woman	42	Neither Non-	Extremely Ag	Aggressive	Aggressive	Aggressive	Non-Aggress	Neither Non-	Neither Non-	Aggressive	Extremely Ag	Non-Aggress	Neither Non-	Extremely Nc	Aggressive	Aggressi
10	R_3nTbhl6PHTfH4RD	Woman	27	Neither Non-	Extremely Ag	Aggressive	Aggressive	Extremely Ag	Neither Non-	Non-Aggress	Non-Aggress	Aggressive	Extremely Ag	Neither Non-	Non-Aggress	Non-Aggress	Neither Non-	Non-Agg
11	R_3iwCLmUkxPEGa7z	Woman	41	Aggressive	Aggressive	Aggressive	Non-Aggress	Aggressive	Extremely Nc	Extremely Nc	Non-Aggress	Neither Non-	Aggressive	Aggressive		Extremely Nc	Neither Non-	Extreme
12	R_3oED0oVvtMCYRZH	Woman	35	Non-Aggress	Extremely Ag	Aggressive	Neither Non-	Extremely Ag	Non-Aggress	Non-Aggress	Neither Non-	Extremely Ag	Aggressive	Extremely Nc	Non-Aggress	Extremely Nc	Neither Non-	Non-Agg
13	R_2ayOQdtLepFZaru	Woman	35	Aggressive	Aggressive	Extremely Ag	Aggressive	Extremely Ag	Neither Non-	Aggressive	Neither Non-	Non-Aggress	Non-Aggress	Non-Aggress	Non-Aggress	Extremely Nc	Extremely Nc	Aggressi
14	R_1dcZ3w15Njeizhv	Woman	53	Non-Aggress	Extremely Ag	Aggressive	Neither Non-	Extremely Ag	Non-Aggress	Extremely Nc	Extremely Nc	Extremely Ag	Extremely Ag	Aggressive	Extremely Nc	Extremely Nc	Aggressive	Non-Agg
15	R_2aailQoezsj0itu	Woman	32	Aggressive	Aggressive	Aggressive	Aggressive	Extremely Ag	Neither Non-	Neither Non-	Neither Non-	Neither Non-	Neither Non-	Non-Aggress	Non-Aggress	Neither Non-	Neither Non-	Neither
16	R_3PFQg8zAvGS6zLB	Woman	30	Aggressive	Aggressive	Non-Aggress	Neither Non-	Extremely Ag	Aggressive	Neither Non-	Neither Non-	Extremely Ag	Aggressive	Extremely Nc	Aggressive	Aggressive	Extremely Nc	Aggressi
17	R_3ez7GBEXfOWLvZU	Woman	30	Aggressive	Aggressive	Aggressive	Aggressive	Extremely Ag	Aggressive	Neither Non-	Non-Aggress	Extremely Ag	Aggressive	Non-Aggress	Aggressive	Aggressive	Extremely Nc	Neither
18	R_3oENLhIZxhY7ehZ	Woman	39	Aggressive	Extremely Ag	Aggressive	Aggressive	Extremely Ag	Non-Aggress	Non-Aggress	Aggressive	Extremely Ag	Extremely Ag	Extremely Ag	Neither Non-	Non-Aggress	Aggressive	Aggressi
19	R_3JLvlvuwCawlVCd		34	Aggressive	Extremely Ag	Aggressive	Neither Non-	Extremely Ag	Non-Aggress	Neither Non-	Aggressive	Extremely Ag	Aggressive	Neither Non-	Non-Aggress	Aggressive	Non-Aggress	Aggressi
20	R_1rIlKYZdco5fJjJ	Woman	30	Aggressive	Extremely Ag	Extremely Ag	Aggressive	Extremely Ag	Neither Non-	Neither Non-	Aggressive	Extremely Ag	Extremely Ag	Aggressive	Non-Aggress	Extremely Nc	Aggressive	Neither
21	R_30jmYdh7XFsKKSi	Woman	38	Neither Non-	Extremely Ag	Aggressive	Neither Non-	Extremely Ag	Neither Non-	Non-Aggress	Neither Non-	Aggressive	Extremely Ag	Aggressive	Neither Non-	Non-Aggress	Neither Non-	Non-Agg
22	R_27QCOxhHqGrntJs	Man	34	Aggressive	Extremely Ag	Neither Non-	Non-Aggress	Extremely Ag	Neither Non-	Non-Aggress	Neither Non-	Aggressive	Extremely Ag	Aggressive	Aggressive	Neither Non-	Extremely Ag	Neither
23	R_2UabFFZYG2Za2x5	Woman	34	Aggressive	Extremely Ag	Aggressive	Extremely Ag	Extremely Ag	Aggressive	Neither Non-	Neither Non-	Extremely Ag	Extremely Ag	Neither Non-	Neither Non-	Neither Non-	Aggressive	Neither
24	R_3iQrc3IRLR7s6qD	Woman	32	Aggressive	Extremely Ag	Aggressive	Neither Non-	Aggressive	Aggressive	Neither Non-	Neither Non-	Aggressive	Aggressive	Non-Aggress	Neither Non-	Neither Non-	Extremely Nc	Neither
25	R_21ApF4BBgKMESNG	Woman	44	Aggressive	Extremely Ag	Aggressive	Neither Non-	Extremely Ag	Aggressive	Neither Non-	Neither Non-	Extremely Ag	Extremely Ag	Aggressive	Neither Non-	Neither Non-	Aggressive	Neither
26	R_ptmWSId1YZ4qBPj	Woman	31	Aggressive	Extremely Ag	Aggressive	Extremely Ag	Extremely Ag	Non-Aggress	Non-Aggress	Non-Aggress	Extremely Ag	Aggressive	Aggressive	Neither Non-	Neither Non-	Aggressive	Non-Agg
27	R_3QQ84QvEkTFig4g	Woman	47	Neither Non-	Extremely Ag	Aggressive	Aggressive	Extremely Ag	Neither Non-	Non-Aggress	Non-Aggress	Aggressive	Extremely Ag	Non-Aggress	Extremely Nc	Extremely Nc	Neither Non-	Non-Agg
28	R_3fBkWZ6zvyw12Er	Woman	42	Aggressive	Extremely Ag	Aggressive	Aggressive	Extremely Ag	Neither Non-	Neither Non-	Aggressive	Extremely Ag	Aggressive	Aggressive	Neither Non-	Neither Non-	Aggressive	Neither
29	R_3PY49Zoh8BRpNkq	Woman	34	Aggressive	Extremely Ag	Aggressive		Extremely Ag	Non-Aggressive		Non-Aggress	Aggressive	Aggressive		Extremely Nc	Extremely Nc	Neither Non-	Non-Agg
30	R_2rlYcshFanROIVH	Woman	43	Neither Non-	Extremely Ag	Aggressive	Aggressive	Extremely Ag	Extremely Nc	Non-Aggress	Non-Aggress	Aggressive	Extremely Ag	Neither Non-	Non-Aggress	Extremely Nc	Aggressive	Neither
31	R_2wKvydC6vgCkfWb	Woman	36	Neither Non-	Extremely Ag	Aggressive	Aggressive	Extremely Ag	Non-Aggress	Extremely Nc	Neither Non-	Aggressive	Aggressive	Aggressive	Extremely Nc	Non-Aggress	Aggressive	Extreme
32	R_5yHYxTvnl98W241	Woman	49	Aggressive	Extremely Ag	Aggressive	Aggressive	Extremely Ag	Aggressive	Aggressive	Aggressive	Neither Non-	Extremely Ag	Aggressive	Non-Aggress	Non-Aggress	Extremely Ag	Non-Agg

Figure 7.7 After an initial scrub of the exported data, the survey data is already looking cleaner.

> **note**
>
> The last step in Excel will be to create a metafile that lists the question ID and its corresponding wording, as well as other helpful information, like how respondents were asked to answer question (that is, Likert, rank, yes/no/maybe). This provides a key to the survey that will support your analysis in Tableau. You should remove the question wording contained in row 2 here, but let's put this information aside for now and revisit in a later step.

Step 2: Creating a Numeric Copy

The next step is to create a copy of the Text worksheet with its numeric partner. To begin, copy and paste the entire Text worksheet into a new tab, and retitle the tab Numeric.

To encode text responses as numeric fields in Excel, you can use a simple find-and-replace operation. For example, in the survey, respondents were asked in Question 11 to rank each *Harry Potter* character on a scale of Extremely Non-Aggressive (1) to Extremely Aggressive (5). Using find and replace in Excel, you can replace the text answer in this field with its numerical equivalent (see Figure 7.8).

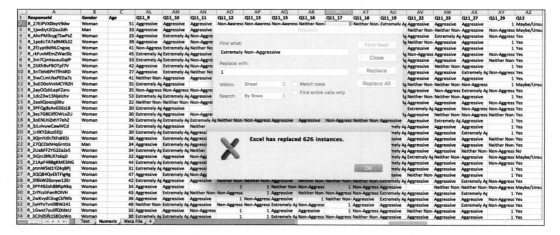

Figure 7.8 Use find and replace in Excel to swap text values for numeric.

Numerically coding demographic data fields is not necessary. As you complete this process, take care to be consistent in how you encode text as numeric responses. For example:

- No = 0
- Yes = 1
- Maybe = 2
- True = 1
- False = 0

In addition, survey questions that are "select all" or that otherwise group multiple responses (such as rankings) into one field must be separated so that each option is contained in its own column. This makes the visualization process much more efficient in later steps.

You use the numeric codes, along with the question and wording data, to compile the metafile in the final step.

> **note**
>
> Later, you use this metafile to replace the headers of your Question ID field by blending the two in a sheet by right-clicking on the value label and selecting Make Primary Label.

After you complete this process, your Numeric worksheet table should look similar to the one shown in Figure 7.9.

	Responseid	Gender	Age	Zipcode	Q4	Q5	Q6	Q7	Q10_1	Q10_2	Q10_3	Q10_4	Q10_5	Q10_6	Q10_7	Q10_8	Q10_9	Q10_10
2	R_27EiPVX0lxyV9dw	Woman	51	22903	5	21	8	1	18	32	29	19	33	14	15	8	22	
3	R_1jwdJyt2QJsuZdh	Man	33	77019	8	13	7	0	1	2	3	4	6	5	7	8	10	
4	R_AhcPM3cygTSwPsZ	Woman	25	24060	5	15	4	1	3	32	16	17	33	4	9	10	21	
5	R_1poEcTA7a9MKk2Z	Woman	39	45419	4	14	4	0	25	31	26	33	30	11	14	29	21	
6	R_2f1yptBdNLCngoq	Woman	41	40324	1	21	21	0	1	2	4	5	3	15	13	24	29	
7	R_rkFuvMEmZWacSlz	Woman	45	90245	2	14	1	1	15	33	20	17	30	7	8	10	29	
8	R_3m7CJmtausuGqlP	Woman	33	19072	2	25	4	1	17	33	22	23	30	16	15	11	29	
9	R_2SXfr8vF9OTpf7V	Woman	42	47404	16	15	1	0	13	32	21	24	25	7	10	12	26	
10	R_3nTbhI6PHTfH4RD	Woman	27	5403	5		7	0	2	1	4	5	8	6	3	7	9	
11	R_3iwCLmUkxPEGa7z	Woman	41	8816	3	13	21	0	18	21	20	9	16	5	6	7	10	
12	R_3oED0oVvtMCYRZH	Woman	35	4605	5	11	7	0	12	32	23	19	33	10	11	4	30	
13	R_2ayOQdtLepFZaru	Woman	35	78130	20	12	7	0	15	20	16	17	21	3	6	12	4	
14	R_1dcZ3w15Njeizhv	Woman	53	62650	5	7	21	0	5	20	13	10	21	9	1	2	17	
15	R_2aailQoezsj0itu	Woman	32	24060	5	14	1	0	15	20	17	13	21	3	4	14	10	
16	R_3PFCgBzAvGS6zL8	Woman	30	80304	5	12	7	1	2	5	19	9	1	7	8	10	3	
17	R_3ez7GBEXfOWLvZU	Woman	30	58102	5	12	4	0	15	19	12	16	21	13	9	5	20	
18	R_3oENLhIZxhY7ehZ	Woman	39	97330	5	21	4	0	6	20	9	12	21	3	5	7	19	
19	R_3JLvluvuCawfVCd		34	45013	2	21	7	0	7	1	19	20	2	17	16	8	3	
20	R_1rIlKYZdco5fijJ	Woman	30	18106	2	14	4	0	7	21	16	8	20	4	6	10	19	
21	R_30jmYdh7XFsKKSi	Woman	38	2474	2	13	15	0	9	21	14	13	20	10	6	7	18	
22	R_27QCOxhHqGrntJs	Man	34	18106	2	13	7	0	6	1	12	14	2	15	20	16	8	
23	R_2UabFFZYG2ZaZxS	Woman	34	2915	2	22	4	1	9	1	7	3	2	12	10	13	5	
24	R_3iQrc3iRLR7s6qD	Woman	32	77018	2	21	7	0	20	21	17	3	19	14	7	9	12	
25	R_21ApF4BBgKMESNG	Woman	44	85704	2	21	1	0	11	1	8	12	2	14	16	17	6	
26	R_ptmWSId1YZ4qBPj	Woman	31	60615	16	21	4	1	8	20	6	11	18	2	3	4	19	
27	R_3QQ84QvEkTFig4g	Woman	47	1136	5	21	4	0	9	20	12	11	21	7	4	5	18	
28	R_3fBkWZ6zvyw12Er	Woman	42	78610	2	21	4	1	8	21	14	12	20	3	2	9	19	
29	R_3PY49Zoh8BRpNkq	Woman	34	95673	5	14	13	1	11	21	14	5	20	12	10	6	18	
30	R_2rIYcshFanROlVH	Woman	43	16801	2	6	1	1	9	21	15	13	17	1	4	7	16	
31	R_2wKvydC6vgCkfWb	Woman	36	31909	2	13	1	1	8	21	14	9	20	5	2	6	16	
32	R_5yHYxTvnl98W241	Woman	49	60613	2	22	1	1	10	21	4	11	19	5	6	9	7	

Figure 7.9 After being fully coded, the numeric file should only include text answers in the demographic fields.

TEXT *AND* NUMERIC?

You might wonder why you want *both* text and numeric responses. The answer is simple. Most surveys include questions that ask respondents to select a value for a question. Consider a Likert scale question, with a universe of possible values on a one-to-five (more common) or one-to-seven (less common) scale. For example, a common survey Likert scale question could be, "On a scale of 1–5, with 1 being "extremely dissatisfied" and 5 being "extremely satisfied," how would you rank your dining experience?" These numeric values could also be a range of "strongly agree to strongly disagree" or "extremely unimportant to extremely important." Without having both numeric and text results you will have to write a lot of IF/CASE statements and add unnecessary burden to the analytic process.

Step 3: Creating the Meta Helper File

The final step is to create a meta helper file that will help you understand the data and facilitate analysis in Tableau. Unfortunately, this file is not something that (most) survey tools provide, so its completion is a manual process. Use Figure 7.10 as a guide in building your meta helper file. You are looking for four key elements:

- QuestionID (Q1, Q2, Q3, and so on)
- Question Wording (The original question's text—what was asked.)

- Question Type (Rank, Likert, Select One, and so on)
- Coding (How the data was coded, i.e. 1=Strong Disagree, 2=Disagree, etc.)

	QuestionID	Wording	Question Type	Code
2	Q4	In my opinion, ___ is the most aggressive character in Harry Potter.	Select One	1=harry, 2=voldemort, 3=draco, 4=snape, 5=
3	Q5	In my opinion, ___ is the least aggressive character in Harry Potter.	Select One	1=harry, 2=voldemort, 3=draco, 4=snape, 5=
4	Q6	In my opinion, ___ is the most heroic character in Harry Potter.	Select One	1=harry, 2=voldemort, 3=draco, 4=snape, 5=
5	Q7	I believe magical creatures are equally as violent as human characters in Harry Potter.	True/False	True = 1, False = 0
6	Q10_1	Please rank the following characters in order from least aggressive to most aggressive. - Harry Potter	Rank	1=harry, 2=voldemort, 3=draco, 4=snape, 5=
7	Q10_2	Please rank the following characters in order from least aggressive to most aggressive. - Lord Voldemort (Tom Riddle)	Rank	1=harry, 2=voldemort, 3=draco, 4=snape, 5=
8	Q10_3	Please rank the following characters in order from least aggressive to most aggressive. - Draco Malfoy	Rank	1=harry, 2=voldemort, 3=draco, 4=snape, 5=
9	Q10_4	Please rank the following characters in order from least aggressive to most aggressive. - Severus Snape	Rank	1=harry, 2=voldemort, 3=draco, 4=snape, 5=
10	Q10_5	Please rank the following characters in order from least aggressive to most aggressive. - Bellatrix Lestrange	Rank	1=harry, 2=voldemort, 3=draco, 4=snape, 5=
11	Q10_6	Please rank the following characters in order from least aggressive to most aggressive. - Ron Weasley	Rank	1=harry, 2=voldemort, 3=draco, 4=snape, 5=
12	Q10_7	Please rank the following characters in order from least aggressive to most aggressive. - Hermione Granger	Rank	1=harry, 2=voldemort, 3=draco, 4=snape, 5=
13	Q10_8	Please rank the following characters in order from least aggressive to most aggressive. - Albus Dumbledore	Rank	1=harry, 2=voldemort, 3=draco, 4=snape, 5=
14	Q10_9	Please rank the following characters in order from least aggressive to most aggressive. - Antonin Dolohov	Rank	1=harry, 2=voldemort, 3=draco, 4=snape, 5=
15	Q10_10	Please rank the following characters in order from least aggressive to most aggressive. - Barty Crouch Jr.	Rank	1=harry, 2=voldemort, 3=draco, 4=snape, 5=
16	Q10_11	Please rank the following characters in order from least aggressive to most aggressive. - Peter Pettigrew	Rank	1=harry, 2=voldemort, 3=draco, 4=snape, 5=
17	Q10_13	Please rank the following characters in order from least aggressive to most aggressive. - Arthur Weasley	Rank	1=harry, 2=voldemort, 3=draco, 4=snape, 5=
18	Q10_15	Please rank the following characters in order from least aggressive to most aggressive. - Quirinus Quirrell/Voldemort	Rank	1=harry, 2=voldemort, 3=draco, 4=snape, 5=
19	Q10_16	Please rank the following characters in order from least aggressive to most aggressive. - Minerva McGonagall	Rank	1=harry, 2=voldemort, 3=draco, 4=snape, 5=
20	Q10_17	Please rank the following characters in order from least aggressive to most aggressive. - Rubeus Hagrid	Rank	1=harry, 2=voldemort, 3=draco, 4=snape, 5=
21	Q10_18	Please rank the following characters in order from least aggressive to most aggressive. - Remus Lupin	Rank	1=harry, 2=voldemort, 3=draco, 4=snape, 5=
22	Q10_19	Please rank the following characters in order from least aggressive to most aggressive. - Dolores Umbridge	Rank	1=harry, 2=voldemort, 3=draco, 4=snape, 5=
23	Q10_22	Please rank the following characters in order from least aggressive to most aggressive. - Sirius Black	Rank	1=harry, 2=voldemort, 3=draco, 4=snape, 5=
24	Q10_23	Please rank the following characters in order from least aggressive to most aggressive. - Alastor Moody	Rank	1=harry, 2=voldemort, 3=draco, 4=snape, 5=
25	Q10_27	Please rank the following characters in order from least aggressive to most aggressive. - Lucius Malfoy	Rank	1=harry, 2=voldemort, 3=draco, 4=snape, 5=
26	Q10_29	Please rank the following characters in order from least aggressive to most aggressive. - Neville Longbottom	Rank	1=harry, 2=voldemort, 3=draco, 4=snape, 5=
27	Q11_1	On a scale of 1 to 5, with 1 extremely non-aggressive and 5 being extremely aggressive, please rate each of the following characters. - Harry Potter	Likert	Extremely Non-Aggressive = 1, Non-Aggressi
28	Q11_2	On a scale of 1 to 5, with 1 extremely non-aggressive and 5 being extremely aggressive, please rate each of the following characters. - Lord Voldemort (Tom Riddle)	Likert	Extremely Non-Aggressive = 1, Non-Aggressi
29	Q11_3	On a scale of 1 to 5, with 1 extremely non-aggressive and 5 being extremely aggressive, please rate each of the following characters. - Draco Malfoy	Likert	Extremely Non-Aggressive = 1, Non-Aggressi
30	Q11_4	On a scale of 1 to 5, with 1 extremely non-aggressive and 5 being extremely aggressive, please rate each of the following characters. - Severus Snape	Likert	Extremely Non-Aggressive = 1, Non-Aggressi
31	Q11_5	On a scale of 1 to 5, with 1 extremely non-aggressive and 5 being extremely aggressive, please rate each of the following characters. - Bellatrix Lestrange	Likert	Extremely Non-Aggressive = 1, Non-Aggressi
32	Q11_6	On a scale of 1 to 5, with 1 extremely non-aggressive and 5 being extremely aggressive, please rate each of the following characters. - Ron Weasley	Likert	Extremely Non-Aggressive = 1, Non-Aggressi

Figure 7.10 The metafile helps guide analysis by summarizing text and numerical worksheets.

note

Remember to code your Likert data in the same logical order as asked. The same applies to ranking questions—be sure to code them numerically in the order they were listed (that is, if you have a list of 25 items to rank, code them as 1–25 in order of their appearance on the list).

note

In the example, I have broken apart multi-select questions with an _ (underscore). However, this approach can introduce errors in Tableau because it might not recognize underscores. Another approach is to use a letter addendum; that is, Q10**a** instead.

After you begin working in Tableau, the metafile should be your first sheet (see Figure 7.11). You can "visualize" the column in your metafile to provide a quick-glance legend to your survey data, prevent toggling back and forth between Tableau and Excel to double-check the questions you want to explore and how responses were recorded.

Sheet 1			
Question ID	**Wording**	**Question Ty..**	**Code**
Q4	In my opini..	Select One	1=harry, 2=voldemort, 3=draco, 4=snape, 5=bellatrix, 6=ron, 7=hermion..
Q5	In my opini..	Select One	1=harry, 2=voldemort, 3=draco, 4=snape, 5=bellatrix, 6=ron, 7=hermion..
Q6	In my opini..	Select One	1=harry, 2=voldemort, 3=draco, 4=snape, 5=bellatrix, 6=ron, 7=hermion..
Q7	I believe ma..	True/False	True = 1, False = 0
Q10_1	Please rank..	Rank	1=harry, 2=voldemort, 3=draco, 4=snape, 5=bellatrix, 6=ron, 7=hermion..
Q10_2	Please rank..	Rank	1=harry, 2=voldemort, 3=draco, 4=snape, 5=bellatrix, 6=ron, 7=hermion..
Q10_3	Please rank..	Rank	1=harry, 2=voldemort, 3=draco, 4=snape, 5=bellatrix, 6=ron, 7=hermion..
Q10_4	Please rank..	Rank	1=harry, 2=voldemort, 3=draco, 4=snape, 5=bellatrix, 6=ron, 7=hermion..
Q10_5	Please rank..	Rank	1=harry, 2=voldemort, 3=draco, 4=snape, 5=bellatrix, 6=ron, 7=hermion..
Q10_6	Please rank..	Rank	1=harry, 2=voldemort, 3=draco, 4=snape, 5=bellatrix, 6=ron, 7=hermion..
Q10_7	Please rank..	Rank	1=harry, 2=voldemort, 3=draco, 4=snape, 5=bellatrix, 6=ron, 7=hermion..
Q10_8	Please rank..	Rank	1=harry, 2=voldemort, 3=draco, 4=snape, 5=bellatrix, 6=ron, 7=hermion..
Q10_9	Please rank..	Rank	1=harry, 2=voldemort, 3=draco, 4=snape, 5=bellatrix, 6=ron, 7=hermion..
Q10_10	Please rank..	Rank	1=harry, 2=voldemort, 3=draco, 4=snape, 5=bellatrix, 6=ron, 7=hermion..
Q10_11	Please rank..	Rank	1=harry, 2=voldemort, 3=draco, 4=snape, 5=bellatrix, 6=ron, 7=hermion..
Q10_13	Please rank..	Rank	1=harry, 2=voldemort, 3=draco, 4=snape, 5=bellatrix, 6=ron, 7=hermion..
Q10_15	Please rank..	Rank	1=harry, 2=voldemort, 3=draco, 4=snape, 5=bellatrix, 6=ron, 7=hermion..
Q10_16	Please rank..	Rank	1=harry, 2=voldemort, 3=draco, 4=snape, 5=bellatrix, 6=ron, 7=hermion..
Q10_17	Please rank..	Rank	1=harry, 2=voldemort, 3=draco, 4=snape, 5=bellatrix, 6=ron, 7=hermion..
Q10_18	Please rank..	Rank	1=harry, 2=voldemort, 3=draco, 4=snape, 5=bellatrix, 6=ron, 7=hermion..
Q10_19	Please rank..	Rank	1=harry, 2=voldemort, 3=draco, 4=snape, 5=bellatrix, 6=ron, 7=hermion..
Q10_22	Please rank..	Rank	1=harry, 2=voldemort, 3=draco, 4=snape, 5=bellatrix, 6=ron, 7=hermion..

Figure 7.11 The metafile provides a handy first sheet in Tableau to guide analysis.

Pivoting Data from Wide to Tall

A very common data prep task is to transform data from "wide"—meaning many, many columns—to "tall" (or "narrow")—meaning many, many rows. The difference lies in readability: Entering data into a spreadsheet in the wide form is generally easier, but computers prefer to read data in the tall form. In this regard, Tableau is similar. Reading "tall" data is preferable within the Tableau environment for use in visual analysis as well as building and sorting charts dynamically.

In plain terms, exported survey data is, by nature, very wide. Each respondent's answers to each question are captured in one row. However, you are analyzing questions and their answers, not respondents. So, you need the survey data to be tall—you need to see every question's answer from every respondent. Reshaping survey data to be tall enables you to look at each question, and distributes each respondent's answers to each question over many rows.

To analyze the survey data, you need to reshape it from "wide" to "tall" before you can look at it meaningfully within Tableau. For these next preparation tasks, you need to bring the data into Tableau and continue from there.

Reshaping Survey Data with Tableau 10

Among its many additions and improvements, Tableau v10 brought about the ability for analysts to prepare survey data without having to either use external tools or spend countless hours engaged in a manual cleaning process.

Keeping this process bundled within Tableau provides many benefits:

- It lessens overhead costs to invest in additional tools.
- It reduces the need to learn multiple pieces of software.
- It enables you to join all three of the created data sources directly within Tableau.

That said, there are also some drawbacks:

- The process is clunky and not intuitive.
- Tableau exhibits some strange behavior that necessitates users to repeat some steps.
- Users might need to create and routinely extract data.

Utilizing the three Excel worksheets created earlier (Numeric, Text, Meta), let's continue this process in Tableau.

> **note**
>
> Tableau Zen Master and Iron Viz Champion Steve Wexler maintains an excellent blog on reshaping survey data for Tableau, including using Excel, Tableau v9 and v10, and Alteryx. His work includes many clearly delivered tutorials and presentations specifically on survey data and is an excellent resource. Visit Steve's blog at http://www.datarevelations.com/surveyjustso.html.

Step 1: Creating Extracts

To create extracts, follow these steps:

1. Open Tableau and connect to your Excel workbook created in the previous step.
2. Drag the Text sheet into the "Drag Sheets Here" Connect to Data screen, as shown in Figure 7.12. (Ignore the Go To Worksheet prompt. It is not time yet.)
3. To select out the demographic data, leave the demographic fields alone (in this example, keep ResponseID, Gender, Age, and Zipcode) and select the remainder of the columns relating to survey question data. To select a column, click its column header. To select multiple columns, you can:

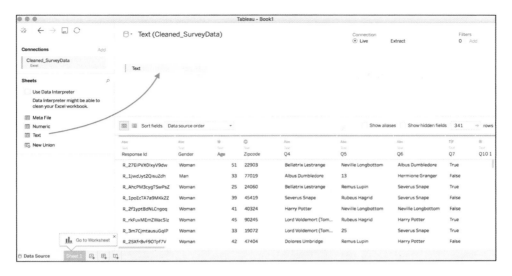

Figure 7.12 Drag your first sheet, Text, to the Connection window.

Hold the Shift key and click each individual column of interest, or

Hold the Shift key and use the scroll bar to scroll to click the last column.

4. Right-click (or click the drop-down arrow) on any of the selected columns and click Pivot
    from the context menu (see Figure 7.13).

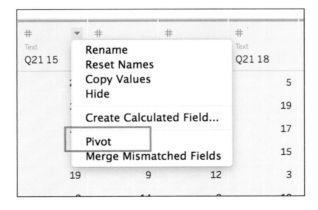

Figure 7.13 Select Pivot from the drop-down menu to pivot your fields.

Two new columns appear at the front of your data, named Pivot Field Names and Pivot
Field Values (see Figure 7.14).

Abc	Abc
Pivot	Pivot
Pivot Field Names	**Pivot Field Values**
Q11 19	Aggressive
Q11 19	Aggressive
Q11 19	Extremely Aggressive
Q11 19	Aggressive
Q11 19	Extremely Aggressive
Q11 19	Extremely Aggressive
Q11 19	Extremely Aggressive
Q11 19	Extremely Aggressive

Figure 7.14 You have to rename these new fields.

5. Using the drop-down arrow on each column, rename them as follows:

    Pivot Field Names to QuestionID

    Pivot Field Values to Text

6. Create the first extract by choosing Extract as the Connection type (on the upper right of the screen). To save the extract, click the Sheet1 tab (see Figure 7.15).

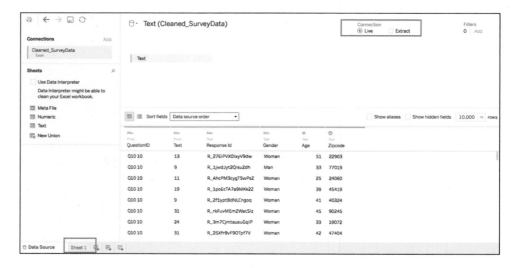

Figure 7.15 Click Sheet1 to generate the Extract dialog.

note

For more on Tableau extracts, visit http://onlinehelp.tableau.com/current/pro/
desktop/en-us/extracting_data.html.

7. In the dialog box that appears, save your new extract as SurveyData_text. The file extension will be .tde. Be sure to note where you are saving your extract.

   You need to repeat this step with the other two Excel sheets (Numeric and Meta); however, the steps are not quite identical.

8. From the Tableau menu at the top of your screen, select Data>New Data Source. Again, navigate to your Excel workbook and click Open.

9. This time, connect to the Numeric sheet by dragging it onto the Connection pane.

10. Because you already selected out the demographic data, you don't need to do it again. However, you do need to leave a field for the join you will eventually do. In this example, ResponseID is the join field. Thus, you should:

   a. Hide the additional demographic fields (in this example, this includes Gender, Age, and Zipcode) by selecting the unneeded demographic fields, right-clicking, and selecting Hide from the drop-down menu (see Figure 7.16).

Abc	Abc	#	⊕	▼	#	#	#	#
Numeric	Numeric	Numeric	Numeric					Numeric
Response Id	Gender	Age	Zipcode	**Rename**				Q7
				Copy Values				
R_27EiPVX0IxyV9dw	Woman	51	22903	Hide			8	1
R_1jwdJyt2QisuZdh	Man	33	77019	Create Calculated Field...		7		0
R_AhcPM3cygTSwPsZ	Woman	25	24060				4	1
R_1poEcTA7a9MKk2Z	Woman	39	45419	Pivot			4	0
				Merge Mismatched Fields				
R_2f1yptBdNLCngoq	Woman	41	40324		1	21	21	0
R_rkFuvMEmZWacSlz	Woman	45	90245		2	14	1	1
R_3m7CjmtausuGqIP	Woman	33	19072		2	25	4	1
R_25Xfr8vF9OTpf7V	Woman	42	47404		16	15	1	0

Figure 7.16 Hide unnecessary demographic fields.

   b. Select the remaining columns, right-click, and select Pivot (for help, see steps 3 and 4).

11. Two new columns appear—Pivot Field Names and Pivot Field Values— but because Tableau does not automatically rename these fields, you must rename them. Using the drop-down arrow on each column, rename them as follows:

   Pivot Field Names to QuestionID

   Pivot Field Values to Numeric

12. Repeat steps 6 and 7 to create your second extract. This time, name the field SurveyData_ numeric.

    You are ready to create the third and final extract with the metafile.

13. Again, from the Tableau menu at the top of your screen, choose Data>New Data Source. Navigate to your Excel workbook and click Open.

14. This time, drag the Meta sheet to the Connection pane.

15. You do not need to pivot any fields within this sheet. You only need to create an extract. Repeat step 12, this last time naming the file SurveyData_meta.

Step 2: Joining Data Sources

At this point you have created three separate Tableau extracts, one for each of the three data sources. In the next step, you will use Tableau 10's ability to join files from different data sources to bring these extracts together and create an extract from the joined files.

1. From the New Data Source menu, click the More option under the To a File header (see Figure 7.17).

Figure 7.17 Select More to add a New Data Source.

2. Navigate to where you saved your exports earlier, and select your Text file (SurveyData_ text). Click Open.

3. Add a connection, and select SurveyData_numeric following the same pathway described in step 1.

4. Tableau will automatically join these two data sources, but they are **not** joined correctly. By clicking the join icon, you will see that Tableau has created an inner join on the field Number of Records (see Figure 7.18). **This is not the field you want to use to join these two data sources.**

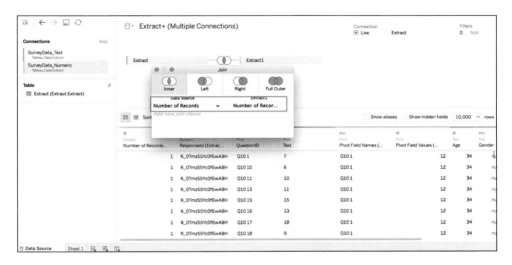

Figure 7.18 Bad join! You do not want to join on Number of Records. This is meaningless.

5. Click Number of Records on both sides of the join and change these fields to ResponseID (see Figure 7.19).

> ### note
> On the left join, this field will appear correctly as ResponseID. On the right join, this field will appear named ResponseID(Extract1). I have received reports from students that _ (underscore) titled fields are not recognized as expected when joining data in Tableau. This has been resolved by replacing underscores with hyphens (-) in field formats.

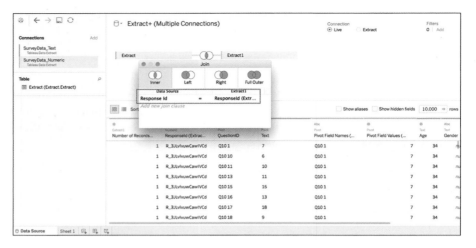

Figure 7.19 Good join! Joining on ResponseID connects a meaningful field.

6. You are not quite finished with the join. You also need to join the QuestionID field (see Figure 7.20):

    a. From the left data source, select QuestionID.

    b. From the right data source, select Pivot Field Names(Extract 1). (Although you previously renamed this column in your pivoting work, Tableau can only track the alias names for fields in the first .tde file, and reverts to the original field name in additional extract files. This will not affect your visualizations or analysis later.)

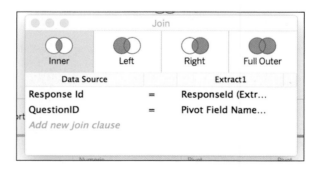

Figure 7.20 The Text and Numeric sheets, fully joined.

7. Click Add, then More, and select your metafile—SurveyData_meta.

8. Click on the new join and remove any fields that may be automatically joined.

9. Before joining the correct fields, you need to make one small adjustment in the field names. A current Tableau issue prevents using two instances of the same field name from

the same table in multiple joins. To work around this issue, before editing any of the new join information, rename the field in question in the Data pane at the bottom of the screen so that the common field has a different name in each table. You can then complete the join (see Figure 7.21):

a. On the columns associated with the Meta sheet, rename QuestionID to QuestionIDNEW.

b. From the left data source, select QuestionID.

c. From the right data source, select QuestionIDNEW.

Figure 7.21 This last join takes a few extra steps to get right.

> **note**
>
> This behavior is related to Tableau known issue ID 651428, which is currently under investigation. After it has been resolved, you should simply be able to join using the QuestionID fields on both left and right.

10. The multiple connection join creates some superfluous fields in the data preview that you need to hide and/or rename:

Hide both Number of Records fields.

Hide the field ResponseID (Extract1).

Hide QuestionIDNEW (or the second QuestionID field).

Hide Pivot Field Names (Extract1).

Rename Pivot Field Values to Value (or Numeric Value).

11. You need to create one more extract. Change the Connection type in the upper right to Extract and click Sheet1 to generate the Extract dialog box.

12. Name this sheet SurveyData_joined.

13. You are almost ready to visually explore your data, but there is one more step to streamline how your field names are grouped. After creating the extract, Tableau automatically groups field names by data source. I find this confusing. Click the drop-down arrow on the Data pane and select Group by Folder to reorganize your field names in a more intuitive manner (see Figure 7.22).

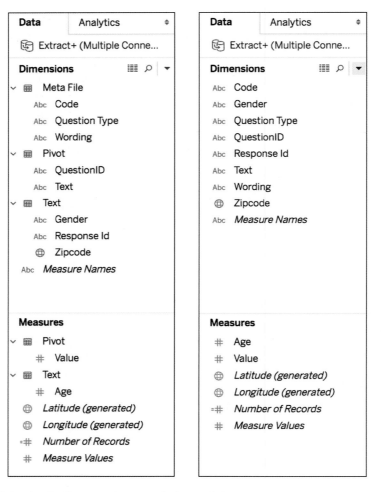

Figure 7.22 Sorting the Data pane by group: before and after.

RESHAPING SURVEY DATA WITH ALTERYX

While Tableau's native functionality will work just fine with shorter surveys or with surveys where either labels or numeric values will work, Alteryx is a great fit for more complex surveys that have a good bit of data and where both text and numeric values are critical. A self-service data analytics platform, Alteryx was ranked as a Challenger in Gartner's 2017 Magic Quadrant for Data Science Platforms. The tool allows analysts to connect to and cleanse data from data warehouses, cloud-based applications, spreadsheets, and other sources; prep, blend; and then prep, blend, and analyze data in a repeatable workflow. For more on Alteryx, visit www.alteryx.com.

One of the reasons I enjoy working with Alteryx is its visual, drag-and-drop workflow canvas. It may look a little complicated at first glance, but it works similar to flowcharting and decision tree-type tools (for example, Microsoft Visio): Actions are color coded and connect to each other by joining logic.

Although this text doesn't cover the Alteryx workflow, Figure 7.23 provides a quick glance at the Alteryx workflow needed to finish the preparation of this data for analysis in Tableau. Notice that this workflow makes use of the three worksheets you created earlier.

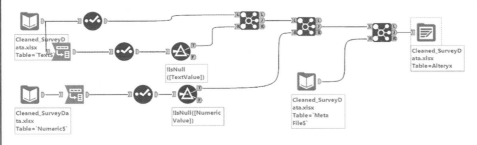

Figure 7.23 The Alteryx workflow we'll be building later.

Summary

At this point, you're ready to take your data into Tableau and begin visually exploring and building your data story. You'll continue working with the reshaped Harry Potter data set in Chapter 8.

STORYBOARDING FRAME BY FRAME

This chapter picks up where the previous chapter left off by looking deeper at the process of constructing a data narrative by visually exploring data, building purposeful visualizations, and organizing them to tell a story. This chapter covers how to build a sequence of data visualizations, reviews how to build dashboards and organize them as well as individual visualizations in story points, and discusses how to make use of some of Tableau's storytelling features.

In an August 2017 episode of "The Nerdist" podcast, celebrated American astrophysicist—and phenomenal data storyteller—Neil DeGrasse Tyson, spoke of the importance of learning how to process and understand today's waterhose of information, commenting, "[we need to understand] how to turn data into information, information into knowledge, and knowledge into wisdom." In my opinion, this is exactly what we are doing when we build visual data stories.

This chapter explores storytelling as a process, considering mechanisms available in Tableau for building and delivering your complete story and the steps you should take to build the appropriate framework for your narrative. You will apply what you've learned in subsequent chapters to building a story frame by frame, from curating visuals to storyboarding the visual narrative, and completing a compelling, presentation-ready story to deliver to your audience based on a dataset explored throughout this book. Along the way is a review of some additional formatting capabilities that support visualizations as you complete that part of the storyboarding process.

> note
>
> You can build stories using Tableau sheets (individual visualizations), dashboards (multiple visualizations), or story points (multiple sheets and/or dashboards). Which mechanism you pick is up to you—and your audience, your display, your presentation style, and other context. Overloading a dashboard is a real concern, particularly in non-narrated or guided presentations, as is trying to cram too much detail into a single visual or a story. In this chapter we approach storyboarding from the perspective of building a narrative, rather than formatting a delivery system. That said, the chapter does cover a few basic aspects of working with dashboards and stories that support your storytelling process.

Understanding Stories in Tableau

Earlier chapters distilled the difference between exploratory and explanatory visualizations, and the obligation of visual data storytellers to focus on building and sharing explanatory visualizations that support the story. Like events in any narrative, visualizations should compound on each other and lead the audience through a series of events, insights, or other information that allows them to reach the goal you have decided on upfront.

Building stories in Tableau is comprised of three primary mechanisms; the following sections provide a quick review.

> best practice
>
> Although all three of these mechanisms can support great visual data stories, be strategic in how you use them. Be aware of the impact of sizing, layout, and positioning, and make sure the view you've curated on your screen is consistent with your audience's. The Device Preview functionality in Tableau supports this practice.

Individual Visualizations (Sheets)

Sometimes one visual is all you need, particularly if it is layered with rich tooltips or annotations. Or, you might want to export simple, static visuals for use in other presentation software. Within the Tableau environment, you can bring individual visualizations (as sheets) into dashboards or story points to build a storytelling framework. A sheet is the building block for any story as it is the place where visualizations are built (and where we've been working to build all our visualizations thus far in this book—revisit Chapter 3, "Getting Started with Tableau," for more detail on the Tableau UI).

> **note**
>
> Many analysts use PowerPoint to present visualizations, but this requires exporting static images of your visuals, instead of letting them stay within their native format and keep any interactive functionality. Instead of this approach, try Tableau Reader, which is a simple, free download that lets everyone appreciate Tableau views at their best, including the ability to "touch" your data as you present. Additionally, views can be shared to Tableau Public.

Dashboards

In Tableau, a dashboard is a collection of several worksheets shown in a single screen so that you can compare and monitor a variety of data visualizations simultaneously, and often with the ability to filter and highlight all visualizations with the use of a single dashboard action. Dashboards, like visualizations, can achieve many purposes, and can be designed to explain, explore, or tell stories. Storytelling dashboards, like ours, seek to weave together a series of visuals that show how something unfolds, and should be constructed aligned to narrative flow.

You can create a dashboard in Tableau by clicking the dashboard button (see Figure 8.1).

Figure 8.1 Dashboard button.

In terms of a delivery mechanism for visual analysis, similarly to visualizations you can create several types of dashboards—explanatory, exploratory, and so on. Storytelling dashboards are not like other dashboard forms, in that they are primarily intended to *present* a story. Thus, compared to other forms of Tableau dashboards, storytelling dashboards tend to:

- Have more descriptive titles and lead-in paragraphs, often including legends (like color or size) within their design
- Have simplified and streamlined views of a fewer number of visualizations

- Include prominent legends, simplified color schemes, and limited views of data, including only that which supports the narrative (that is, filters or parameters)

- Be devoid of interactive elements that might affect the narrative, such as quick filters or other actions (this often depends on whether the presentation will be narrated or left to the audience)

- Include explanatory annotations to point out specific "story points" the narrator deems of interest to the audience

Figure 8.2 shows an example of a storytelling dashboard.

This dashboard leaves little guesswork up to the audience as it tells the story of survey demographics in a regional school cyberbullying survey by bringing in several visualizations that speak to the responder's age, gender, and other distinguishing characteristics. The dashboard features clear titles and image captions, consistent color schemes, and simple visuals with appropriate labels, annotations, and legends.

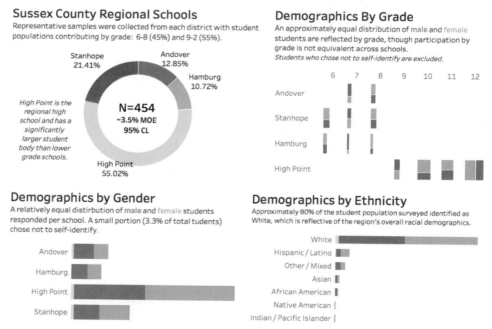

Figure 8.2 Storytelling dashboard example using survey data.

THE DASHBOARD WORKSPACE

Figure 8.3 presents an annotated view of the Tableau dashboard workspace.

Figure 8.3 An annotated view of the Tableau dashboard workspace.

Here is a breakdown of some of the functionality of the Tableau dashboard workspace:

- **Device Preview:** This option allows you to see your dashboard as it will appear on the form factor selected in Size.

- **Size:** This is an important aspect to think about *before* you start building a dashboard, and these options let you select from a pre-programmed list of fixed display sizes (that is, desktop browser, laptop browser, tablet) while the Canvas adjusts accordingly. An "Automatic" option allows the dashboard display to dynamically resize to any display it is presented on, but this has certain ramifications for things like floating legends, because these will move around as the screen resizes.

- **Sheets:** This area provides you with a list of all sheets in the workbook.

- **Objects:** This area offers a list of additional elements, such as logos or images, that you may elect to add into your dashboard from outside of Tableau.

> **note**
>
> This section just provides a basic overview of dashboard functionality. You can find more information on creating a dashboard, including adding views, objects, and interactivity at http://onlinehelp.tableau.com/current/pro/desktop/en-us/dashboards_create.html.

Story Points

Story Points was introduced in Tableau in version 8.2 as a way to "build a narrative from data." Story Points is similar to other presentation software in it provides a presenter with the ability to highlight certain insights or provide content, as well as break the story into pieces using visualizations (whether as worksheets or dashboards) in a series of click-through sequences for easy consumption. A story is a sheet, so the same methods you would apply to create, name, and manage visualizations in worksheets also apply to stories.

The benefit to using Tableau Story Points, rather than using PowerPoint or similar, is that with it, interactivity remains in the story. They are not static images: Presenters or audiences can explore or expand on the data using actions such as quick filters within the narrative. (Note: Currently these actions only affect the visual in the story point and do not filter across all visuals or dashboards in a story.) Additionally, Story Points updates live as the underlying visualizations or data updates, reducing the need for reworking or re-exporting worksheets.

You can create a story in Tableau by clicking the story button (see Figure 8.4).

Figure 8.4 Story button.

You present stories (in Tableau Desktop only) by clicking the Presentation Mode button (see Figure 8.5) on the toolbar.

Figure 8.5 Presentation Mode button.

Figure 8.6 shows an example of Tableau Story Points in action using presentation mode.

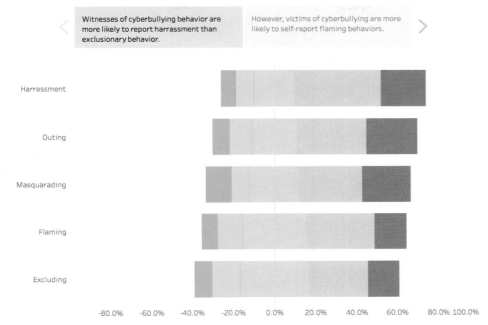

Figure 8.6 Story Points in presentation mode.

note

To find more information on creating a story, including layout options, formatting, and presentation go to https://onlinehelp.tableau.com/current/pro/desktop/en-us/story_create.html.

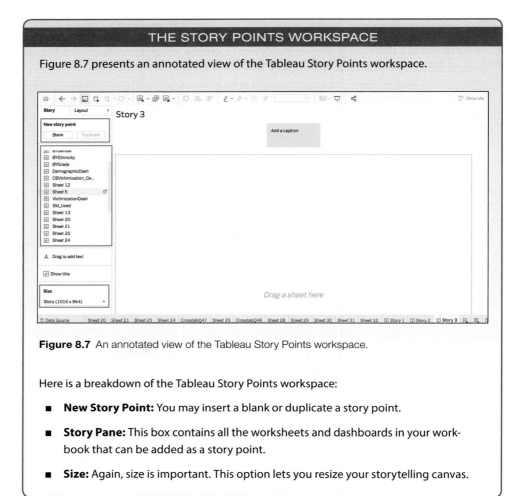

THE STORY POINTS WORKSPACE

Figure 8.7 presents an annotated view of the Tableau Story Points workspace.

Figure 8.7 An annotated view of the Tableau Story Points workspace.

Here is a breakdown of the Tableau Story Points workspace:

- **New Story Point:** You may insert a blank or duplicate a story point.

- **Story Pane:** This box contains all the worksheets and dashboards in your workbook that can be added as a story point.

- **Size:** Again, size is important. This option lets you resize your storytelling canvas.

The Layout pane provides further options intended to help you format the style of navigation for the text boxes. Navigation can be formatted as Caption Boxes (default), Numbered, or Dots (see Figure 8.8).

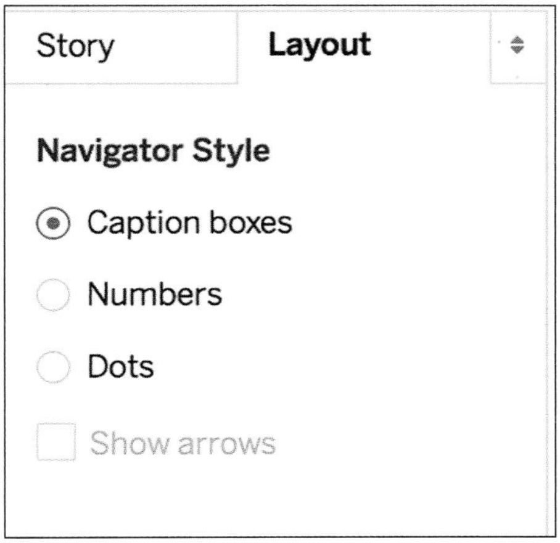

Figure 8.8 Format navigation in the Layout pane within story points.

THE STORYTELLING CHECKLIST

Before building a story, make sure to complete the Storytelling Checklist and answer as many questions as possible before moving into the storyboarding process to make sure the story aligns to its goals. You can then start sketching out the story outline for guidance during development of the narrative.

- **Who: The Data's Audience**

    - Who is your audience?
    - What do they want?
    - What do they need?
    - How might they be feeling?
    - What action do they need to take?
    - What type of communication do they prefer?
    - How well do they know the data?

- **You**

    - How well does the audience know you?
    - Does the audience trust you? Do they find you credible?
    - How well do you know the data?
    - Do you have any pre-conceived notions or bias about the data?

- **What: The Data's Context**
  - What is the data?
  - What is it about?
  - Is the data complete?
  - Do you have enough data to tell a complete story?
  - Is the subject matter general or specialized?
- **Why: The goal**
  - Why are you telling this story?
  - What action do you want the audience to take?
- **How: The Data's Presentation Mode**
  - Is this story static or interactive?
  - Will you be narrating the story?
  - Do you want to explore or expand the story while narrating?
  - Will it be presented in a small group or a large setting?
  - Will the audience be live or virtual?

The Storyboarding Process

Like all aspects of data visualization, crafting a perfect visual data story is a process of ongoing iteration and refinement. Luckily, crafting a data story is much like crafting any other narrative, and after taking the time to clean and explore your data, you can take advantage of a rather linear process to build a complete visual data story (see Figure 8.9).

Figure 8.9 This linear process can help you craft the best visual data narrative.

Planning Your Story's Purpose

Whichever mechanism you are using, as you begin planning your story, taking some time to reflect on the purpose of the story and the narrative you are attempting to share with your captivated audience is critical. Defining this purpose is the most important step of the planning stage in the storytelling.

Chapter 4, "Importance of Context in Storytelling," discussed the seven types of data stories. Pick one. **ONE**. Regardless of the type of story you are telling, your story should have one goal and one only. The clarity of your story is just as important as the clarity of each visualization within it. Audiences shouldn't have to guess to understand the salient point you are trying to make with your presentation.

In addition to the Storytelling Checklist, think like an author and consider the following:

- **Plot:** What story are you trying to tell? What is its purpose, and what is your goal or the action you want the audience to take when you roll the credits, figuratively speaking, at the end of your story?

- **Characters:** Think of your data as your main character, and its context as the story's setting. Your filters, parameters, limitations, even external data sources, are all supporting characters in your story, and each contributes to the overall narrative. It's your job to identify how.

- **Audience:** Consider each of the questions in the Storytelling Checklist. Like any good storyteller, you should know who is going to be listening to or reading your story.

Storyboarding Your Data Story

As you begin constructing your story, considering order and flow and how the pieces of your story fit together is important. You've already seen the importance of understanding the data's context and of audience analysis and how the story's purpose is supported by understanding its plot, characters, and audience. You've also reviewed several common types of data visualizations and how to curate them to make them more intuitive, focused, and compelling. Your story will, when complete, tie together all of these into a cohesive whole.

It's important to note that stories may be comprised of various views of a single visualization, of a series of compounding similar visualizations, or of a series of unique visualizations that support different aspects of an analysis. There is no single correct way to build a story. The example in this chapter tells a story about survey data, and in doing so shows how to work through a series of unique visualizations that support the story structure and take advantage of several of the chart types explored in this book.

Although many different types of narrative structures exist to consider, the one I have found most effective for consistently telling compelling and meaningful visual data stories regardless of the type of story is the three-act structure.

Let's review how this structure functions:

- **Act One—The Setup (or, the Exposition):** This is where you, as the narrator, lay the groundwork for your story. It's where you explain the purpose, introduce the plot, establish the characters and their relationships, and finish with your dramatic question or inciting incident. This is the catalyst; it's the type of story you are telling. Are you going to explore a change over time? Zoom into detail on something that happened? This act ends with your hypothesis, or what question you are exploring or answering within your story.

- **Act Two—The Rising Action:** This is the meat of your story. It's where you combine plot, characters, and audience as you guide them through the data. In a film or play, this act typically depicts a protagonist's attempt to resolve a problem or the escalation of an issue, and who experiences character development along the way. In a visual data narrative, this is your opportunity to perform a curated version of your own analysis, capitalizing on the insights you have found that support your narrative's purpose—and making your audience believe in your discoveries as they experience the story for themselves.

- **Act Three—The Climax:** Finally, you've reached your grand reveal. Your audience has absorbed the plot point and is ready for their call to action via a final viz that ends the story.

> **note**
>
> You can use many techniques to build your storyboard. One of the most common—and the one I use in my classroom—is the sticky note approach. This process involves using color-coded sticky notes (that is, yellow for Act One, pink for Act Two, green for Act Three) and treating each sticky note as a view in your story. You can easily adjust and rearrange your storyboard based on audience feedback and as you fine-tune the visuals and supporting narrative.

Building a Story

Keep in mind that the process of building a story begins with thorough exploratory visual analysis to help you find the data's story, decide what's meaningful, and curate the best visuals to tell the story and deliver on your goal. After you've finished this process you can then structure these visuals into the right format for your presentation delivery.

Stories are magical, so it's only fitting to put this process into practice and get hands on with storytelling in Tableau by using the Harry Potter dataset referenced throughout this text as an example (particularly in Chapter 7, during the transformation of the raw dataset from a jumble of messy survey data into well-prepped data for visual analysis in Tableau). Not only is this data a perfect fit for the storytelling process, but it's fun data, too, and a solid example of how to move through the data visually to uncover its story.

In this section, we take a very limited view of this dataset to work on telling a short story about the data: who took the survey, and what their answers were to the most important survey question (who do readers perceive as the most and least aggressive characters in the *Harry Potter* series?).

> **note**
>
> This data story was presented at the 2017 6th Annual *Harry Potter* Conference at Chapel Hill University. Learn more about the conference, as well as view the full presentation, at www.harrypotterconference.com.

Making Meta Meaningful

Remember the Meta worksheet you manually created in Chapter 7 as you scrubbed survey data in Excel? Now is the time to make it useful in Tableau. This sheet provides a key to the data within Tableau and eliminates the need to switch back and forth between Tableau and your data source by providing a data legend directly within the analysis environment. Regardless of the data you are working with, having a complete understanding of what data you have (and don't have), how it's structured, and how it's coded is critical.

Building a simple data table can help to visualize the helper Meta worksheet created in Chapter 7. To do this, drag the Dimension pills that represent your meta key—in this case, Question ID, Wording, Question Type, and Code—to Rows in Tableau to create a text table (see Figure 8.10).

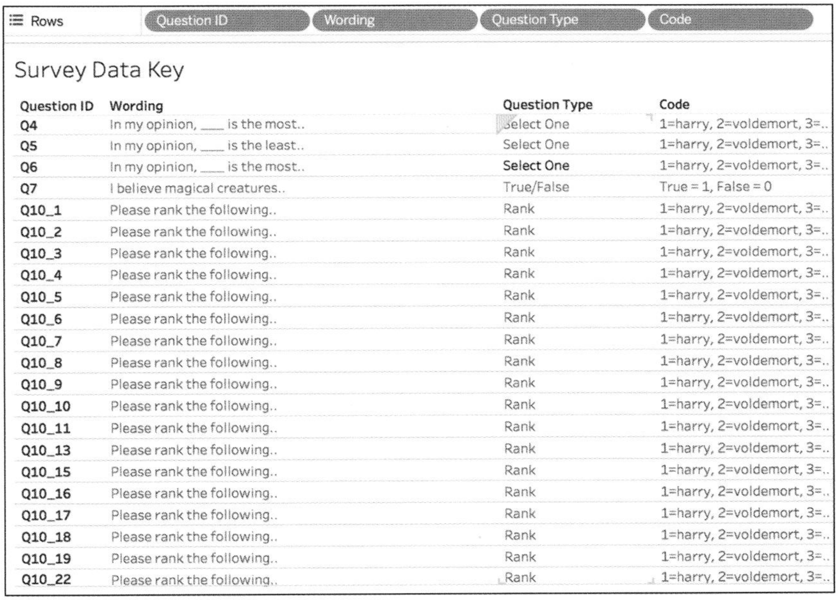

Question ID	Wording	Question Type	Code
Q4	In my opinion, ___ is the most..	Select One	1=harry, 2=voldemort, 3=..
Q5	In my opinion, ___ is the least..	Select One	1=harry, 2=voldemort, 3=..
Q6	In my opinion, ___ is the most..	Select One	1=harry, 2=voldemort, 3=..
Q7	I believe magical creatures..	True/False	True = 1, False = 0
Q10_1	Please rank the following..	Rank	1=harry, 2=voldemort, 3=..
Q10_2	Please rank the following..	Rank	1=harry, 2=voldemort, 3=..
Q10_3	Please rank the following..	Rank	1=harry, 2=voldemort, 3=..
Q10_4	Please rank the following..	Rank	1=harry, 2=voldemort, 3=..
Q10_5	Please rank the following..	Rank	1=harry, 2=voldemort, 3=..
Q10_6	Please rank the following..	Rank	1=harry, 2=voldemort, 3=..
Q10_7	Please rank the following..	Rank	1=harry, 2=voldemort, 3=..
Q10_8	Please rank the following..	Rank	1=harry, 2=voldemort, 3=..
Q10_9	Please rank the following..	Rank	1=harry, 2=voldemort, 3=..
Q10_10	Please rank the following..	Rank	1=harry, 2=voldemort, 3=..
Q10_11	Please rank the following..	Rank	1=harry, 2=voldemort, 3=..
Q10_13	Please rank the following..	Rank	1=harry, 2=voldemort, 3=..
Q10_15	Please rank the following..	Rank	1=harry, 2=voldemort, 3=..
Q10_16	Please rank the following..	Rank	1=harry, 2=voldemort, 3=..
Q10_17	Please rank the following..	Rank	1=harry, 2=voldemort, 3=..
Q10_18	Please rank the following..	Rank	1=harry, 2=voldemort, 3=..
Q10_19	Please rank the following..	Rank	1=harry, 2=voldemort, 3=..
Q10_22	Please rank the following..	Rank	1=harry, 2=voldemort, 3=..

Figure 8.10 The Meta sheet created in Excel provides a handy survey data key in Tableau.

Visualizing Survey Demographics

Before you can craft a meaningful story about survey data, you need to set the stage and build your story's setting by scripting in the people and places who will contribute to the events in later acts. In this use case using survey data, you should know exactly who your respondents were, as this could have relevant implications or offer valuable insight into your survey data as well as its story. This involves exploring and visualizing the demographic questions to get a good grasp of who is represented in the responders, and see what interesting things might rise to the top when looking at demographics.

Determining Who Took the Survey

The obvious first question that comes to mind in understanding how many survey responses you received is just that—how many? However, reshaping the survey data from wide to tall essentially created an entry for every question response per survey respondent, so a simple count or Number of Records function will not work here.

In the survey data, the Response ID field identifies each person who took the survey. You can use this field to produce a distinct Count() function to "count" the number of survey responders; however, notice that Response ID is currently a dimension in the Data pane. You need to convert it to a measure to do this calculation.

1. Drag the Response ID dimension pill to the Columns shelf.
2. Right-click the pill.
3. Choose Measure>Count (Distinct) as shown in Figure 8.11.

> **note**
>
> Because this storytelling example uses survey data, it provides a nice headstart on Act One by looking—rather literally—at "who" the story is about. Although this example is used for teaching purposes, in reality you might not have much demographic information, and therefore, there could be other ways to start out exploring the data—if it's not who provided the data, it could be who the data is about (customers, athletes, and non-persons like housing prices, and so on), or your initial thesis statement or research question that prompted the analysis.

Figure 8.11 We can convert the Response ID to a measure and use the Count() function to count survey responses.

You can now see that this survey has 341 responses (see Figure 8.12).

Figure 8.12 The first job in understanding survey data is to know how many responses were received.

From here, you can explore the other demographic fields by dragging and dropping fields to the canvas. This survey collected data on gender, age, and location, so let's take a look at these fields and get to know the responders a little better. Perhaps there will be something interesting to find.

Understanding Gender

By adding the field Gender to the Rows pane, you can quickly see that the vast majority of survey respondents were women (see Figure 8.13). This is, actually, not surprising. Many sources that have looked deeply into the demographic makeup of people who voluntarily complete online surveys (a challenging group of people to definitively diagnose due to a number of fluid factors) have discovered that most survey responders, in general, tend to be disproportionately women.

> **tip**
>
> Add a quick table calculation to change this view from a simple count of responders to a percent of total by right-clicking the Response ID pill, and then selecting Quick Table Calculation > Percent of Total.

> **note**
>
> In this dataset, one survey responder chose not to answer this question, resulting in a null response. For the sake of simplicity, you can filter out this null by clicking it and then excluding this response.

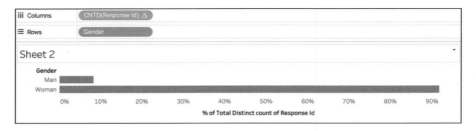

Figure 8.13 It may appear surprising that the survey respondents were more than 90% women, but given the context of both the survey and the subject matter (and as discussed later), that might not be as insightful as we would like to believe.

Understanding Age

Let's remove Gender from the canvas and look at another demographic field—Age.

This survey asked respondents to enter their age numerically, which provides Age as individual values rather than categories. Thus, this data is organized as a Measure by Tableau.

A couple of different ways to look at this data (Figure 8.14) include the following:

- Convert Age to a dimension, and change the field type to String to view a count of responders per age.
- Convert Age to a dimension and see a sparkline of ages.

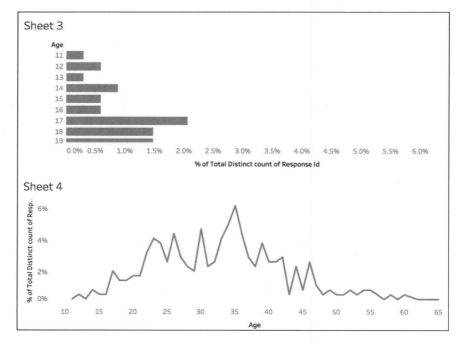

Figure 8.14 This quick age dashboard shows a couple of options for looking at survey responders' ages, although neither is particularly helpful.

Although both of the approaches in Figure 8.14 would help you see a basic count of survey responders by their ages as well as identify any age-oriented clusters, averages, or so forth, looking by age (with a range from 11 to 65, in this case) is a bit overwhelming. Another potential way to look at this element of the demographic data in Tableau to identify more general trends is *groups*.

GROUPS

One potential way to look more productively at the ages of survey respondents is to group individual ages together and take a generational approach.

Luckily, Tableau enables you to quickly group dimensions with just a few clicks.

note

You can create groups from a dimension in the Data pane. Whenever you create a group, a group field is added to the Data pane and designated with a paperclip icon. A default name is automatically constructed using the combined member names. You can rename the group by right-clicking it and clicking Rename at the bottom of the dialog box. If you create multiple groups from one dimension, you can rename each alias as appropriate.

Before moving on to grouping, let's clearly define what the generational "groups" will be. Because this data is relevant to a pop culture fandom that spans many generations, let's set our own generations rather than bucketing by the proper generational age ranges (GenX, millennials, and so on). It's hard to define an age range for the huge *Harry Potter* fandom, but we can make a general guess by keeping in mind that the first *Harry Potter* book—aimed to readers around age 11—hit U.S. bookshelves in 1998 (it released in the UK in 1997) and the final book arrived in 2007. Thus, those readers who first read and "grew up" with Harry (who turned 11 himself in the first book) would currently be around 32 years old. Therefore, we could loosely pinpoint the "prime" *Harry Potter* age to be around 32—let's see how this looks in the data.

Here are the groups to create:

- Young Adult: 11–18
- Adult: 19–35
- Mature Adult: 36–54
- Senior: 55–65

To create a group, select all fields you want to group and click the paperclip icon on the toolbar (see Figure 8.15).

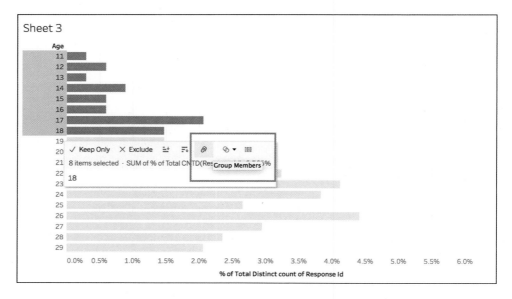

Figure 8.15 To create a group, select all desired items and "paperclip" them together.

When you've finished creating the groups, you can further fine-tune your view of the age groups by:

- Editing each alias and renaming it to the generational range (refer to Figure 8.15)
- Sorting how the Age groups appear on the canvas so that they are in the correct order
- Showing a Filter box to toggle between generations included in the view

When you've finished, your screen should appear similar to the one shown in Figure 8.16. You should now see a few things:

■ A new dimension Age(Group) should appear on your list of Dimensions. It will include the paperclip icon.

■ Your segmented group should appear named by alias, and in order, on your canvas.

■ A filter box for Age should be visible.

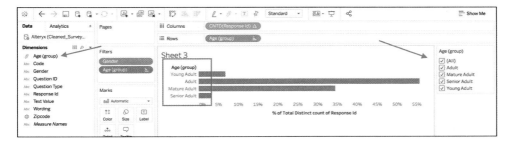

Figure 8.16 Fine-tuning your new groups provides a clearer view of trends in the survey respondents' age demographic.

> **note**
>
> The *Harry Potter* prime age of 32 fell within the 55.59% majority of Adults. However, 35 was actually the most prolific age, at just over 6% of total responders.

Repeat this exercise with any other demographic categories that interest you and continue to curate your visuals until you have a thorough understanding of how demographics—or other data fields—contribute to your story's setting.

Act One: Demographic Dashboard and Key Question

With the demographic data comprising Act One of the storyboard, let's build a quick dashboard to show this part of the story. I've used some of the methods described in this book to build a simple, storytelling dashboard to visualize this part of the story (see Figure 8.17).

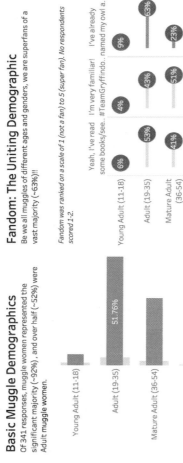

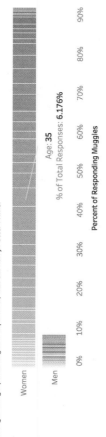

Basic Muggle Demographics

Of 341 responses, muggle women represented the significant majority (~92%) , and over half (~52%) were Adult muggle women.

Fandom: The Uniting Demographic

Be we all muggles of different ages and genders, we are superfans of a vast majority (~63%)!!

Fandom was ranked on a scale of 1 (not a fan) to 5 (super fan). No respondents scored 1-2.

Harry Potter Prime

The largest single percentage of respondents, was **35**: Harry Potter Prime.

Figure 8.17 This explanatory dashboard is the first part of the *Harry Potter* survey story, explaining the demographic characteristics of survey respondents.

Act Two: Questioning Character Aggression

Act Two digs into the heart of the survey by exploring respondents' answers to questions exploring perceptions of character aggression and who readers perceive as the most heroic and villainous characters in the series.

Using the methods described in this book, I've built a series of visualizations exploring responses to various questions asked within the survey. A few selected visualizations are shown in Figures 8.18 and 8.19. These are intended to highlight various "scenes" of key importance in the survey responses to build toward the reveal—in this case, the answer to our question—in Act Three.

The Nice Guy, the Villain, and the Hero

Nice Guy (Most Non-Aggressive) and Villain (Most Aggressive) characters were distinct. However, Hero is a little more ambiguous.

Characters who scored very lowly or not at all across all three categories were exluded.

Neville Longbottom	40%	0%	13%
Bellatrix Lestrange		52%	
Harry Potter	2%	1%	27%
Hermione Granger	5%	0%	24%
Rubeus Hagrid	26%	0%	0%
Lord Voldemort		27%	
Severus Snape	1%	2%	24%
Dolores Umbridge		13%	
Minerva McGonagall	7%		4%
Albus Dumbledore	4%	1%	5%
Remus Lupin	9%		1%
Ron Weasley	6%	1%	1%
Draco Malfoy	1%	3%	

Figure 8.18 This lollipop chart displays survey responses for Least Aggressive, Most Aggressive, and Most Heroic character.

Wizarding Heroes, According to Women

Women's view of herodom had many names in the goblet. Younger women saw Harry as the clear hero, but favor moved to Hermione before returning back to Harry. Senior women shared herodom between Harry and Snape, who increased in favor with age.

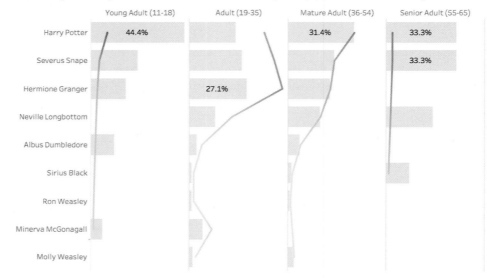

Figure 8.19 This bar chart looks at how women's perception of the most heroic character changes depending on respondent age.

Act Three: The Reveal

In this survey, the goal is to answer the question of which character is perceived as most heroic, and which is perceived as most villainous. The previous two "acts" set the stage for this ending by helping the audience get to know the responders and exploring how they look at this question through the lens of who they are, and what variables might affect their answers. Now, it is time to finish the story by answering the question.

The first step is to set up a final visualization to position the answer (see Figure 8.20) and then one to end the story (see Figure 8.21).

Are Potterheads "okay" with the Level of Violence in Harry Potter?

Figure 8.20 These side-by-side donut charts, designed intentionally to look like Harry's glasses, give some context to the reveal and pique audience interest for a grand finale.

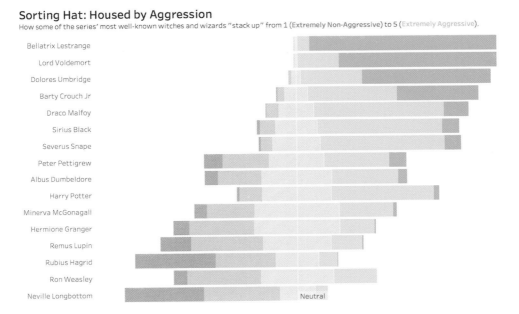

Figure 8.21 This modified Gantt chart, displaying Likert data (covered further in Chapter 9) provides a perfect ending to this story by thoroughly answering the question and providing a rich visual ending.

Figure 8.22 shows how the storyboard worked out using sheets and dashboards. These individual elements can be brought into story points to deliver a complete presentation.

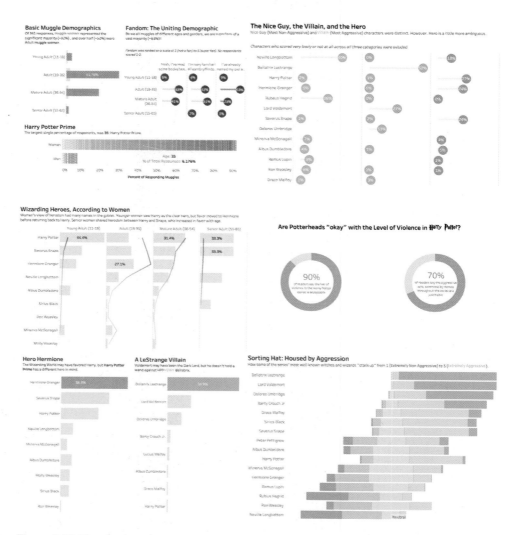

Figure 8.22 The storyboard.

Summary

This chapter reviewed mechanisms for building visual data stories, including understanding the narrative structure; visually exploring the data while building out story acts; and using sheets, dashboards, and story points to deliver a visual presentation. The next chapter provides a look at a few advanced visualizations to help visualize your story's data.

CHAPTER 9

ADVANCED STORYTELLING CHARTS

This penultimate chapter explores advanced strategies for visual data storytelling beyond the basic charts and graphs provided in Tableau's core functionality. You will learn how to create advanced charts that require additional formatting and calculations, including timelines, Likert scale charts, lollipop charts, and more.

As discussed in Chapter 5, many fantastic data visualization options are available to create from the menu of charts presented in the Show Me card in Tableau. These require little manual formatting beyond tidying up visualizations and cover most of the common chart types used in traditional data visualization and basic visual storytelling.

This chapter goes beyond these basic options and takes a look at how to create several advanced charts step by step in Tableau. These advanced charts require the use of more calculated fields and formatting to build; however, they offer deeper, more dynamic views into data and can be beneficial in supporting more complex visual data stories. These charts include:

- Timelines
- Bar-in-bar charts
- Likert scale visualizations
- Lollipop charts
- Word clouds

Timelines

A timeline chart can be a useful way to depict when events occur over time, whether to analyze patterns in notable events, or to show dates of interest. Although a timeline isn't a graph that can be built out of the box in Tableau, creating one in a few simple steps is easy, and it is a useful visual that can support storytelling when discussing important events over time.

I keep a timeline graphic on my website to visually display upcoming conferences, speaking events, and client on-site visits to website visitors (in addition to a more detailed list), as shown in Figure 9.1.

Figure 9.1 A snapshot of a finished visual timeline.

To create this visualization requires, at minimum, a very simple dataset (see Figure 9.2). In this case I have connected to a small, simple Excel dataset that lists the date of the event, the type of event, its title, and its location.

Date	Event Type	Event Title	Location
Sheet1	Sheet1	Sheet1	Sheet1
10/1/2017	Academic Conference	IEEE InfoVis	Phoenix, AZ
10/9/2017	Industry Conference	Tableau UC 2017	Las Vegas, NV
10/20/2017	Academic Conference	Harry Potter Confere...	Philadelphia, PA
10/30/2017	Academic Conference	ASIS&T	Washington, DC
11/15/2017	Client On-Site	Private	Washington, DC

Figure 9.2 A simple timeline requires minimal data: the date of the event and the event itself. You can use additional detail to enhance the visualization.

Before beginning, in your Sheet make sure that your date is recognized by Tableau as a *continuous* date. If it is not, you can change it by right-clicking the field on the Dimensions pane, and selecting Convert to Continuous on the list of options (see Figure 9.3).

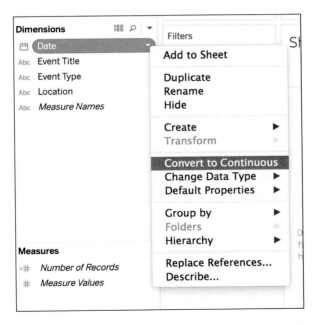

Figure 9.3 Adjust your date to continuous if it is not already. This allows you to view an event over a span of time, rather than in isolation.

The key to creating a timeline in Tableau is to create a calculated field that will form the horizontal axis of the timeline and allow all of your dates to line up on a straight line. Think of this field as an anchor to hold your events to time.

> ## note
>
> Calculated Fields can be created easily in Tableau to extend your analysis by creating a new field (or column) that is not already contained in your data source. To create a new calculated field, in a Tableau worksheet select Analysis > Create Calculated Field. A dialog box will open, called the Calculation Editor, which prompts you to give the calculated field a name and provide a formula. Formulas can be created using a combination of functions, fields, and operators. Once created, the new Calculated Field will appear as a new Measure in the Data Pane, and be designated with an equal (=) sign that precedes the field name.

1. Create the Anchor calculated field by following these steps: MIN(0).

2. Drag the newly created Anchor calculated field to the Rows shelf to provide a starting point for your timeline. At this point your visualization is simply a horizontal axis line with a zero line (see Figure 9.4)

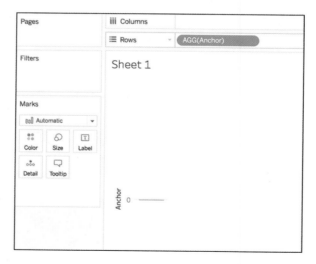

Figure 9.4 The Anchor placeholder gives a straight axis to begin plotting your events.

3. Drag your Date field to the Columns shelf. Right-click the Date pill and select Exact Date. This prompts Tableau to recognize each of the exact dates listed in your dataset of events and lays the foundation of the timeline by displaying a flat, solid, colored line (see Figure 9.5). Because there is no additional data, this is correct.

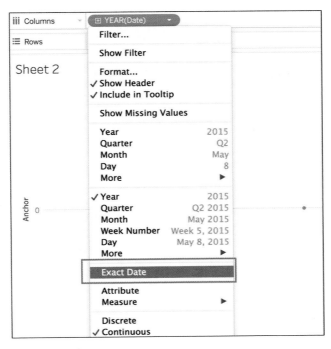

Figure 9.5 Adding the Date field to the Columns shelf provides the foundation of a timeline.

With the baseline set, you can now add dated events and begin formatting the timeline to look more traditional. To do this:

1. Drag the Date dimension from the Data pane again, this time dropping it on the Details Marks card. Initially, the timeline continues to appear flat. This is because Tableau automatically looks at the largest segment of the date, in this case, Year. You need to prompt Tableau to look at a more granular view of the date.

2. Click the + icon to expand the date to its lowest level, in this case, Day. Your timeline should now display each of the events in your dataset as individual dots (see Figure 9.6).

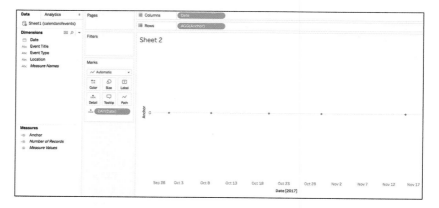

Figure 9.6 With event dates added to the baseline, the timeline begins to take form.

A bit of additional formatting can enable this timeline to tell a more detailed story about the events displayed. In Figure 9.7, I have used Event Category to color-code the events, as well as adjusted the shape and size of each event point and added a tooltip to provide more information. You can also adjust or delete zero lines, axis rules, and axis ticks as desired.

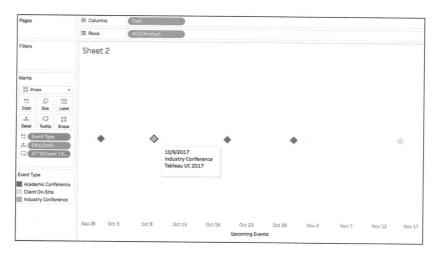

Figure 9.7 A little bit of additional formatting can add more detail and visual impact to your timeline.

A few additional things you can do to spice up a timeline and make it more visually appealing include:

- **Add a timeframe.** With a large number of events to display, adding a relative date filter to show only the events within a certain amount of time might be helpful. To do this, drag the Date dimension to the Filters shelf and choose Relative Dates. You can set the logic to be any subset of dates that you want to dynamically display. In this example, I have limited the range to a mere 30 days (see Figure 9.8).

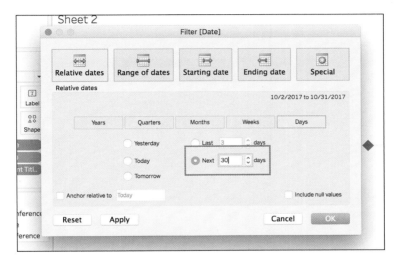

Figure 9.8 Filter the dates in a view to limit the number of events displayed.

- **Add a Reference Line for "Today."** A reference line for the current date can give audiences a visual checkpoint on the timeline. To create a reference line, follow these steps:
    1. Create a new calculated field, Today: TODAY()
    2. Place this newly created calculated field on the Details Marks card. This allows the field to be used as a reference line. Adjust the field from a discrete date by right-clicking the date pill and selecting Exact Date (see Figure 9.9).
    3. To add the reference line onto the timeline, select Reference Line from the Analytics pane. Choose the Today calculated field as the Line Value for the line. Additionally, use the Line Label option Custom to type how you want the line to be labeled on the canvas. Further formatting can also be completed in this box to define how you want the line to visually appear (see Figure 9.10).

Figure 9.9 Adjusting the field for today's date to be Exact Date is critical to achieve a reference line that displays the current date.

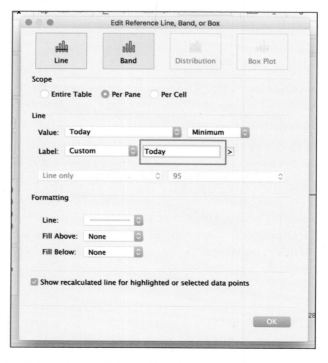

Figure 9.10 Use the Today calculated field to add a reference line to the timeline.

With a few formatting tweaks, you can finalize a visually appealing timeline that makes a great asset to a dashboard or data story.

Bar-in-Bar Charts

Chapter 5, "Choosing the Right Visual," covered several forms of a basic bar chart, including side-by-side and stacked bar charts. Both of these options are available out of the box in Tableau. Another option in the bar chart landscape is a bar-in-bar chart. These can be useful when comparing a measure against a goal or comparing two measures (or discrete dimensions) against one another, with both items starting at the zero line for a precise analysis (see Figure 9.11).

Building a bar-in-bar chart in Tableau is not terribly difficult, but it does require taking a few additional manual steps to help get your bars in the shape you want.

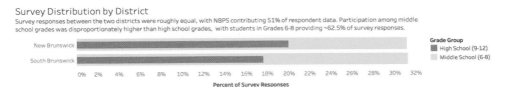

Figure 9.11 This bar-in-bar chart compares the percentage of survey respondents in a two-district cyberbullying survey.

The first step in building a bar-in-bar chart is to create a slightly odd-looking stacked bar chart by dragging one measure and one dimension to the Rows and Columns shelves. Drag your second dimension to the Color Marks card, and then drag this same dimension to the Size Marks card (see Figure 9.12). Now you should see a stacked bar chart with dimensions differentiated by color and by size.

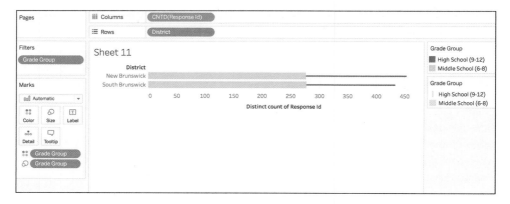

Figure 9.12 A bar-in-bar chart begins with a slightly odd-looking stacked bar chart.

At this point, the two dimensions are stacked together along the x axis of the measure, rather than laid atop each other with both starting at the zero point. This stacking is an automatic function of Tableau that you need to turn off to manually build your bar-in-bar chart. To disable this feature, navigate to the Analysis menu and choose Stack Marks > Off (see Figure 9.13).

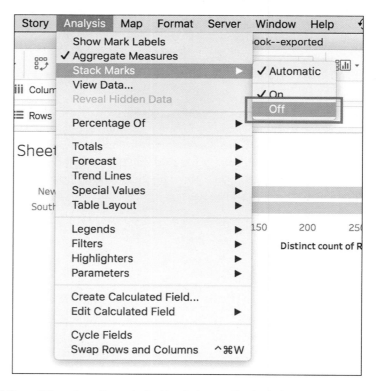

Figure 9.13 Turn off the automatic mark-stacking feature on the Analysis menu to overlay components of stacked bars.

After this step, you should have completed a raw version of your bar-in-bar chart. At this point, you can adjust which dimension is in the foreground and background by dragging and dropping to sort the measures on the Color Marks card filter, if desired. You may also edit the width of the bars by clicking the drop-down menu on the Size Marks card, selecting Edit Sizes, and then adjusting the Mark Size Range slider as desired (see Figure 9.14). Complete your visualization by editing and removing axis headers, titles, and so on (see Chapter 6).

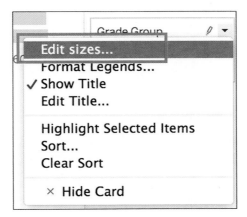

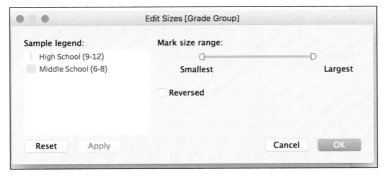

Figure 9.14 Adjust the width of the bars by editing the size range on the Size Marks card menu.

> tip
>
> To make a chart larger on the canvas, hold down Ctrl+Shift and press B several times.

Continue to format as desired to clean up and curate the bar-in-bar chart.

Likert Visualizations

Likert scales are the most widely used approach to scaling responses to gauge sentiment and tendencies, and are a staple of surveys and other types of data collection methodologies. Several ways exist to ask Likert scale questions, as well as several ways to visualize their data. This section provides a look at the two most common Likert scales and the best ways to visualize them: a 100% stacked bar chart and a divergent bar chart.

Before discussing how to build Likert visualizations, let's take a look at what Likert scale data looks like. Figure 9.15 shows an example of a five-point Likert scale using an example from the Harry Potter dataset. Common 5-point Likert scales range values from one extreme to another (for example, Highly Satisfied to Highly Dissatisfied) with a neutral option residing midrange.

On a Scale of 1 to 5, with 1 being Extremely Non-Aggressive and 5 being Extremely Aggressive, how would you rate each of the following Harry Potter characters?

	Extremely Non-Aggressive	Non-Aggressive	Neither Non-Aggressive Nor Aggressive	Aggressive	Extremely Aggressive
Harry Potter					
Hermione Granger					
Severus Snape					
Lord Voldemort					
Ron Weasley					

Figure 9.15 A 5-point Likert scale.

Whereas 5-point Likert scales are commonly used to measure sentiment, 4-point Likert scales are more typically used to measure tendencies. Figure 9.16 shows an example of a 4-point Likert scale using an example from the Cyberbullying dataset.

Have you ever enacted any of the following cyberbullying behaviors?

	Often	Sometimes	Just Once	Never
Posted Rude Comments				
Teased/Threatened Someone Online				
Hacked Into Someone's Account				
Used Information Found Online to Tease/Harass				
Posted Pictures of Someone Without Permission				

Figure 9.16 A four-point Likert scale.

> **note**
>
> When preparing Likert data for analysis, the recommendation is to have both a text and numerical value associated. Chapter 7 discussed the value of having both of these pieces of metadata.

100% Stacked Bar Chart

A stacked bar chart is a simple, straightforward way to visualize Likert questions that does not involve the creation of any calculated fields and little manual work (see Figure 9.17).

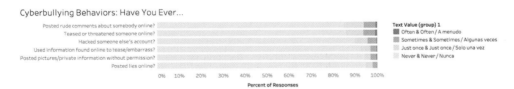

Figure 9.17 A 100% stacked bar chart can be an easy way of visualizing Likert data, although it falls short of the richness that other methods can add to the data's story.

To create this visualization, drag your first dimension to the Rows shelf (this example uses survey data so the field is Wording) and a measure to the Columns shelf. A simple horizontal bar chart with solid color bars of equal length, representing the total *count* of responses for each dimension, appears.

Next, drag your second dimension that represents the Answer value (or the value representing survey responses) to the Color Marks card (see Figure 9.18).

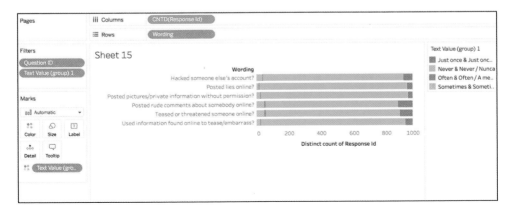

Figure 9.18 A rough stacked bar chart begins to visualize Likert data; however, it requires more curation to be a useful visualization.

A number of things need to be done to improve this basic 100% stacked bar chart to properly visualize the Likert data:

- **Color**: The automatic color scheme in Tableau does little to help us see behaviors that are adjacent (for example, sometimes/often and just once/never). Using the Color Marks card, adjust these to a more suitable color palette.

- **Sort**: Tendencies are sorted in alphabetical order rather than by how often they occur. Manually sort these to reflect the correct order.

- **Totals**: A count of data is an okay option, but a better option (particularly in survey data) may be Percent of Total. Add in the correct table calculation to reflect this.

- **Curate**: Remove unnecessary headers to clean up your canvas.

> ## note
>
> You can apply several types of calculations to transform the values for a measure in Tableau, including custom calculations, table calculations, level of detail (LOD) expressions, and more. For more information on these various types of calculations and how to use them, visit https://onlinehelp.tableau.com/current/pro/desktop/en-us/advanced_overview.html.

With a bit of tweaking, this 100% stacked bar chart can be a decent approach to display Likert responses (see Figure 9.19). You could also add labels onto each category to see percentage of responses per tendency.

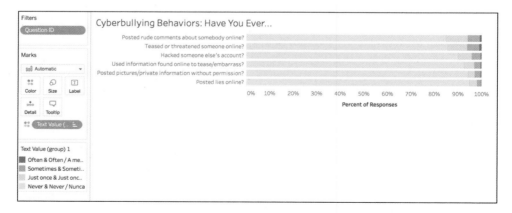

Figure 9.19 With better colors, and sorted, this 100% stacked bar chart does a better job of visualizing the Likert data.

Divergent Stacked Bar Chart

Although the 100% stacked bar chart will *work* to represent Likert data, a better approach is a divergent bar chart, which is not actually a bar chart but a modified version of a Gantt chart. Rather than stacking tendencies or sentiment ratings on a scale of 0 to 100, this approach shows the spread of negative and positive sentiment values (such as Strongly Disagree to Strongly Agree) aligned to each other around the neutral midpoint (see Figure 9.20).

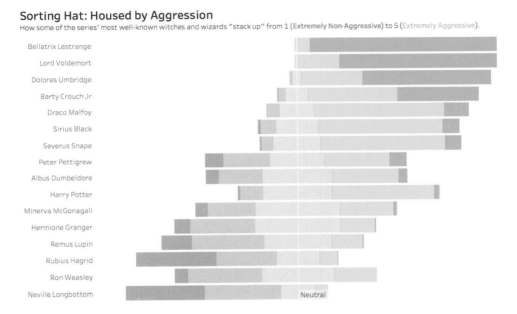

Figure 9.20 Completed divergent stacked bar chart representing five-scale Likert data.

This approach requires the creation of several calculated fields. As such, to begin building this visualization by you must first create a table, or crosstab, in Tableau. This enables you to see the output of each of the calculations you build and troubleshoot any calculation errors before moving into visualizing them.

> **note**
>
> For this challenging chart, you will use the Harry Potter dataset used in previous chapters. Download the dataset to follow along.

In this table, first drag the QuestionID and Text Value dimensions to the Row shelf. (In this example, the QuestionID has been renamed to match the character name for readability.) Because we included both the text and the numeric coding for each Answer field, we can avoid writing any calculations at this point (the Numeric Value for each response will become useful in the next steps). However, notice that when you add this dimension the Text Values are not in the sequence they should be. Click the drop-down menu on the Text Value dimension on the Rows shelf, select Sort, and manually adjust these so that they display in the correct ranking order (minimum to maximum, or 1 to 5). Then, drop the Number of Records Measure (SUM) onto the Text Marks card. Your table should appear similar to Figure 9.21.

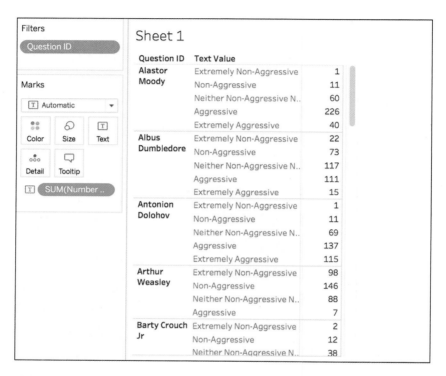

Figure 9.21 After this step, you can see for each question asked (in this case, each character ranked) how many respondents chose each option on the Likert scale.

The next step is to create a series of calculated fields and add them onto the table.

Calculated Field #1: Negative Sentiment

The first calculated field will calculate how many negative sentiment responses were received for each question (or item ranked) and should appear as negative values and below (or to the left of) the dividing line of 0 in the divergent stacked bar chart. To do this we need to count the number of responses received for the two lowest selections on the scale (in this case 1—extremely non-aggressive and 2—non-aggressive) as well as *half* of the neutral selection (in this case, 3—neither non-aggressive nor aggressive). Because neutral responses in a survey are neither positive nor negative, we want to split them in half to distribute them across the bars in the chart as to not unfairly weight one side of the data.

Create this calculated field, named Negative Sentiment:

IF [Numeric Value] < 3 THEN 1 ELSEIF [Numeric Value] = 3 THEN 0.5 ELSE 0 END

Add this calculation onto the canvas. Your screen should appear as in Figure 9.22; the Number of Responses in the two negative sentiment ranks should match the count in the Negative Sentiment column. The neutral response count in Negative Sentiment should be half the count of Number of Responses, and the two positive sentiment ranks should appear with a count of 0 in the Negative Sentiment column.

Question ID	Text Value	Number of Records	Negative Sentiment
Alastor Moody	Extremely Non-Aggressive	1.0	1.0
	Non-Aggressive	11.0	11.0
	Neither Non-Aggressive N..	60.0	30.0
	Aggressive	226.0	0.0
	Extremely Aggressive	40.0	0.0
Albus Dumbledore	Extremely Non-Aggressive	22.0	22.0
	Non-Aggressive	73.0	73.0
	Neither Non-Aggressive N..	117.0	58.5
	Aggressive	111.0	0.0
	Extremely Aggressive	15.0	0.0

Figure 9.22 This calculated field counts the number of negative sentiment responses that will appear on the negative side of the dividing 0.

Calculated Field #2: Total Negative Sentiment

The next step is to create a calculated field to calculate the percent of negative values per question.

Create this calculated field, named Total Negative Sentiment:

TOTAL(SUM([Negative Sentiment]))

This calculated field is a default table calculation; however, we need to manually change the field being used to compute the calculation. From within the calculated field editor box, click the blue text Default Table Calculation. Then, select Text Value from the list (see Figure 9.23).

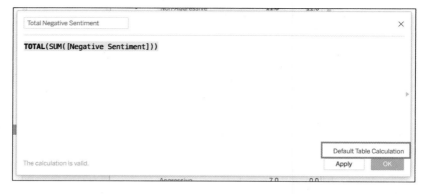

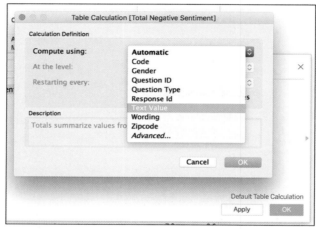

Figure 9.23 This calculated field calculates the percent of negative values per question.

After you add this calculated field to your crosstab, it should appear similar to Figure 9.24. Notice that the Total Negative Sentiment value is the same for each QuestionID. This function simply sums the values in the Negative Sentiment column for each item scored. For example, Alastor Moody has a Negative Sentiment Count of 1 + 11 + 30 = 42. This total sentiment appears in the Total Negative Sentiment column.

Question ID	Text Value	Number of Records	Negative Sentiment	Total Negative Sentiment
Alastor Moody	Extremely Non-Aggressive	1.0	1.0	42.0
	Non-Aggressive	11.0	11.0	42.0
	Neither Non-Aggressive N..	60.0	30.0	42.0
	Aggressive	226.0	0.0	42.0
	Extremely Aggressive	40.0	0.0	42.0
Albus Dumbledore	Extremely Non-Aggressive	22.0	22.0	153.5
	Non-Aggressive	73.0	73.0	153.5
	Neither Non-Aggressive N..	117.0	58.5	153.5
	Aggressive	111.0	0.0	153.5
	Extremely Aggressive	15.0	0.0	153.5

Figure 9.24 The Total Negative Sentiment function sums the individual count of negative responses per question scored.

Calculated Field #3: Total Sentiment Scores

Now that we have the percent of the total for the negative values, we need the percent of the total for the entire bar and add up the responses for each item scored.

Create this calculated field, named Total Sentiment Scores:

TOTAL(SUM([Number of Records]))

You will need to change the default table calculation to Text Values.

Added to the crosstab, this calculated field will sum the number of responses per question. If your dataset is nice and clean and all questions were answered, the value in this column should be the same all the way down. For datasets where not every question was answered, such as this one, you will see variations in the count of responses in this column (see Figure 9.25).

Question ID	Text Value	Number of Records	Negative Sentiment	Total Negative Sentiment	Total Sentiment Scores
Alastor Moody	Extremely Non-Aggressive	1.0	1.0	42.0	338.0
	Non-Aggressive	11.0	11.0	42.0	338.0
	Neither Non-Aggressive N..	60.0	30.0	42.0	338.0
	Aggressive	226.0	0.0	42.0	338.0
	Extremely Aggressive	40.0	0.0	42.0	338.0
Albus Dumbledore	Extremely Non-Aggressive	22.0	22.0	153.5	338.0
	Non-Aggressive	73.0	73.0	153.5	338.0
	Neither Non-Aggressive N..	117.0	58.5	153.5	338.0
	Aggressive	111.0	0.0	153.5	338.0
	Extremely Aggressive	15.0	0.0	153.5	338.0
Antonion Dolohov	Extremely Non-Aggressive	1.0	1.0	46.5	333.0
	Non-Aggressive	11.0	11.0	46.5	333.0
	Neither Non-Aggressive N..	69.0	34.5	46.5	333.0
	Aggressive	137.0	0.0	46.5	333.0
	Extremely Aggressive	115.0	0.0	46.5	333.0
Arthur Weasley	Extremely Non-Aggressive	98.0	98.0	288.0	339.0
	Non-Aggressive	146.0	146.0	288.0	339.0
	Neither Non-Aggressive N..	88.0	44.0	288.0	339.0
	Aggressive	7.0	0.0	288.0	339.0

Figure 9.25 This calculated field counts the total number of scores for each question in order to calculate the length of the entire bar.

Calculated Field #4: Gantt Start

The next step is to create a calculated field that will determine the percentage offset, or how far into the negative to begin building the bar chart. Remember, what we are creating is a modified Gantt chart, so this calculated field is really intended to be the first data point in the Gantt chart.

Create this calculated field, named Gantt Start:

−[Total Negative Sentiment]/[Total Sentiment Scores]

Because this number will be expressed as a percent, we need to adjust the number format. Do this by right-clicking on the Measure and choosing Default Properties > Number Format (see Figure 9.26). Select percentage from the menu and enter the number of decimal points.

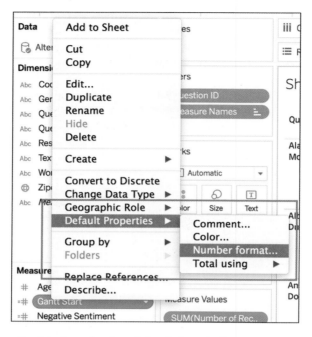

Figure 9.26 Change the default number format directly from the Data pane.

You can spot-check the Gantt Start calculated field after it's added into the crosstab by comparing it against the number of positive and negative responses. The higher the count of negative responses, the larger the Gantt Start percentage will be (see Figure 9.27).

Calculated Field #5: Percent of Gantt Sizing

The next step is to build a calculated field to determine the size (how wide) each section of the Gantt chart should be.

Create this calculated field, named Percent of Gantt Sizing:

SUM([Number of Records])/[Total Sentiment Scores]

Again, this is a percentage, so you must adjust the default number format for this calculated field, too.

Question ID	Text Value	Number of Records	Negative Sentiment	Total Negative Sentiment	Total Sentiment Scores	Gantt Start
Alastor Moody	Extremely Non-Aggressive	1.0	1.0	42.0	338.0	-12.4%
	Non-Aggressive	11.0	11.0	42.0	338.0	-12.4%
	Neither Non-Aggressive N..	60.0	30.0	42.0	338.0	-12.4%
	Aggressive	226.0	0.0	42.0	338.0	-12.4%
	Extremely Aggressive	40.0	0.0	42.0	338.0	-12.4%
Albus Dumbledore	Extremely Non-Aggressive	22.0	22.0	153.5	338.0	-45.4%
	Non-Aggressive	73.0	73.0	153.5	338.0	-45.4%
	Neither Non-Aggressive N..	117.0	58.5	153.5	338.0	-45.4%
	Aggressive	111.0	0.0	153.5	338.0	-45.4%
	Extremely Aggressive	15.0	0.0	153.5	338.0	-45.4%
Antonion Dolohov	Extremely Non-Aggressive	1.0	1.0	46.5	333.0	-14.0%
	Non-Aggressive	11.0	11.0	46.5	333.0	-14.0%
	Neither Non-Aggressive N..	69.0	34.5	46.5	333.0	-14.0%
	Aggressive	137.0	0.0	46.5	333.0	-14.0%
	Extremely Aggressive	115.0	0.0	46.5	333.0	-14.0%

Figure 9.27 The Gantt Start calculated field tells each bar in the Gantt chart where on the axis to begin.

Calculated Field #6: Gantt Percent Line

The last calculated field to build will tell Tableau where to draw each line after the original Gantt Start data point and separate the sentiment value categories.

Create this calculated field, named Gantt Percent Line:

> PREVIOUS_VALUE([Gantt Start]) + ZN(LOOKUP([Percent of Total Sizing],−1))

You need to change the default table calculation to Text Values, and adjust the default number format to be a percentage.

The Gantt Percent Line is the trickiest of all the calculated fields needed to create the divergent stacked bar chart. Essentially, in plain English, the calculated field begins with the table calculation Previous Value and tells Tableau to look to the previous row of the calculation we've just made. However, there is no previous row for the first line in the table, so instead we are directing Tableau to Gantt Start instead (−12.4%). We then tell Tableau to add the previous row, this time on Percent of Total Sizing, and minus one. However, again, because there is no previous value, we've directed Tableau to zero nulls (ZN), and so the first value in this column is −12.04%. In the next row, we can see this formula begin to work more smoothly (see Figure 9.28).

Gantt Start	Percent of Gantt Sizing	Gantt Percent Line
-12.4%	0.3%	-12.4%
-12.4%	3.3%	-12.1%
-12.4%	17.8%	-8.9%
-12.4%	66.9%	8.9%
-12.4%	11.8%	75.7%
-45.4%	6.5%	-45.4%
-45.4%	21.6%	-38.9%
-45.4%	34.6%	-17.3%
-45.4%	32.8%	17.3%

Figure 9.28 The Gantt Percent Line calculated field creates a new calculation using the values generated from previously created calculated fields.

After all five of these new calculated fields have been created and added into the view, the crosstab for the divergent stacked bar chart is complete (see Figure 9.29). We are now ready to begin building the visualization in a new sheet.

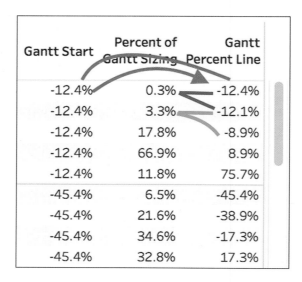

Figure 9.29 Although it's a long process, this crosstab creates the foundation for our eventual Likert visualization.

In a new sheet, drag the Question dimension to the Rows shelf and the Gantt Percent Line measure to the Columns shelf. ***Tableau will break immediately***, flagging the measure in red and giving the error message that a critical field used to create this calculation is missing from the view (see Figure 9.30).

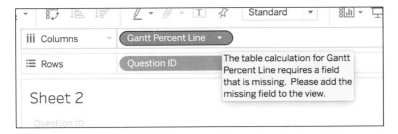

Figure 9.30 The first step in creating this Likert visualization throws an error—but that's okay!

The missing field is Text Value, which is the field we calculated everything over in the crosstab. Bring this dimension into the view and drop it on the Color Marks card (you might need to filter and then add depending on how many options there are for this dimension).

Immediately we see a divergent stacked bar chart begin to appear! However, as we're actually creating a Gantt chart, we still have quite a bit of work to do:

1. Change the mark from Automatic to Gantt chart (see Figure 9.31). This adjusts the view from bars to lines that separate each section of the Gantt chart.

Figure 9.31 Changing the mark from the automatic bar to Gantt begins the Gantt chart transformation.

2. You need to manually re-sort your text value options, the same way discussed when making the crosstab table, but this time by clicking the sort option on the Color Marks card and manually adjusting so that text values display in the correct ranking order (minimum to maximum, or 1 to 5).

3. Drag and drop the Percent of Gantt Sizing calculated field on the Size Marks card. Now, the visualization is beginning to take shape.

4. Now to address color: Tableau has used the automatic color palette, which is intended to make things look very different; however, for this example, make the colors look more like a standard blue-orange diverging palette by changing the colors to a colorblind palette, and manually selecting better color choices (see Figure 9.32).

Because this scale is from Extremely Non-Aggressive to Extremely Aggressive, I used color choices that reflect the severity of character aggression. You could use other color scales depending on the context of the story and the takeaway intended.

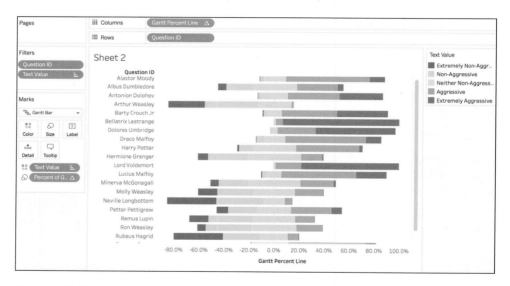

Figure 9.32 With a few quick clicks, leveraging the calculated fields already made, and making smart color choices, the divergent chart is beginning to take shape.

5. Now, to fix the axis: Because we know that the axis can range from a −1 to 1, adjust it by right-clicking on the x axis, selecting Edit Axis, and then changing the fixed range from −1 to 1 (see Figure 9.33). This shifts the bars slightly so that everything is centered on the zero midpoint.

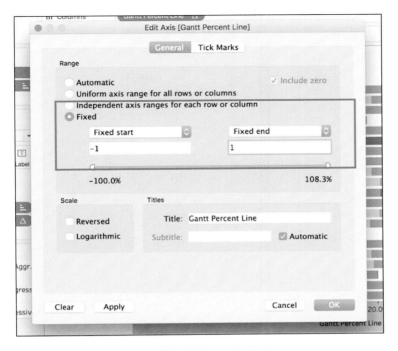

Figure 9.33 Shifting the axis allows everything to line up nicely at zero.

A few more clicks to simplify and remove headers and clean up the visualization delivers a stunning divergent bar chart that displays the Likert scale sentiment data nicely. (The final result will look like 9.20, shown earlier in the chapter.)

Lollipop Charts

The lollipop chart, while not native to Tableau, is a hybrid chart that combines a traditional bar chart and a Cleveland dot plot. It is simply a dual axis chart that superimposes a circle on top of a very thin bar chart (see Figure 9.34). However, it's a fun way to spice up a bar chart to give it more visual appeal without reducing its analytical integrity.

> note
>
> Lollipop charts are a helpful way to visualize many bars of the same length while avoiding the Moire effect discussed in Chapter 6.

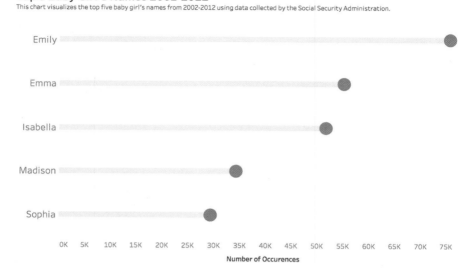

Top 5 Baby Girl's Names 2002-2012
This chart visualizes the top five baby girl's names from 2002-2012 using data collected by the Social Security Administration.

Figure 9.34 Completed lollipop chart.

A lollipop chart is great for comparing multiple measures because it helps the reader to align categories to points without drowning the graphic in ink. It typically contains categorical variables on the y axis measured against a second (continuous) variable on the x axis, although these can be plotted on the y axis. With either orientation, the emphasis is on the circle, as it is a visual cue to draw the audience's attention to the specific value in each category. The line (or bar) itself is meant to be a minimalistic approach to tie each category to its relative point without drawing too much attention to the line itself.

To begin:

1. Build a basic bar chart in Tableau (see Figure 9.35). In this example, I am using the Top Baby Names dataset provided by Tableau. This dataset contains the most popular male and female names in each state for each year from 1910–2012 via the Social Security Administration.

2. Duplicate your dimension on the same shelf you are currently using to display dimensions (in this example, the Columns shelf). This creates a side-by-side view of two identical bar charts (see Figure 9.36).

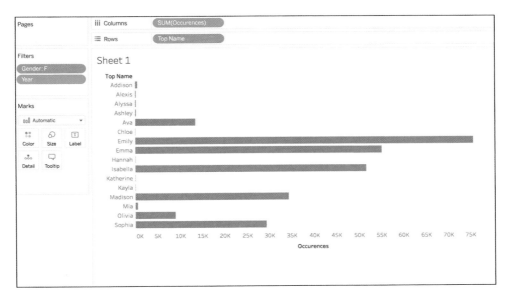

Figure 9.35 To tell a story about the top baby girl names over a decade, I have filtered the dataset to include only girl's names from 2002 to 2012.

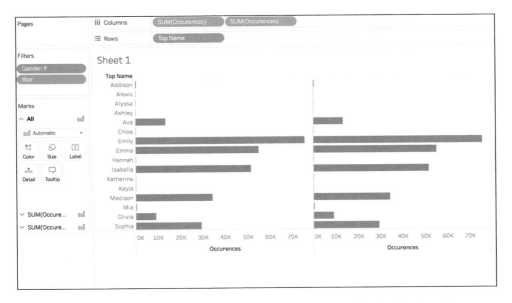

Figure 9.36 A little messy at first, duplicating your dimension creates a side-by-side view of two identical bar charts.

3. Using the duplicated measure, adjust to a dual axis by right-clicking the second measure (or second axis) and selecting Dual Axis (see Figure 9.37). Because the mark Type is set to Automatic, Tableau will likely convert both visualizations to circle charts.

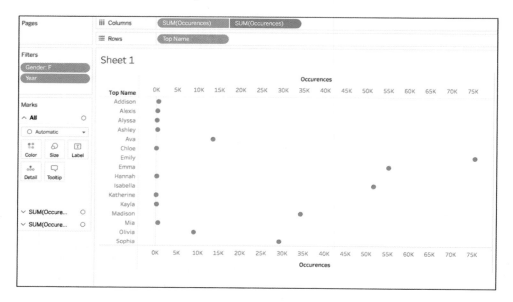

Figure 9.37 Converting to a dual axis adjusts the marks, but you can now change the Marks formatting for each dimension.

4. Using the Marks card, change the first occurrence of your dimension to a bar. Use the Size slider to slim down the line and the Color Marks to adjust the color of the bar as appropriate. I typically use a lighter gray (see Figure 9.38).

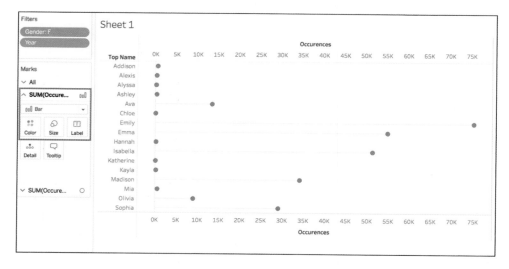

Figure 9.38 With your first marks adjustment the lollipop charts begins to take shape.

5. To adjust the second dimension occurrence, using the Size Marks card, enlarge the circles as appropriate (see Figure 9.39).

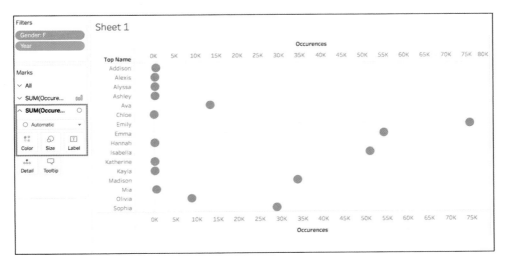

Figure 9.39 The bars and circles of the lollipop chart can be changed individually in size and color to curate your chart.

With the basis of the lollipop chart built, it's time to clean up the visualization.

6. Make sure your axes line up correctly. Right-click the second measure axis (the one on top) and choose Synchronize Axis to make the axes equal. Right-click the axis again and uncheck Show Header.

7. Tidy up the visual by sorting bars and excluding any data that might not be pertinent to your story. I have sorted in Descending order and excluded everything but the Top 5 names. (You will likely need to readjust the Marks Sizing after this step.)

8. Continue removing headers and axis titles as well as adjusting titles as appropriate until you are happy with the visualization.

Labeled Lollipops

You might elect to remove the bottom axis header and use the circles to encode their value.

To do this, drag the measure to the canvas for a third time, this time dropping it on the Label card on the second occurrence. Adjust the Label alignment to be centered and Automatic, and make sure the checkbox to allow marks to overlap other labels is selected (see Figure 9.40).

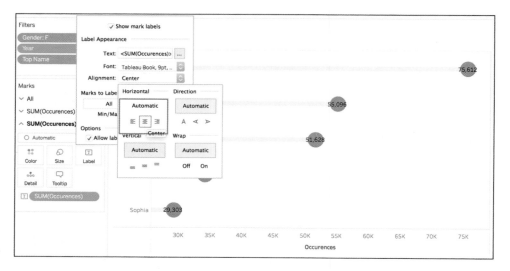

Figure 9.40 Carefully formatting mark labels can embed additional data in your lollipop chart, and eliminate the need for axis headers.

Right-click on the dimension on the Labels shelf to format the number and text color, and then remove axis headers and tweak as necessary (see Figure 9.41).

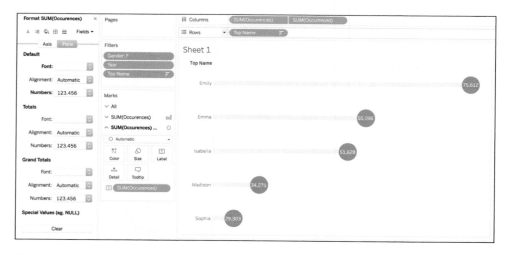

Figure 9.41 With proper size, color, and label adjustments, a lollipop chart can be a richer visual alternative to a classic bar chart.

Other options to embellish your lollipop charts include color-coding the circles based on a measure or changing circles to custom shapes.

Word Clouds

A word cloud is an image composed of words in which the size of each word indicates its frequency or importance (see Figure 9.42). While not particularly analytically astute and not recommended for analytical purposes, these types of visualizations can be a powerful way to display textual data and can be an attention-grabbing technique for the purpose of data storytelling and visual impact. In fact, word clouds can make great bookends to presentations to incite interest or leave a lasting impression on an audience.

The good news is that word clouds are quick and simple to create in Tableau.

Keyword Word Cloud
Keywords used in computing journal articles.

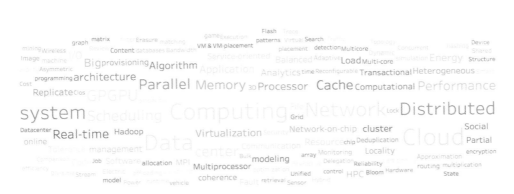

Figure 9.42 A word count of article keywords created in Tableau.

Creating a word cloud in Tableau essentially requires using your Text dimension in a variety of marks. First, on a blank canvas, drag the desired dimension to the Text Marks card, and then drag the same dimension to the Size Marks card. At this point your canvas should look similar to Figure 9.43, displaying a simple list of your words in increasingly larger size. Depending on the number of words in your list, this size differential may be more immediately noticeable, or may be subtler as in Figure 9.43, which contains a rather long list of keywords.

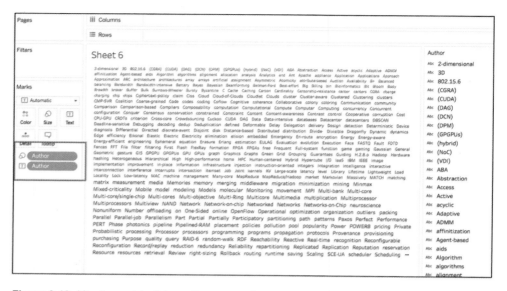

Figure 9.43 After two quick clicks on the canvas, the structure of a word cloud begins to form.

At this point you are ready to transform this view into something that better resembles your expectation of a word cloud. To do this, right-click on the dimension on the Size card and select Measure > Count (see Figure 9.44).

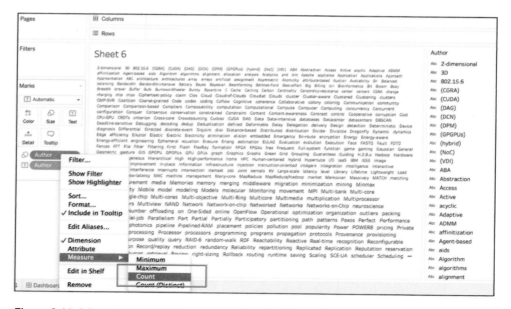

Figure 9.44 Adjust the dimension to a measure to resize the words based on their count.

This step converts your initial word cloud structure to something that looks like a tree map of a single color. Change the Mark type from Automatic to Text and your word cloud will re-form (see Figure 9.45).

Figure 9.45 Changing the Mark type from Automatic to Text reshapes the tree map into something more akin to a word cloud.

You might need to do some additional work to clean up your word cloud, including removing extraneous words, performing deduplication, or streamlining the words included.

To add color to the word cloud, drag the same dimension to the Color Marks card. Now, your word cloud is complete (see Figure 9.46).

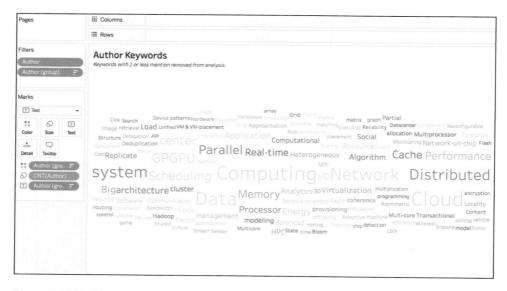

Figure 9.46 To finish your word cloud, add color.

Summary

This chapter provided a look at how to create a few advanced chart types that are not available on the Show Me card in Tableau. These charts require a little more hands-on manipulation but can be excellent candidates to add some variety into dashboards or visual presentations. Many more advanced charts exist, too, that can be learned and built in Tableau. Some fun ones to try on your own might be waffle charts or hexbin map charts, or you can explore the use of spark lines. There are always more charts to learn—explore and have fun!

CHAPTER 10

CLOSING THOUGHTS

We've covered a lot of ground in this book—from
understanding the value of visual data storytelling
to practicing how to build visual data stories
using basic and selected advanced charts and
graphs in Tableau.

The lessons in this book are a huge step in the right direction, but still only the first step. Becoming a seasoned visual data storyteller takes time.

The best visual data storytellers recognize that learning how to apply fundamental data visualization best practices and tell meaningful, effective stories is a skill learned over time with practice, experience, and a good, realistic dose of trial and error. These practices are ever-evolving areas, spurred onward with new technologies and inspiring new creatives who have the courage and curiosity to experiment with new approaches and new ideas. We then, as visual data explorers and storytellers, need to commit to continuous learning, both with visualization and with tools, including Tableau, as they introduce new capabilities that facilitate deeper visual analysis.

As Neil DeGrasse Tyson says, "as the area of your knowledge grows, so too does the perimeter of your ignorance." We never know everything, we can only keep learning and trying to know more.

In that spirit, this last chapter recaps the main lessons covered throughout the text. It also serves as a resource kit for life beyond the book by providing checklists of best practices and practical suggestions for continuing to master data storytelling, as well as discusses additional resources available to support the text.

Five Steps to Visual Data Storytelling

In his book, *Beautiful Data*, Yau noted that today's visual data stories are "Something in-between the textbook and the novel." In a similar sentiment, a 2010 article in *The Economist* asserted that today's visual narratives "meld the skills of computer science, statistics, artistic design, and storytelling."

Here are five steps to guide you as you work to build a perfect data story.

Step 1. Find Data That Supports Your Story

The first step in telling a data narrative is to find or collect data that supports the story you want to tell. The storytelling process is, in many ways, more similar to the scientific process than to any literary one. After all, as an analyst and storyteller you are tasked with asking questions, performing background research, constructing and testing one or many hypotheses, and analyzing results to draw a conclusion.

Finding data to support a story doesn't necessarily require scientific data. Ultimately, the data chosen to tell a story should support the story it is telling in context, complexity, and depth. In other words, find a story you're interested in telling. Then, make sure you understand your data and respect its limitations, knowing the story your data *can* logically support, and where you might need to add additional data to fill gaps or answer additional important questions.

Step 2. Layer Information for Understanding

After you have the goals of your story clearly in mind and your data in hand, script your story by layering information to build a framework around a narrative with a clear beginning, middle, and end, as well as a clear message fitted for your audience. In writing terms, think of this as constructing your story's outline and plot.

Remember, knowledge is incremental. Every piece of information we learn is founded on something we have already learned before. Thus, layering information is critical: it's a tool you can use to guide your audience as a narrator. In data storytelling, you can achieve this by compounding builds in visualization or by sequencing different types of visualizations, providing annotations or interactive capabilities on a dashboard, drilling deeper into a single visualization, and so on.

Step 3. Design to Reveal

As tools, charts can't do it all. Data visualizations can't be relied upon to tell the story for you. Likewise, various types of visualization can present the data properly, but still fail to tell a story. Thus, choose your data and your visual form carefully so that the two work in tandem toward communicating one accurate and meaningful message. Then, put the right dialogue into place to guide your audience through a story.

Start by stripping out unnecessary information and design the data story in a way that leaves the audience with a single, very potent, message. Focus on the most powerful elements; however, understand that these aren't always the most obvious trends or elements. And remember: there is not always one truth in data, and this is where context becomes a critical element of a data story.

Step 4. Beware the False Reveal

A false reveal can be a dangerous thing. It can incite the audience to draw the wrong conclusions or take an incorrect action. It can also damage the effect of the data itself, and your credibility as a storyteller. As a visual data documentary, data stories should be engaging and entertaining, but should focus foremost on sharing truth.

Whether we do it intentionally or inadvertently, we can force the data to tell the story we want it to, even if it's the wrong—or inaccurate—one. With visual narratives, we are tasked not only with telling a story, but also with making it interesting, engaging, and inspiring storytelling. But data stories aren't works of fiction. Think of a visual story as a documentary: a nonfiction work, based on a collection of data, told in a visually compelling way.

Step 5. Tell It Fast

Stories have an inherent amount of entropy, and have the most potency when they are happening. Data journalists are taking this to heart in models that keep track of events as they happen in real time (like political elections or disaster scenarios). The timestamp on when data is reported—or a visualization story released—can be a big difference in how the story is interpreted or on the impact it makes, and so can your narration as a storyteller.

One way to tell a data story fast is by sharing with mobile. Mobile has been a game changer for data visualization in many ways and will be even more so in the years ahead. However, mobile requires wise editing. Be aware of form factor limitations and rethink the way storytelling via mobile devices happens.

The Important Role of Feedback

In June 2015, when I was still in my Radiant Advisors years, I developed and brought to market a concept called the Data Visualization Competency Center (DVCC). At its heart, this methodology described the framework for a permanent, formal organizational structure tasked with advancing and promoting the effective use of data visualization as information assets within the business.

Among its tenets, one of the most critical to the DVCC is the need for feedback. As with any type of information, data visualization created and used in isolation can become its own version of a data silo. We should not overlook the need to collaborate and engage in group critiques before publishing new visuals or presenting new data stories.

Successful data visualizations should be able to be understood by their intended audience from a position of personal insight and experience—this is the ability for the visualization to tell a meaningful story. Collaboration helps ensure the visualization does tell a story—and the one the author anticipated it to tell.

This need for feedback is applicable both at an organizational level and at an individual one. All data storytellers should user-test their visualizations and stories to ensure that the message they are working to communicate is the same one being received by its intended audience.

Here are a few ways to test the usability of your visualization:

- Give a mock presentation to colleagues or friends to see whether they "see" the same insights you do.
- Ask a member of your intended audience if she can explain the message in the visualization.
- Have someone get hands-on with your visualization and see whether he can navigate the filters, actions, or annotations in your visual.

Frankly, the process of user-testing a data visualization or story is easier said than done, and feedback can be a fickle friend. We invest a significant amount of time and energy into building visualizations and crafting narratives, and—like any creation—become attached to them, and maybe even a little blind to their potential flaws. Still, feedback can be validating or constructive, and if collected consciously can help us engage audiences and perfect our data stories.

The old phrase "everyone's a critic" is well and alive in data visualization. I've created many that have not been as brilliant as I initially thought they were. Tableau guru Steve Wexler, in his blog *Data Revelations*, wrote a similar sentiment, even describing moments of anger or depression that accompany less than enthusiastic feedback about a new visualization. Being resistant to or wary of feedback is *normal*. Instead of dwelling on negative feedback, use it as a way to improve your visualization, corrective learning, and new information to add into your visual data storytelling skillset for your next project.

> **note**
>
> For more on the Data Visualization Competency Center, check out the Visual Imperative or the whitepaper from Radiant Advisors, available at https://radiantadvisors.com/our-research/new-research-the-data-visualization-competency-center.

Ongoing Learning

Practice and receiving audience feedback are important ways to continuously learn and perfect your skills as a visual data storyteller. Alongside these, many additional resources, both those that accompany this text and those you can find out in the wild, are available to aid you in ongoing training and skills development.

Teach Yourself: External Resources

A bevy of incredible information assets beyond this book can expand and deepen your knowledge and understanding of the concepts we approached from a pragmatic stance in this text. The following are some of the resources I recommend.

Blogs

Blogs have two great qualities: there are many, and they are constantly adding new material and new ideas. Here are a few of my favorites that I believe offer unique and compelling galleries of visual data storytelling in action by some of the most prominent voices in data visualization and storytelling today.

- **Flowing Data** (http://flowingdata.com): This blog, run by data visualization author and statistician, Nathan Yau, explores how we can use analysis, visualization, and exploration to understand data and ourselves.

- **Eager Eyes** (https://eagereyes.org): This blog devoted to visualization and visual communication belongs to Tableau research lead Robert Kosara, and explores what we know and what we don't know—so we can be less wrong about visualization.

- **The Pudding** (https://pudding.cool): The Pudding is a weekly journal of visual essays produced by Polygraph (http://polygraph.cool), an "incubator for visually driven storytelling." Using code, animation, and data visualization, these stories tackle a wide range of interesting topic matter, from insights in politics, cinema and art, and science.

- **Info We Trust** (http://infowetrust.com): This website belongs to RJ Andrews, an independent creative whose visualizations provide a striking lesson in how to use design and science to humanize complex information using analysis, illustration, motion, and interactive design.

- **Bora Beran "On Anything Data"** (https://boraberan.wordpress.com): This website belongs to Tableau's Bora Beran and takes a unique look at more technical aspects of data visualization, including building extremely complex visuals, like sunburst diagrams, in Tableau, as well as using languages like R and Python to collect and prepare data for visual analysis.

- **Data Revelations** (http://www.datarevelations.com): Run by Tableau Zen Master and Training Partner Steve Wexler, this blog provides practical training and hands-on guidance on using Tableau to properly and creatively visualize data.

- **Information is Beautiful** (http://www.informationisbeautiful.net): This blog by data journalist David McCandless, is focused on distilling the world's data, information, and knowledge into beautiful and useful graphics to help everyone make better, clearer, more informed decisions about the world.

Books

Many books, old and new, are available on the market that take deep dives into many of the concepts covered in this text, as well as provide valuable additional insight from other leading voices in the field. Here are a few of the titles I use as reference, both in and out of my classrooms:

- *The Visual Imperative* by Lindy Ryan
- *Storytelling with Data* by Cole Nussbaumer Knaflic
- *The Functional Art* by Alberto Cairo
- *Data Points* by Nathan Yau
- *Communicating Data with Tableau* by Ben Jones
- *Tableau Your Data* by Daniel Murray

Tableau Resources

Tableau has a rich and expansive set of resources, including blogs, white papers, visualization galleries, webinars, training videos, and more on its website that are available to the general public. Additionally, educators and students can access relevant, in-depth materials, including datasets, through its community forums and special interest groups.

Companion Materials to This Text

Along with the external resources outlined earlier, there are also several companion materials designed to accompany this text and provide additional hands-on support for practitioners and educators. These are available to you at no additional cost, and are freely available online:

- **Website** (www.visualdatastorytelling.com): This website acts as an information hub to share all companion materials, including lecture decks, datasets, and more. It is continuously updated and also features a timeline of upcoming events that I'll be speaking or teaching at, as well as a video library of presentations and papers, new and upcoming research, current projects, and more.

- **Datasets**: All publically available datasets used in this text are available either from their original source (that is, the CDC Lyme Disease dataset), through www.VisualDataStorytelling.Com, or on Github at https://github.com/deepwatermedia. New datasets are added as they become available. Additionally, Tableau catalogs a wide array of datasets that can be used to practice, teach, or otherwise engage with data visualization.

- **Curricula**: Designed for entry to mid-level analysts, as well as undergraduate and graduate students, select lecture materials and assignments to support this text are also available. These can be found on the website. They are incrementally updated and include recommended readings and videos. Guest lecturing services are also available to university faculty, as well as corporate training workshops for industry professionals.

- **Connect with Me**: Reach out to me directly on any social media. I love to engage with you and see what stories you are telling with data!

  - **Twitter:** @lindy_ryan
  - **Tableau Public**: https://public.tableau.com/profile/lindyryan#!/
  - **LinkedIn**: https://www.linkedin.com/in/lindyryan/
  - **Online**: https://www.visualdatastorytelling.com

INDEX